Pat Collins CM

intimacy

and the Hungers of the Heart

The Columba Press, Dublin • Twenty-Third Publications, Mystic, Connecticut

1991

First edition, 1991, published in Ireland by
THE COLUMBA PRESS
93 The Rise, Mount Merrion, Blackrock, Co Dublin

Reprinted 1992

ISBN 1 85607 027 1

And in the United States of America by
TWENTY-THIRD PUBLICATIONS
185 Willow Street
P.O. Box 180
Mystic, CT 06355
203-536-2611
800-321-0411

ISBN 0-89622-497-X
Library of Congress Catalog Card No. 91-75410

Cover by Bill Bolger
Origination by The Columba Press
Printed in the United States of America

Contents

To Angela, Pat and Marie
the three graces

Foreword

Nearly twenty years ago I heard Mother Teresa of Calcutta describing her work for the destitute and dying in India. Like the others present at that lecture in a London training college, I was deeply moved and impressed. Towards the end of her talk she said, 'I suppose that some of you are feeling that you would have to buy a plane ticket and travel to India if you were to give effective help to the poor. There is no need she said. The poor are right here in your own country. In the third world there is often a famine of the stomach due to lack of food, but the people are rich in love. They share what little they have with one another. In developed nations like yours there is an abundance of food. But here there is often a famine of the heart due to a lack of love. The victims of this famine of love are the new poor. And who are these poor people?' she asked dramatically, 'They are the people sitting next to you.'

When I returned to Ireland I often thought about what Mother Teresa had said. I decided, rather naïvely as it turned out, that I would become a latter day Good Samaritan by trying to help those of the new poor that I met as a priest. However, I realised rather quickly that, in spite of my good intentions, I didn't seem to have much to offer. I became disillusioned and frustrated, wondering what was wrong. Then one day I was reading the scriptures and came across these words: 'You say, "I am rich and well off; I have all I need." But you do not know how miserable and pitiful you are! You are poor, naked and blind.' (Rev 3:17) All of a sudden the penny dropped. In spite of the fact that I had a secure home, a happy upbringing, and a good education, I was one of the new poor. I was often troubled by feelings of anxiety, and a fear of being unlovable and unappreciated. As I came to terms with my poverty of spirit in this way, I began to have a deep-seated desire for a spiritual awakening, one that would enable me to experience God's great love for me. Suffice it to say that my prayers were answered in a wonderful way sometime later when I experienced an outpouring of the Holy Spirit.

That was many years ago. But I have never lost the desire to be a famine relief worker, by helping people to discover the renewing and healing power of love in their lives. This book is animated by that general intention. It attempts to bring together a number of disparate topics that have preoccupied me for a long time.

Ever since I was a child, I have been blessed by a recurring intimation of a unity that lies beyond the apparent multiplicity of everyday experience. As a result, while I have always been fascinated by the amazing discoveries and achievements of modern science, I have often felt that its methods and conclusions were alien to my intuitive sense of a mysterious reality that sustains all things in being. However, in recent years I have been encouraged to find that the so-called new science is not only less hostile to the religious outlook, it often seems to be influenced by it.

In adult life, I have not only been attracted by the ideal of friendship, I also experienced this kind of love in a few committed relationships. As I have read what philosophers and spiritual writers have said about this subject, they have reinforced a conviction, based on personal experience, that, in Christian as in all spiritual friendships, human and divine love coalese in a uniquely wonderful way. Over the years, I have taught courses on this subject and intended to write a book about it. But the more I thought about the matter, the more I realised that something wasn't right, some key ingredient was missing.

Then a few years ago I began to reflect on the meaning of intimacy. It became increasingly clear to me that, properly understood as self-disclosure and loving attention, intimacy is a key, not only to all kinds of human relationships, but also relationships between people and nature and people and God. Gradually I began to see how the religious sense, the experience of interpersonal love and the insights of modern science could be brought together under the umbrella concept of intimacy. The resulting synthesis has its limitations of course, but it does attempt to provide a framework within which psychological and spiritual development can be understood in an integrated way. While being at home in the modern world, so to speak, it continues to point beyond it to the transcendent Source of all existence, life and love.

Intimacy and the Hungers of the Heart opens with an introductory chapter which outlines some of the main ideas in the book. It is followed by three sections, each devoted to a different aspect of intimacy. The first deals with the importance of self-intimacy, or self-awareness. The second focuses on the dynamics of inter-personal intimacy. I may say, in passing, that the chapter on intimacy as loving attention is of pivotal importance. The third section shows how the first two forms of intimacy are a prerequisite for intimacy with God.

If you are, or have been a famine victim like me, I hope that this book will provide you with some manna for your life's journey.

CHAPTER 1

Intimacy in the age of experience

Contemporary society has experienced an unprecedented growth in human knowledge. What was known about the world doubled between the time of Christ and the mid-eighteenth century. It doubled again between 1750 and 1900. Nowadays it takes less than ten years for another doubling to take place. The practical application of this ever-growing body of information has transformed our contemporary society. In doing so, it has also undermined some of the most basic values, beliefs and assumptions of Western culture.

We have entered an on-going transitional crisis. The symptoms are obvious. In spite of improved standards of living, health care and life expectancy, many people suffer from a growing sense of alienation, anxiety and anger. In an environment where 'the centre cannot hold' the incidence of mental illness, violent crime and social unrest continues to increase. The responsibility is ours. To discover a new world-view to replace the one that is currently disintegrating, we will have to identify the basic issues that lie at the heart of the often bewildering and disconcerting changes we have been living through.

I believe that one of the most important interpretative keys to this complex phenomenon is the fact that, in our culture, the centre of gravity has been shifting from *the experience of authority* to *the authority of experience*. This important paradigm shift is the culmination of a process that has been going on for a long time.

Agents of change

The Middle Ages lasted nearly a thousand years. They reached a high point in the twelfth century with the formation of what was later known as the medieval synthesis. St Thomas Aquinas was its chief architect. He integrated the philosophical and scientific insights of the Greeks with the dogmatic teachings of the Catholic Church.

With the emergence of experimental science in the six-teenth century, the authority of this medieval overview was under-mined and finally replaced. While men like Nicolas Copernicus (1473-1543) and Francis Bacon (1561-1626) were its precursors, Galileo Galilei (1564-1642) was the true father of the scientific revolution. By observing Jupiter and its satellites with a newly invented telescope, he said that he could prove that the earth revolved around the sun. This confirmed what Copernicus had previously suggested in a hypothetical way in his book, *On the Revolution of the Heavenly Bodies* .

The reaction of the Church was both rapid and harsh. Because Galileo's empirical observations contradicted the author-itative teaching of Ptolemy and the scriptures, he had to be in error. After all, Joshua 10:12 had stated that, during an Old Testa-ment battle, 'The sun stood still, and the moon stopped.' This verse confirmed the prevailing common-sense view that the heavenly bodies revolved around the earth. So, under the threat of prison and possible torture, Galileo was forced to make a public recantation. In private, however, his views remained unchanged. In one of his letters, he explained why he saw no nec-essary conflict between the claims of religious authority and those of empirical experience: 'I think that in discussions of physical problems we ought to begin not from the authority of scriptural passages but from sense-experience and necessary demonstra-tions, for the whole Bible and the phenomena of nature proceed alike from the same divine Word.' [1]

If the Church had been prepared to accept this enlight-ened distinction, it could have avoided the evolutionary contro-versy in the nineteenth century. In 1832, Charles Darwin joined the crew of *The Beagle*. For five years he conducted scientific research in the South Atlantic and the Pacific. Among other things, he noticed that there were slight variations between the species of flora and fauna to be found on the Galapagos Islands. Having reflected for twenty-five years on the theoretical implications of these discoveries, he published his findings in *The Origin of Species* in 1859. It was followed, twelve years later, by a companion vol-ume entitled, *The Descent of Man*. In these two important books, Darwin challenged the prevailing view, that the world was essentially static and unchangeable. He maintained that humankind had evolved from the animal kingdom, by means of natural selection, over a period of millions of years.

This theory challenged important Christian beliefs about the purposefulness of the world, the unique dignity of human beings and the drama of their special creation and fall. Because his views challenged the authoritative teaching of Genesis, Catholic and Protestant churchmen alike said that Darwin had to be wrong. Time has shown, however, that, broadly speaking, Darwin, like Galileo, was correct. Consequently, the twentieth century Church has had to modify and refine its teachings. It now accepts that the scriptures teach theological rather than scientific truth. As such they should be interpreted in an allegorical way.

The success of the scientific method has had an important effect. People today are not impressed by authoritative teachings as such. Just as scientific claims have to be supported by empirical evidence, so religious claims have to be authenticated at the level of personal experience. As the scientific outlook has permeated our culture, it has been augmented by a number of changes which have reinforced the shift from *authority* to *experience*. We will look at four of them: the growth of democracy, the influence of modern psychology, the contribution of existentialist philosophy and the advent of feminism.

The growth of democracy

In Britain and Ireland during the eighteenth century, only men with property had the right to vote. Because members of parliament received no salary, only those with private means could be elected. As a result, relatively small elites held a monopoly of power. They commanded and the people obeyed. In the nineteenth century this paternalistic view of authority began to weaken with the growth of an educated middle class and an extension of the franchise. At the end of World War I adults in many Western countries were free to vote and the secret ballot was introduced. It helped to ensure that workers and tenants were not unduly influenced by either landlords or employers. From that time on, elected representatives were expected to carry out the will of the people, instead of arbitrarily imposing their own as heretofore. This growth in popular democracy was matched by increased investment in education. Its aim was to equip the people to carry out their new-found political and social responsibilities and to cope with the demands of an increasingly complex industrial society.

Since then, the growing numbers of people attending colleges and universities, the availability of cheap travel and the all-pervasive influence of the mass media have had a number of knock-on effects. Not only are people better informed, they are exposed as never before to ideas, values and beliefs which differ from their own. In an increasingly pluralistic world of this kind, the authoritative and sometimes paternalistic claims of church and state are judged on the basis of their intrinsic meaning and relevance. Those that make experiential sense are accepted, those that fail to do so are rejected.

The influence of modern psychology

The shift from the experience of external authority to the authority of inner experience has been explored and reinforced by modern psychology. Until the twentieth century, Western culture had invested great faith in the authority of human reason. It was thought to be objective, realistic and reliable. But Sigmund Freud and his followers questioned this belief. When they examined hysterical patients, people under hypnosis, the meaning of dreams, etc, they discovered that besides the rational mind there was also the pre-rational realm of the unconscious. From it's hidden depths it could exert a powerful but often unrecognised influence on rational attitudes, beliefs and choices. As Freud wrote, 'Thinking is indeed nothing but a wish emanating from the unconscious.' This awareness led to what Paul Ricoeur has called the 'hermeneutic of suspicion,' i.e. a tendency to be sceptical about people's conscious motives and intentions, no matter how good and sincere they might seem to be. So, for example, if a Bishop said that he was against the ordination of women for theological reasons, many people might suspect that his attitude was motivated by an irrational but unconscious fear of feminine sexuality.

The contribution of existentialist philosophy

Twentieth century existentialism is a style of philosophising that moves away from the traditional way of looking at reality.

Instead of knowing about truth in an objective and dispassionate way, it stresses the importance of being grasped by the truth in a decisively subjective manner. It emphasises themes such as finitude, guilt, alienation, despair, and death. Classical philosophy maintained that *existence* followed *essence*. So for example, the *essence* of a building must originate in an architect's mind before it can find expression in concrete *existence*. However some contemporary existentialists, such as Sartre and Heidegger, believe that in the case of human beings, existence *precedes* essence. Men and women create their own *essences*, both by the choices they make and the actions they take . Not surprisingly, therefore, existentialists tend to oppose any ideology, or regime, that would attempt to overide the claims of subjective experience in the name of some abstract dogma or truth. Atheistic and Christian existentialists alike have had widespread influence on most aspects of modern cultures, from psychiatry through literature to ethics.[2] Not only have they reflected the paradigm-swing from authority to experience, they have accelerated it.

The advent of feminism

Until recently, Western society was dominated by men. But with the advent of universal suffrage, better educational opportunities for all, and the increasing need for skilled women in the work force, the *status quo* has been changing. For years now, the ranks of the women's movement have been growing. Feminist scholars have been formulating a telling critique of the unjust assumptions, dynamics and effects of patriarchal authority. Not only does it oppress women and prevent them from developing their unique potential, paradoxically it deprives their male oppressors of the kind of women they will increasingly need. I'll try to explain why.

Research has shown that, in our culture, there are some identifiable differences between men and women. For example, when it comes to the understanding of human relationships, a man will see a problem that requires a solution, while a women will see a process that requires understanding.[3] Carol Gilligan has argued persuasively[4] that where moral issues are concerned, men are drawn to the 'ethics of duty.' They evaluate moral dilemmas

13

in the light of abstract notions of justice and ask, 'what would be the *right thing* to do in these circumstances?' For their part, women expouse the 'ethics of responsibility.' They evaluate moral dilemmas in the light of concrete relationships and perceived needs, and go on to ask, 'what would be the *most caring thing* to do in these circumstances?' It would seem then, that the characteristically male attitudes are suited to a static model of society based on authority – usually male authority – whereas the characteristically female attitudes are suited to a dynamic model of society based on experience. As the women's movement gains strength, it will tend to reinforce the shift from patriarchal authority to shared experience. In the future, when men find it harder to cope with the demands of a changing culture, they will have to rely more and more on the increasingly relevant insight, skills and adaptability of women.

The Church in a changing world

The cultural transformation we are living through has enormous implications for contemporary Christianity. While revelation is complete and unchangeable in itself, each generation has to adapt the Gospel message to meet the changing needs of society. This is what happened in the Middle Ages. We have already noted that while St Thomas remained true to the teachings of scripture and the Church, he expressed Christian belief in terms derived from the objective categories of Greek philosophy. Evidently they suited the needs of a relatively static feudal society. The task of transposition and adaptation has to be undertaken once again, if the message of Christ is to be incarnated in modern culture.

Because he was aware of this, Pope John XXIII convened the Second Vatican Council. In 1961 he outlined his purpose in a letter to his bishops: 'Today the Church is witnessing a crisis under way in society. While society is on the verge of a new era, tasks of great importance await the Church. It is a question in fact of bringing the modern world into life-giving contact with the Gospel.'[5] By 1965 the Council fathers had drawn up an inspired blueprint for change and renewal. When he returned from Rome, John Charles McQuaid said reassuringly to the Catholics of Dublin,

'No change will trouble the tranquility of your Christian lives.' Events at home and abroad were soon to show that this was wishful thinking on the Archbishop's part.

After an initial phase of enthusiasm and hope, the implementation of the conciliar decrees ran into trouble. Structures were changed, but hearts were harder to change. Instead of renewal there were often disputes, divisions, and disillusionments. A more obvious sign of this on-going crisis, has been the fall in vocations and the large number of priests and religious who have returned to the lay state or left the Church altogether. The crisis has been obvious among the laity also. In spite of the Church's teaching on divorce and artificial forms of contraception, it is striking that the statistical incidence of both has been much the same for Catholics as it has been for those who do not share our faith. Sad to say, many lay people have lapsed in recent years. Even in Ireland, where Church attendance is unusually high, the practice rate is as low as ten per cent in some large urban parishes.

As we look at the evidence, it becomes increasingly clear that the Church, like secular society, is in the midst of a crisis of change. Understandably some people interpret our present difficulties in terms of a struggle between Gospel values and those of the world. There is a lot of truth in this point of view. But surely, that kind of choice has been crucially important in every generation since New Testament times. It remains so today, but is it the root problem that would enable us to understand the present crisis? I don't think so.

I believe that we will only come to terms with what is going on when we grasp the fact that in modern Catholicism, the centre of gravity is shifting from *the experience of religious authority* to *the authority of religious experience*. I should say in passing that while the authority of religious experience is being emphasised nowadays, it doesn't mean that authoritative Church teaching is irrelevant. Both are important. While dogmatic faith unsupported by personal experience remains dead, mere personal experience unrelated to the faith of the Church remains blind.[6] As a result, the orthodoxy of a religious experience, from a Catholic point of view, can only be discerned in the light of Church teaching.

There are a number of factors which have contributed to

this state of affairs. As members of contemporary society, Christians, like everyone else, are influenced by the current swing from authority to experience. As members of the Church, Catholics are influenced in particular by two teachings of the Vatican Council which, rightly or wrongly, have tended to put an end to the days of blind, unquestioning obedience to ecclesiastical authority.

Before the Vatican Council, the Church was seen as an organisation, a hierarchical pyramid with the Pope at the top, the bishops and priests in the middle, and the mass of the laity at the bottom. This led to a paternalistic view of ecclesiastical authority. As one fifties textbook put it: 'The position of leadership extends pre-eminence to the clergy, which is not given to the laity ... A pre-requisite to the use of power as shepherds is the submission of those who are inferior, i. e. the laity.'[7] After the Council, the Church was seen as an organism, a graced union of all the baptised, priests and people alike. Instead of being 'inferior' recipients of clerical ministry, lay people are seen as those who are gifted to play their part in building up the Church in love. Significantly, the conciliar documents point out that the right and duty of the laity to do this is derived from their baptism and not from the ecclesiastical authorities.

The Council also stressed the primary importance of religious freedom and the rights of conscience. 'Deep within his conscience,' said one document, 'man discovers a law which he has not laid upon himself, but which he must obey.' Increasing numbers of Catholics are motivated by their inner convictions, rather than by the external obligations imposed upon them by the institutional Church.

Taken together, these points imply a less authoritarian model of obedience. In any case, that is the way a growing number of lay people actually see things. This was highlighted with the publication of Paul VI's encyclical in the late sixties. Among other things, it condemned all forms of artificial birth control. During the intervening years, millions of conscientious Catholics have dissented from the Pope's teaching, either in principle or in practice. Nevertheless, the majority of them continue to attend church and to receive the sacraments.

In retrospect, I think that it is clear that the *Humanae Vitae* controversy was a watershed. It indicated that a combination of secular and religious influences had conspired to shift the centre of gravity in modern Catholicism. Things would never be the same again. Repeated surveys in a number of countries have confirmed the subjective impression that increasing numbers of Catholics accept the authority of the Church to the extent that it seems meaningful and relevant in their personal lives. [9]

The nature of intimacy

If the shift from authority to experience is the interpretative key to the religious crisis of our times, I believe that the experience of intimacy, which is open to transcendence, is the interpretative key to all genuine religious experience.

In our culture, where eroticism is all pervasive, the word *intimacy* is often used as a euphemism for sexual intercourse. In this book however I'm using it in its strict etymological sense. The words *intimacy, intimate* and *to intimate* in English are derived from two Latin words. *Intimus* refers to that which is 'innermost'. The word *intimare* means 'to hint at, announce, publish or make known.' Combining the meaning of the two Latin terms, the words *intimate* and *intimacy* mean 'to hint at, to publish or make known that which is innermost.' So the concept of intimacy implies some sort of revelation or disclosure of the innermost truth of something.

In this connection, I was interested to discover that in Greek the word for truth is *aletheia,* meaning 'to unveil, to uncover that which is hidden.' In that sense, every experience of intimacy is an epiphany, a manifestation of the unseen. So we are intimate with a person or the world of nature when we go beyond outward appearances to discover their inner truth. Encounters of this kind can have a religious dimension, as we shall see.

Intimacy as a way of seeing the world

Intimacy is the fruit of a particular way of contemplating the world, one that is rare enough in modern society. The French philosopher, Gabriel Marcel, has shown how the world can be looked at as a problem or as a mystery.[10] The distinction can firstly be illustrated by a concrete example: I have a small scientific instrument called a radiometer. It consists of a sphere of glass which looks rather like a light bulb. Inside, in a virtual vacuum, stands a steel pin. Suspended on the top is a device with four small, black and white panels, protruding outwards. When they are exposed to bright light, they spin on top of the needle. The more light there is, the faster the rotation, thereby illustrating how radiant energy can be transformed into mechanical force. Normally I leave this gadget on a windowsill in my office. When visitors see it for the first time, they invariably ask, 'What's that?' 'A radiometer,' I reply, while going on to explain how the light of the sun, stars and galaxies enables it to turn. The next question is also predictable: 'But what is it for?' There was only one exception over a period of twenty years. When I explained what it was, one ninety-six-year-old priest stood for a while in awed silence and said, 'Isn't that just wonderful!' While everyone wanted to know what the radio-meter was, their reasons were different. Most people were motivated by a problem-centred curiosity which wanted to know what use they could make of such a thing. Only the elderly priest was motivated by a mystery-centred wonder which admired the instrument and what it represented, for its own sake.

Viewed as a problem, nature is something to be understood, mastered and exploited by means of rational enquiry. This detached and objective approach is characteristic of the scientific attitude and is very common in our culture. As we know, science continues to lay bare the inner structure of animate and inanimate things. Although it often does this in stunning detail, scientific knowledge, as such, doesn't foster the sense of connection that is typical of intimate knowing. On the contrary, it has tended to sever the umbilical cord of intuitive wonder that can put us in touch with the inner nature of things.

The consequences of lacking intimacy

The extent to which we lose touch with the inner nature of things, is the degree to which alienation replaces intimacy as the normal way of relating to the world. As our sense of oneness declines, is it any wonder that we go on to ravage and pollute the natural world? So, at the heart of the grave ecological crisis of our time, lies a crisis of intimacy.

I also believe that the moral and religious crisis we are

living through is due, in large part, to a lack of intimacy. As our sense of human solidarity declines, it is not surprising that there is a loss of meaning which expresses itself in a deep-seated sense of anxiety. That anxiety, in turn, can lead to an obsessional pursuit of power, wealth and pleasure as substitutes for transcendental intimacy.

It is also my belief that the extent to which we suffer a famine of genuine intimacy, is the extent to which society will be plagued by forms of pseudo-intimacy, such as a vicarious identification with fictionalised relationships, the cultivation of romantic infatuations, and a permissive attitude to sexual behaviour.

The consequences of enjoying intimacy

When the world is viewed as a mystery, the normal distinction between subject and object breaks down. The basic intuition that informs this attitude is the wonder that something, rather than nothing, exists and that I am an integral part of that something. It transcends the normal modes of perception. As a thinking reed on the shore of existence, the wonder-filled person realises that he or she is comprehended by the mystery contemplated. This way of looking at things is typical of artists, poets, seers and children. Instead of uncovering scientific facts, it establishes a sense of relationship with the qualities of reality, such as beauty, goodness and truth, which disclose its inner value.

Trancendental intimacy

It is my belief that everything that exists has two outstanding characteristics, that of *inwardness* and that of *relatedness*, The simpler the structure of a material thing, the more elementary its level of inwardness will be. So obviously a plant, a living thing, has more inwardness than an inanimate stone. But a dog, which is conscious of the world around it, has more inwardness than either a stone or a plant. The greater the level of inwardness, the greater the ability of the object to relate to the world about it. A stone is related to everything else by gravity, but as living things, plants adapt to the world about them, e. g. there are flowers that can capture insects by closing their petals. They then go on to digest their victims by means of a chemical process. As a conscious creature, a dog can relate to the world about it, to other dogs, and to its owner.

19

According to science, the apparent solidity of material things is deceiving. In reality everything that exists is made up of countless atomic and sub-atomic particles. Einstein went even further when he suggested that the apparent solidity of things is deceptive. His famous formula $E=MC^2$ implied that material things were in fact so many manifestations of different forms of *created energy*. This seems to be the power that makes both inwardness and relatedness possible in animate and inanimate things.

I suspect that created energy, and the dynamics of its activity and manifestations, is made possible by the uncreated energy of the Holy Spirit. It 'fills the whole world,' as Wisdom 1:7 assures us. Indeed, priest-scientist Teilhard de Chardin has written: 'Without any doubt there is something which links material energy and spiritual energy together and makes them a continuity. In the last resort there must somehow be one single energy active in the world.'[11]

I believe that in all true intimacy the Spirit 'which searches everything,' (1 Cor 2:10) enables us human beings to know the innermost truth of people and things. I will try to explain what I mean. Proportionate to its degree of inwardness, everything that exists possesses an inner secret, a mysterious truth of its own. I believe that all created things have a God-given ability to disclose their innermost value by means of their discernible qualities. As persons capable of self-awareness and rational reflection, human beings have the greatest degree of inwardness and the most highly developed capacity for relating to the world around them. As they do so, they activate their own latent capacity for greater degrees of conscious subjectivity. To do this, however, they have to learn how to look at reality in the proper way.

This learning involves having to escape from the gravitational pull of self-absorption in order to pay sustained and loving attention to the world about them. To do this, they have to stop theorising about it. They have to withdraw their projected ideas, feelings and symbolic meanings, in order to allow things to be themselves. Finally, they have to wait patiently until that which is innermost in reality, is manifested and made known. The late Max Scheler has said that this kind of contemplative attitude is 'not merely an activity of the knowing subject who penetrates into the already present object, but is, at the same time, a responsive answer of the object itself; a 'self giving' and 'opening' of the object, i. e. a genuine self-revelation of the object. It is 'love's question' as it were, to which the world 'answers'insofar as it opens itself and therein first comes to its fullest being and value.' [12]

I believe that the Holy Spirit prompts both the desire for such intimacy, and the contemplative attitude which makes it possible. When they are informed by a desire to know God, the Lord's presence can be manifested in and through the things the Creator has made. As St Paul has written: 'Ever since the creation of the world, God's eternal power and divine nature, invisible though they are, have been understood and seen through the things he has made.' (Rom 1:20) An experience is religious, therefore, insofar as it leads to a conscious sense of relationship with the Mysterious Other who is revealed in and through our everyday intimacies.

Evaluating experience

I suggested earlier that the centre of gravity in our culture is moving *from authority to experience*. This isn't necessarily a good thing. Indeed it is fraught with danger. Benevolent authority, of whatever kind, is inclined to restrain people's worst impulses, to foster laudable values and beliefs, and to channel social energy toward worthwhile goals. But as the influence of those authorities is weakened, as is the case in our culture, the whole situation becomes problematical. Unless experience is informed and guided by the dynamics of a type of intimacy which is open to transcendence, it can lead to narcissism, moral relativism, social fragmentation, and a release of the demonic and destructive forces latent in the personal and social unconscious.

Besides being aware of these 'signs of the times,' Christians need to avoid two unhelpful reactions which are all too common nowadays. The Church will become increasingly alienated from our culture if it tries to influence this often disturbing situation by resorting to out-dated modes of paternalistic authority. On the other hand, it will become part of the problem instead of being part of the solution, if it immerses itself in an uncritical way in the culture of subjective experience.

As followers of the Lord, Christians are called to be a leaven in the dough of society. The Lord wants us to be in the world but not of it; to save society and not to judge or condemn it. It's my belief that we will only do this to the extent that we can foster genuine forms of intimate knowing which are open to transcendence. The orthodoxy and authenticity of religious experiences, which are associated with this kind of redemptive relationship, have to be assessed in the light of the dogmatic teaching of the Church.

Implicit in the Greek word for dogma, is the notion of testing something to see if it seems good or not. So the apostles were 'dogmatic' in this sense, when they said, 'It seems good to us and the Holy Spirit' in Acts 15:18. Understood in this way, dogma is not something to be arbitrarily imposed on people by the Church authorities. Rather it is a gift to be used in an act of service by the Church. In the light of its dogmatic teachings, bishops and people alike can discern together whether experiences are truly from God and in accord with Christian revelation.

I'm also convinced that evangelisation will only be effective in our culture if it is rooted in the experience of redemptive intimacy. So in the future, the bishop, priest, or lay person who substitutes the authority of objective religious truth for the authority of subjective but orthodox religious experience, will contribute by default to the demise of the Church.

Three intimacies

It will be apparent by now that I'm not intending to confine the notion of intimacy to interpersonal relationships. It will be used in this book to describe a contemplative way of relating to reality, whether that of nature, people or God. It will be informed throughout by a number of convictions which are worth noting at this early stage.

I suspect that consciousness of intimacy, love and the Holy Spirit are closely related, and are synonymous with one another in genuine religious experiences. I have also come to the conclusion that human intimacy is only fulfilled when it transcends itself by means of a personal relationship with God. That being so, the people of our time will get no closer to the divine than they are to the reality of their true selves and the world of people and things around them. This book, therefore, will be divided into three interrelated sections. Although we will have to look at each one separately, it's important to emphasise just how closely intertwined and interdependent they actually are.

In the first, we will look at *self-intimacy*, the way in which people can get in touch with that which is innermost in their own experience. There is something paradoxical about intimacy with oneself. While it is an indispensable requirement for intimacy with people, nature and God, it is at the same time dependent upon both. In a well-known poem, Wordsworth tells us how he enjoyed the sight of a host of golden daffodils. Sometime later he lay on his couch, in vacant or in pensive mood, and the daffodils flashed upon his inward eye, to bring him bliss in his solitude. We know that this kind of reflection in tranquility helped him not only to deepen his appreciation of beautiful things, but also to grow in self-awareness. In the opening chapters of this book, I will be advocating the importance of devoting time to this kind of reflective self-awareness. By focusing the spotlight of attention on the personal implications of the presence or absence of intimate relationships of all kinds, it avoids the dangers of self-absorbed naval-gazing.

In the second part of the book, we will look at the dynamics of *interpersonal intimacy*. In the final section we will examine how intimacy with self, others and nature, enables us to be intimate with the One who is the Beyond in the midst of our everyday lives. In this way, hopefully, we will have the makings of a spirituality which will be relevant to what Bernard Lonergan has called the 'contemporary age of interiority.'[13]

Notes
1. Quoted from 'Concerning the Use of Biblical Quotations in Matters of Science,' by J. Bronowski & B. Mazlish, in *The Western Intellectual Tradition*, Pelican, London, 1963, 153.
2. cf. J. Macquarrie, *Existentialism*, Pelican, 1973, 203-219.
3. cf. L. Rubin, *Just Friends*, Harper & Row, N.Y., 1985, 161.
4. *In a Different Voice*, Harvard University Press, Cambridge, 1982.
5. Humanae Salutis', in Abbott's, *Documents of Vatican II*, Geoffrey Chapman, London, 1966, 703.
6. Joseph Ratzinger's foreword to *Renewal & the Powers of Darkness*, by L. Suenens, DLT, London, 1983.
7. Quoted from Eichman & Morsdorf's *Manual of Canon Law*, by A. Bittlinger, *Gifts and Ministries*, Hodder & Stoughton, London, 1974, 25.
8. 'The Church Today', par. 16, Abbott, *op. cit.*, 213.
9. Fogarty, Ryan, Lee, (eds) *Irish Values and Attitudes: The Report of the European Value Systems Study*, Dominican Publications, Dublin, 1984, 8-12.
10. *Etre et Avoir*, Paris, 1935, 145.
11. Pensee, 13, in *The Hymn of the Universe*, Collins, London, 1965, 87
12. Quoted by Ed Vacek, 'Scheler's Phenomenology of Love,' *The Journal of Religion*, Vol 62, No. 2, April 1982, 168.
13. *Method in Theology*, DLT, London, 1971, 327-328.

PART I

self-intimacy

'Self-knowledge would certainly be maintained by me to be the very essence of knowledge, and in this I agree with him who dedicated the inscription, "Know thyself!" at Delphi.'

(Plato, *Charminides*, 164B)

CHAPTER 2

The journey inward

In his *Confessions*, St Augustine wrote, 'Men go abroad to admire the heights and mountains, the mighty billows of the seas, the courses of rivers, the vast extent of the ocean, the circular motion of the stars, and yet pass themselves by.'[1] If that was true over fifteen centuries ago, it's even more true today.

For hundreds of years now, our extroverted culture has become increasingly fascinated by the external world. Motivated by an insatiable desire to understand the whole of created reality, a growing number of scientists, in an ever-expanding number of disciplines, have engaged in a relentless study of everything from sub-atomic particles to the most distant galaxies. Each year their findings are published in tens of thousands of scientific papers, journals and books. Their principal insights are then disseminated by universities, schools and the mass media. Never was so much known, by so many, about such a wide variety of topics. And yet, there is a danger that in learning about external reality we will, in Augustine's words 'pass ourselves by.'

Of course, the human sciences, such as anthropology, sociology, psychology, etc, study men and women from overlapping points of view. And while their findings can increase our self-knowledge, they don't necessarily increase self-intimacy. If anything, they make self-intimacy harder to achieve because they encourage people to look at themselves in an objective, detached sort of way. For example, in 1920 Carl Jung published his monumental study of *Psychological Types*. Some years later, Katherine Briggs and her daughter, Isabel Myers, developed his insights and suggested that there were sixteen basic personality types. In 1962 they published their *Personality Type Indicator*.[2] Like hundreds of thousands of other people, I answered their questionnaire a number of years ago. My 240 replies were fed into a computer and I duly received a helpful print-out which described the nature and characteristics of my personality type. While the test, like all the human sciences, can help a person to grow in self-knowledge, I know from experience that they don't of themselves increase self-intimacy. It is important to pin-point the reason why this is so.

Subjects like psychology and sociology help a person to take an introspective look at himself or herself. They lead to indirect knowledge about the personality and its relationships. But it is only when a person becomes directly aware of himself or herself, by getting in touch with what is innermost in the heart, that self-intimacy can grow. While self-awareness of this kind usually goes on to articulate itself in a conceptual way, thereby becoming a form of self-knowledge, the converse is not necessarily true.

The next three chapters will suggest some ways of growing in self-awareness. But for now, we will take a closer look at the nature of self-intimacy, together with some of the ways in which we can resist the journey inwards for one reason or another.

From the ego to the self

The human personality is mysterious and indivisible. Nevertheless the great spiritual teachers have pointed out in conceptual and imaginative ways that it can be looked at from two points of view. Jesus said that the self-centred, worldly part of the personality has to die like a seed, if the plant of the spiritual self is to grow and bear fruit. (Jn 12:24) St Paul reiterates this point when he talks about getting rid of the old self in order to be clothed with the new self, created according to the likeness of God. (Eph 4:22-24) This scriptural teaching is repeated in various different ways throughout the Christian era. The terminology used may be different, but the substance remains the same. For example, during the Middle Ages Meister Eckhart wrote: 'A man has many skins in himself covering the depths of his heart. Man knows so many things; he does not know himself. Why thirty or forty skins or hides just like an ox's or a bear's, so thick and hard, cover the soul.'[3]

The ego and the self in contemporary spirituality

In the twentieth century Thomas Merton has echoed the traditional teaching in his influential writings. He makes a sharp

27

distinction between two selves. Firstly, there is what he variously calls a true self, deep self, new self, and a hidden identity. Secondly, there is a false self, shadow self, outer self, empirical self, mask, and false identity.[4] He argues repeatedly that the spiritual crisis in Western culture is largely due to the fact that so many people are prisoners of their false individualistic selves with their egotistical desires for satisfaction and fulfilment. Until they get back in touch with their true selves, created as they are in God's image, they will remain absent from the Lord. He wrote: 'There is no real love of life unless it is oriented to the discovery of one's true, spiritual self, beyond and above the level of mere empirical individuality with it's superficial enjoyments and fears.' [5]

For Merton, as for all great spiritual guides, there is a paradox involved in the quest for God. On the one hand he says that in order to find the divine image within, we must first become intimate with our own deepest, truest selves. Then, on the other hand, he believes that the discovery of the in-dwelling of God is only made possible when we become aware of the love of Christ as it is mediated to us through contemplation of such things as people, nature and the scriptures. 'Who am I?' he asked in a conference on prayer, 'My deepest realisation of who I am is – I am one loved by Christ ... The depths of my identity is in the centre of my being where I am known by God.'[6] In other words, by means of transcendental intimacy we have religious experiences whereby we become consciously aware of both God and the true self, immersed as it is in his divine love.

The ego and the self in modern psychology

A number of the great contemporary psychologists have explored this theme, among them Jung, Assagioli, Kunkel and Progoff. In different ways, they say that the human personality is made up of the ego and the self. In his clearest description of this elusive distinction, Jung wrote: 'The self is not only the centre but also the whole circumference which embraces, both conscious and unconscious; it is the centre of this totality, just as the ego is the centre of the conscious mind.'[7] In other words, the self is an archetype, a structuring pattern that guides the unfolding and development of the entire personality, conscious and unconscious. Its function is akin to that of the soul in Christian theology.

The nature and dynamics of the ego

In a Jungian psychology, therefore, the term *ego* normally refers to my conscious sense of identity and, as such, is a part of the self. It includes two related aspects. Firstly, there is the public self. It includes those characteristics that are obvious to others such as gender, height, weight and personal things that one is consciously aware of and prepared to reveal to others. Normally that includes basic information about things like nationality, place of residence, religious affiliation and the like. It may be augmented by personal details which show one up in good light, for example, one's ideals, the fact that one's children are at university, etc. Then there is the private self. It refers to those things that one knows about oneself but which one is not prepared to reveal to other people. Fear is a common motive for this kind of reticence. All of us fail betimes to live up to our ideals, beliefs and values. We can feel ashamed of our weaknesses and so keep them to ourselves in order to retain the good opinion of others. On other occasions, we may keep our cards close to our chests simply because it would be inappropriate or imprudent to reveal them.

The ego, then, consists of the public and private self. As such, it is the focal point of consciousness and decision making. When it is aware of its strengths and limitations, and open to the inner and external truth, the ego has an essential and constructive role to play. When the ego espouses an idealised self-image, which is largely based on inherited beliefs, values and aspirations, it can become closed, arbitrary and unrealistic. In the name of altruism and love, it is often motivated by an egocentric but unacknowledged need for recognition, power, security, privacy and the like. Deep down, the defensive ego is subject to a lot of anxiety, a free-floating fear that its idealised self-image will be tarnished, that its often obsessive needs will not be satisfied. The English word *anxiety* comes from the Latin *angustus* meaning to 'narrow'. The defensive ego tends to be narrow minded. Sandwiched between the threatening worlds of external reality and the unknown or unconscious self, it is inclined to censor any dream, intimation or feeling that might disturb its tenuous sense of equilibrium.

29

The nature and dynamics of the self

It has been said that the mind is like an iceberg, one eighth above the water line of consciousness and seven eighths beneath. So if the ego wants to be at the service of the entire personality, it has to pay sustained attention to the unknown self as it publishes and makes known its innermost secrets. It does this in the form of symbols. They represent inner realities whose meaning is still partially, if not wholly, beyond the ambit of conscious awareness. Without the intervention of reason or will, images charged with energy, feeling and meaning are secreted from the shadowlands of the unconscious in the form of dreams and day time fantasies. All too often, these letters from the unconscious remain un-opened and un-read. But as a person becomes adept at interpreting them, their symbolic meanings can become apparent.

Jungian psychologists maintain that in dreams, myths and fairy tales the self is symbolised by images such as king, prophet, wise old man or woman and in the form of circles, squares and crosses. We will have more to say about the subject of dream interpretation in subsequent chapters. At the moment it's sufficient to note that if the voice of the unknown self is recognised and accepted, it will often challenge the arbitrary and inadequate perceptions, values and beliefs that have sustained the ego. As a result, the ego is invited, time and time again, to surrender cherished illusions in order that something deeper, fairer, and more all-embracing may arise within.

Self-fulfilment and self-trancendence

When the ego and the unconscious are reconciled in this way, the self guides and energises the process. The role of the self is similar to that of the genes that mastermind the formation of the different parts of the body. While each of them has its own separate identity and function, organs like heart, kidneys, bladder and lungs are programmed to work together, thereby promoting their common health and welfare. It's something the same with our inner life. Our deepest self has an innate ability to promote the unfolding of the psyche in a way that activates and integrates its mysterious potential around a transcendental search for meaning, and ultimately for God. So although it may manifest itself in the conscious life of the ego, our desire for intimacy with God originates in the self. It achieves wholeness and fulfilment only insofar as it enjoys a conscious relationship with the Lord.

Just as the unconscious psyche realises its potential by means of symbols, the spiritual self realises itself in terms of God images. Jung wrote: 'The Christ-symbol is of the greatest importance for psychology insofar as it is perhaps the most highly developed and differentiated symbol of the self.'[8] Like Merton, Jung believed that an important paradox was involved in self-transcendence. The extent to which the self reaches out to God by means of the Christ Symbol, and associated Christian images, is the extent to which Christ is revealed in the depths of the self. (cf. 1 Cor 2:9-16; Eph 3:16-18; Gal 2:20)

Because he knew that so many Western Christians were prisoners of their egos, Jung observed somewhere that, 'Too few people have experienced the divine image as the innermost possession of their souls. Christ only meets them from without, never from within the soul.' This is a point of crucial importance. When genuine religious experience is lacking, the inner and outer, the subjective and objective aspects of the Christian religion become alienated from one another. When the dogmas, rituals and morality of Christianity no longer mediate meaning to the self, a number of things can happen. They are either adhered to in a servile way, become a function of the security needs of the inflated ego, or are angrily rejected as something alien and oppressive.

I have already argued that the centre of gravity in our culture is shifting from authority to experience. Unfortunately it is often an impoverished form of ego-centric experience. As self-intimacy declines, it is inevitable that intimate connection with other people and creation will be weakened. Because conscious relationship with God is normally mediated by such intimacies, the sense of true religion declines.

The well-intentioned teachings of humanistic psychologists like Rogers, Fromm and Maslow make a bad position worse. They seem to encourage people to substitute a form of secular self-fulfilment for a Christian form of self-transcendence, i. e. the ability to become absorbed in transcendental meanings or values beyond the narrow confines of the ego.[9] This would be the case if a compassionate young woman sacrificed her career, comfort and marriage prospects in order to work with and for the oppressed in a third world country. In spite of many of its fine sentiments, the self-fulfilment approach is a sickness that mistakes itself for a cure.

The deepest self is orientated towards transcendence rather that fulfilment. If it does experience fulfilment, it is only because its antecedent desire for transcendence has first been satisfied. As soon as the self loses touch with transcendent meaning, the integrating tendencies of the psyche begin to go awry. Instead of the self achieving increasing degrees of healing and wholeness, the negative energies of the unconscious begin to take over, as we shall see in greater detail in chapter four. The embattled ego becomes afflicted by all kinds of obsessions, compulsions and neuroses. No doubt Jung had this point in mind when he wrote: 'In thirty years I have treated many patients in the second half of life, i. e. over thirty-five. Everyone of them fell ill because he or she had lost that which the living religions in every age have given their followers, and none of them was fully healed who did not regain his religious outlook.'[10] It is worth noting that many of Jung's patients were practising Christians. Like agnostics and unbelievers, they could only recover their emotional health when they first learned to relate to transcendent meaning from the self. Otherwise they would remain prisoners of their troubled egos.

Resisting self-intimacy

A German priest who was on the verge of a breakdown went to Dr Jung for help. 'I can't cope with the pressures of a fourteen hour day,' he exclaimed. Following a long and detailed interview, Jung advised: 'If you want to recover, you will have to change your life-style. Work an eight hour day. Have your evening meal. Then remain quietly on your own, until it is time to go to bed.' The priest expressed his gratitude: 'I'll do anything you say, Doctor, if it will help me to get better!' The next day he worked for eight hours, had his supper and retired to his study. Soon he was restless, so he listened to some piano music by Chopin and finished a novel by Herman Hesse. Next day he did much the same, only on this occasion he listened to Mozart and began a novel by Thomas Mann. At bed time this well educated and cultured man felt as bad as ever. The following morning he returned to Jung. 'I carried out your instructions,' he complained angrily, 'but I feel no better.' Having described how he had spent his time, Jung said to the unfortunate cleric: 'You don't seem to have understood. I didn't want you with Chopin or Hess, Mozart or Mann. I wanted you to be all alone, by yourself.' At this, the priest looked alarmed. 'Oh! I can't think of any worse company,' he exclaimed, to which Jung gave this classic reply: 'And yet this is the self you inflict on other people for fourteen hours a day!'

Clearly, Dr Jung could see that his client's problems were due to lack of self-intimacy. But the question arises, why was he reluctant, like so many of us, to come to terms with that which was innermost in his own heart?

Pain can block self-intimacy

I think that fear of pain is the principal reason. It can be obvious in our relationships with others. A few years ago I witnessed a poignant example of this. I was working as a part-time chaplain in an American hospital. One evening before Christmas, a ward sister asked me to see Mike. In spite of his leukemia, he was still a good-looking college student of about twenty. We spoke for a while. He told me about some of his fellow-sufferers who had already lost their fight to live. Then suddenly the door opened. In walked his father and brother. They put some fruit on his bed-side table and began to talk. 'Your mum is looking forward to having you home for the Christmas,' said the father in a cheerful tone of voice. 'I don't think I'll make it,' Mike replied in a subdued whisper. 'Nonsense,' retorted the father, 'the doctors will fix you up like before. You have nothing to worry about.' 'I don't know about that,' said Mike, 'the last remission lasted only two weeks. I feel very low. I don't think I'm going to make it this time.' 'For Christ's sake, Mike, you shouldn't talk like that,' snapped the brother, 'Dad is right. You'll be home for Christmas.' And so this heart-rendering conversation went on, Mike telling his father and brother he was dying, while they continued to dodge the issue with clichés. Not long afterwards they left. They were never to see Mike alive again. He died at 3 a.m. the following morning. Why was it that the father and brother couldn't really listen to what he was saying? Was it lack of love? I'm sure they loved him all right. But their love wasn't strong enough to overcome the fear of losing him.

A Biblical example

The inability to face painful realities is mentioned more than once in the bible. For example, Job is depicted as a wealthy, pious man. Suddenly he suffers one terrible disaster after another. Then his three friends come to see him. While they are moved by his predicament, they can't help suspecting that Job must have committed a terrible sin to warrant such misfortune. He assures them that he hasn't. Indeed he is so confused and frustrated himself that he is close to blaspheming. But instead of facing Job's pain and the way in which it called the religious orthodoxies of the day into question, the three men end up preaching at Job. They cannot let go of the traditional notion that God rewards the good and punishes the wicked, so they resort to religious clichés as a substitute for genuine compassion. Job is quite right when he replies, 'I have understanding as well as you.' (12:23) And again, 'I have heard many such things. I could also speak as you do, if you were in my place.'(16:2) And yet again, 'Oh, that you would keep silent, and it would be your wisdom.'(13:5) Interestingly, the Lord expresses his dissatisfaction with the three so-called friends, but not with the complaining Job. The trio have satisfied their own need for religious security instead of satisfying Job's need for comfort by facing the disconcerting implications of his sufferings. Like the priest and the Levite in the parable of the good Samaritan, they fail to respond to Job's pain, for egocentric reasons.

The pain of childhood

Just as people can close their ears to the still sad music of humanity, so they can they avoid their inner pain. This strategy of denial can usually be traced back to early childhood. My earliest memory goes back to the time I was about one. I was in my dark red pram, in a Summer house at the back of our home. Then my mother came out the back door, walked over to the pram and tucked me in. After a while she turned on her heels to go back into the house. For some reason or another I desperately wanted her to stay with me. No doubt I cried but, unable to speak, I couldn't get my desperate need across; and so my mother kept going. Quite innocently she had gone into the kitchen to make my father's dinner. For my part, I felt the awful pain of abandonment and rejection.

I mention this incident because it illustrates an important point. Small children have all kinds of emotional and physical needs. Many of them go unnoticed because, no matter how loving the parents are, they may be unable to either recognise or to answer them all. As a result, the baby can feel abandoned, isolated and vulnerable. Quite often this sense of hurt can turn to rage against the parents. But the baby is caught in a catch-twenty-two situation. If it expresses its feelings, it fears it might have to forfeit the very love and approval it needs so much. After all, most children get the impression – often it's a mistaken one – that they are loved in a conditional way by mum and dad. Their words, tone of voice and facial features can say to a child, 'We will love you more if ... if you do as you are told ... if you don't cry ... if you don't throw a tantrum ... etc.' In a child's mind, this can give rise to the belief that it is lovable in so far as it can conform to the expectations of the parents. As a result, it learns not even to feel, let alone express emotions and impulses that may be displeasing to others. As it grows older, the child will adopt a set of ideas and attitudes that will reinforce its repression of unacceptable feelings. For example, as a result of its upbringing it may come to the conclusion that all anger is sinful. Boys may come to the conclusion that only weaklings cry.

When our natural reluctance to experience pain of any kind is reinforced by this kind of conditioning, it is not surprising that painful memories and their associated feelings are buried alive by many people, in the unconscious. Remarkable as it may seem, there are, for example, many women and men who are consciously unaware of the fact that they have suffered the trauma of being sexually abused as children. The extent to which people put hurts and painful feelings of this kind into cold storage, is the extent to which their capacity to experience positive feelings will be frozen as well. They are inclined to adopt an apathetic approach to life, one where feelings are ignored in favour of facts and ideas. Is it any surprise that people who consign themselves to such a grey world are prone to varying degrees of depression? This blue plague, the most widespread disease in the Western world, like all neuroses, afflicts those who turn against the self.

Conformism as a block to self-intimacy

Psychology throws light on another reason why many people avoid self-awareness. It sees adult maturity as a movement from conformism to responsible autonomy. Mature people's sense of identity and worth flows from a loving acceptance of their true selves. The sense of identity and worth, characteristic of immature people, tends to depend on two things. Firstly, they have an inner need to win the approval of a moralistic and dictatorial conscience. Secondly, they also have an external need to win the approval of others, especially authority figures such as parents, teachers, employers, peers, etc. When people's sense of identity and worth is dependent on one or both of these forms of authority, they suffer from a largely unconscious preoccupation with things like approval, reputation, status, etc. Instead of being motivated on the basis of the internalised beliefs, values and ideals of the responsible self, they act on the basis of the 'oughts, shoulds, musts and have-tos' of external authority. Psychological research has shown that, as a result of this dynamic, the majority of people in society become alienated from their true selves.[11] By using all kinds of unconscious defence mechanisms they ignore any thought, desire or feeling that might evoke the disapproval of either a demanding conscience or of significant people in their lives. The anxiety that would follow such a punitive withdrawal of love is so fearful that many people prefer hypocrisy to authenticity.

I use the word *hypocrisy* in a descriptive rather than an evaluative sense. In biblical Greek, it has a theatrical background. It literally means, 'to act or to play a part' as distinct from being one's true self. Jung referred to this false self as the person's *persona*. The word is borrowed from Latin. It refers to the mask worn by Roman actors in classical times. Whenever people identify with roles, they hide their true selves by trying to project a positive but unrealistic self-image. Instead of being motivated by their deepest needs, desires, values and convictions, they lose touch with them in an overweening effort to conform to the expectations of other people.

Pride as a block to self-intimacy

From a spiritual point of view the sin of pride may be involved in this form of egocentricity. It is as if the false self says, with the fallen angels, 'I will not serve, I will not obey, I will not submit to any reality that might threaten my sense of security and control.' A proud person is someone who refuses to listen to the voice of truth, especially an inner one. In view of the fact that the Holy Spirit acts in and through the self, pride can lead people to close their ears to an inner 'word,' that might call for conversion and a change of heart. As Jesus said, 'This people's heart has grown coarse, their ears dulled, they have shut their eyes tight to avoid using their eyes to see, their ears to hear, their hearts to understand, changing their ways and being healed by me.' (Mt 13:15-17)

Forms of self-denial

Traditional spirituality speaks of self-denial, the need to restrain worldly and sinful desires. As most of these are the result of egocentricity, it would be more accurate to highlight the need for *ego*-denial. Paradoxically, it is when the fear of pain and the threat of change lead a proud ego to be closed and defensive, that people practise unhealthy forms of self-denial. There are many ways of doing this. We will look at three of the commonest forms: hiding behind ego defences, engaging in escapist activities of all kinds, and addictions.

Defence mechanisms

Freudian psychology has shown how people can resist self-intimacy. With great insight it has uncovered the unconscious defence mechanisms which protect the ego. They are good and helpful in so far as they prevent us from being overwhelmed by temporary threats and traumas, by providing us with a 'breathing space', time in which to come to terms with conflict or find alternative ways of coping, for example, after a sudden and unexpected death in the family. Defence mechanisms become harmful when they persistently shield us from the intimidating implications of self-awareness. Because they are unconscious, these defences are very hard to identify in one's own experience. Things such as psychotherapy, attention to deeper feelings with their associated memories, and dream-analysis can enable a person to recognise and so to outwit these barriers to self-intimacy. At the risk of being a bit technical, we will look at the dynamics of a number of these defences, while illustrating each one with an example.

The ego can repress threatening memories, desires and feelings by *burying* them alive in the unconscious. For example, a five-year-old child could forget its incestuous feelings for one of its parents. The ego also learns to cope with disconcerting feelings about people and events by *displacing* them somewhere else. A case in point: a man is humiliated at work by a supervisor. Although he is hurt and angry, he has to keep his feelings to himself. To do otherwise would risk losing his job. But when he gets home from work he displaces his anger by drinking heavily and shouting at his unfortunate wife and kids. Another strategy employed by the ego is to *deny* any truth that is too painful to accept. I have found that it is the first reaction of many hospital patients when they are faced with the fact that they are suffering from a deadly disease. They explain it away by saying things like, 'they must have the wrong X-Rays because I haven't felt so well for a long time.' Often the ego will avoid facing the truth about itself by means of *rationalisation*. It invents a cover story to excuse the inexcusable, for example: 'When I take money from the firm it's not stealing because they don't pay me enough in the first place.' What's known as *reaction-formation* is another of the ego's coping strategies. At the conscious level the person thinks or feels the opposite to what he or she is thinking or feeling at an unconscious level. So a man with latent homosexual leanings has a dislike of gays and maintains that they are 'disgusting.' One of the ego's most constructive ways of coping is called *sublimation*. The person displaces an unconscious need into some harmless alternative. For example, a man or woman could dissipate sexual or aggressive feelings by becoming involved in sports. The ego can also engage in what's called *introjection,* which is the incorporation of another person into oneself. This is what happens when an adolescent girl, with a poor self-image, admires a sports star or pop singer. By identifying with her hero figure and imitating his or her dress, mannerisms and behaviour, she can bask in the light of reflected glory. What is known as *projection* is the opposite to introjection. The person attributes unwanted feelings and characteristics to someone else. The ego sometimes *regresses* in order to avoid an adult problem. It falls back on a response which would have been appropriate at an earlier stage of life. For example, a woman throws a temper tantrum every time she fails to get what she wants at home.

Escapist activities

The poet T. S. Eliot has written: 'Human kind cannot bear very much reality.' Later in the same poem, he says that people today are 'distracted from distraction by distraction.'[12] I sometimes suspect that we have turned our extroverted culture into one big circus, reminiscent of those that entertained the masses in ancient Roman times. Thanks to the mass media, we live in the age of noise, physical noise, mental noise and the noise of desire. Together they invade those pools of silence which are needed to nurture reflection and self-awareness. We listen to transistor radios at home, to walkmans on the bus or train, and to the stereo when we travel by car. Daily we watch TV or videos for hours on end. We read newspapers, books and magazines in an endless search for knowledge, information and gossip. We go to the sports grounds, theatres, and cinemas to witness the activities and lives of other people. Needless to say, all these things are good in moderation. But they are dangerous when they so absorb our energies and attention that we learn millions of facts about the world around us while remaining ignorant of our true selves. To quote Eliot again, 'Where is the wisdom we have lost in knowledge, and where is the knowledge we have lost in information?'[13]

Besides endless distractions, our attachments, dependencies and addictions can act like an anaesthetic which deadens self-awareness. All of us experience a hierarchy of physical, psychological and spiritual desires. Our physical desire for food and drink, warmth and human touch, together with our emotional desire for love, acceptance, and a sense of belonging, are orientated towards fulfilment. The human spirit has a desire for meaning, transcendence and, ultimately, a conscious relationship with a loving God. We have seen that as far as the self is concerned the desire for self-actualisation is subordinate to the desire for self-transcendence. However, it often happens that our physical and psychological desires lead us to focus our energies on merely human forms of fulfilment. We can develop attachments to people, places, sensations, pleasures, etc. The word *attachment* in English comes from the French, meaning to 'nail down'. So when we become attached to worldly things, the energies of the self are nailed down to things which in themselves cannot satisfy its deepest but repressed desire. Instead of trying to come to a point of self-forgetful transcendence through relationship with the divine, the worldly-self tries to satisfy its needs in and through created things.

The problem of addiction

The dynamic I have been describing often leads to the state of addiction. Gerald May has written: 'Addiction exists wherever persons are internally compelled to give energy to things that are not true desires. To define it directly, addiction is a state of compulsion, obsession, or preoccupation that enslaves a person's will and desire. Addiction sidetracks and eclipses the energy of our deepest, truest desire for love and goodness.'[14] In our culture, where the pursuit of worldly experiences has so often been substituted for the pursuit of transcendental intimacy, it is not surprising that the incidence of all forms of addiction has increased. We all suffer from this kind of enslavement to created things, to a greater or lesser extent. Some of us become hooked by substances like sugar, nicotine and chocolate. Others, like the German priest mentioned earlier, sacrifice relationships and leisure activities by becoming workaholics. One in twelve of the population develops a sexual addiction, which can range from compulsive masturbation to bestiality. Then there is the scourge of addiction to alcohol and chemical substances of all kinds, ranging from tranquilisers to cocaine and heroin. Besides the harmful physical and psychological effects of most addictions, they prevent intimacy with oneself and others. They also repress transcendental desires. No wonder Carl Jung told one of the authors of the twelve steps of Alcoholics Anonymous that addicted people could achieve sobriety by getting in touch with their deep down desire for liberation and through openness to a Higher Power. They would need to go beyond mere wishing, or the feeling that they ought to stop drinking, to desire sobriety with all their hearts. It was then, and only then, that the Holy Spirit, acting in and through their rejected selves could give them the power to do what heretofore was impossible.

Conclusion

Courage is needed to embark on the journey inwards. We have to be prepared to encounter our inner pain, to face challenges to our idealised self-image, and to let go of egocentric attachments. In this way we can imitate the example of Teilhard de Chardin who wrote in his *Le Milieu Divin:* 'We must try to penetrate our most secret self.' He then goes on to describe his own experience: 'For the first time in my life perhaps, although I'm supposed to meditate every day! I took the lamp and, leaving the zone of everyday occupation and relationships where everything seems clear, I went down into my innermost self, to the deep abyss whence I feel dimly that my power of action emanates. But as I moved further and further away from the conventional certainties by which social life is superficially illuminated, I became aware that I was losing contact with myself. At each step of the descent, a new person was disclosed within me of whose name I was no longer sure, and who no longer obeyed me. And when I had to stop my exploration, because the path faded beneath my steps, I found a bottomless abyss at my feet, and out of it came – arising I know not from where – the current which I dare to call *my* life.'[15]

In the following three chapters we will suggest some ways of growing in this kind of self-intimacy.

Notes

1. *Confessions*, 10, 8.
2. Myers & Briggs, *Gifts Differing*, Consulting Psychologists Press, Palo Alto, 1980; Kiersey & Bates, *Please Understand Me*, Prometheus, Del Mar, 1978.
3. Quoted by A. Huxley, *The Perennial Philosophy*, Fontana, London, 1966, 171.
4. Quoted by J. Higgins, *Thomas Merton on Prayer*, Image Books, N.Y., 1971, 59.
5. *Op. cit.*, 62.
6. *Op. cit.*, 59.
7. *Collected Works* 12, par 444.
8. *The Basic Writings Of C. G. Jung*, Modern Library, N.Y., 1959, 449.
9. cf. P. Vitz, *Psychology as Religion: The Cult of Self Worship*, Eerdmans, Grand Rapids, 1977.
10. *Modern Man in Search of a Soul* , 279.
11. cf. V. Dywer, *Lift Your Sails*, Image, N.Y., 1987, 16.
12. Burnt Norton, in *Four Quartets*, Faber, London, 14.
13. *The Rock*, Faber, London, 1934, I.
14. *Addiction and Grace*, Harper & Row, N.Y. 1988, 14.
15. *Le Milieu Divin*, Fontana, London, 1964, 76-77.

CHAPTER 3

Fingerprints of the heart

In Greek society the Stoics encouraged their disciples to imitate God by leading apathetic lives. The word apathy in English is derived from the Greek *apatheia*, meaning 'without feeling'. They believed that God was unmoved emotionally by either the joys or sorrows of human beings, for otherwise God would be subject to change for either better or for worse. But in view of the fact that God was by nature perfect and unchanging, it necessarily followed that the deity was detached and unmoved by the human condition. That being so, the Stoics told their followers that they would be God-like if they remained emotionally unaffected by outward events. If they couldn't be suppressed altogether, feelings like compassion, grief and anger should be ignored. The events of daily life were to be mastered in a dispassionate way, and action motivated by duty and right reason.

Surprisingly, this apathetic attitude has become widespread in Western culture. Until recently, church and state have been dominated by men. Research has confirmed the common sense impression, that unlike women, a majority of males prefer facts to 'mushy', 'sentimental' or 'effeminate' feelings. The scientific method has reflected and reinforced this bias. It has successfully championed a rational, emotionally detached approach to reality. And since the publication of St Thomas Aquinas' *Summa*, which was heavily influenced by the rationalism of Aristotle, Catholic theology has shared in this bias. It has stressed the importance of reason and will at the expense of feelings, which it compared to the weather. Unlike reason, they are changeable, unreliable and often misleading. It can be noted in passing, however, that a good deal of Catholic piety (for example, devotion to the Sacred Heart) had a strong affective dimension.

A theory of the emotions

Happily in recent years, philosophers, theologians and psychologists alike, have been re-examining and rehabilitating the important and complex role of feelings in our lives. We will take a brief look at some of their findings.

The first problem one runs into is linguistic. There seems to be no clear-cut difference in the meaning of such words as emotion, mood, affect, feeling, sensation and passion. Willard Gaylin has suggested[1] that the words emotion, affect and feeling are the important ones. As a psychiatrist he assigns them fixed, if slightly arbitrary and restricted meanings.

An *emotion* refers to a person's feeling tone and the biophysiological and chemical states that underlie the sensations he or she experiences. For example, when a person is angry the hypothalmus, pituitary and adrenal glands are activated, hormones are secreted, digestion slows, the stomach contracts, the heart beats faster, and both respiration and blood pressure increase.

The word *affect* , which was introduced from psychoanalysis, is usually used to describe the dominant emotional tone of an individual. So at a case conference in a psychiatric hospital doctors and nurses will note that the patient's affect was 'depressed', 'elated', 'anxious', etc.

The word *feeling* refers to a person's subjective awareness of his or her own emotional state. This implies that a man or a woman could have an emotion, such as anger, without being consciously aware of it. It would become a feeling as soon as it articulated itself in conscious awareness.

While there are literally hundreds of feeling words in the English language, theorists have tried to isolate the principal ones and to categorise all the others, alongside them, so to speak. In the seventeenth century, Descartes suggested that there were six principal emotions: admiration, love, hate, desire, joy and sadness. For the last hundred years or so researchers such as Wundt, Schlosberg and Osgood have put forward revised lists. In the seventies, Ekman[2] identified six primary emotions, surprise, fear, disgust, anger, happiness and sadness. He suggested that these feelings are recognised by people in every culture when they are shown photos of different facial expressions. In the eighties, Plutchik[3] identified eight primary emotions six of which correspond to Ekman's list. He adds two more, acceptance and expectancy. He suggests that each of these primary emotions can be associated with a stronger and weaker companion. For example rage and annoyance would be the companions of anger. But it could have many other shades or nuances of feeling associated with it, such as antagonism, fury, hostility, scorn, impatience, defiance, sarcasm, exasperation, etc. When primary emotions are mixed, they result in predictable feelings, for example, when anger and disgust come together they express themselves in the form of contempt.

Researchers also suggest that emotions have three components, the subjective experience of happiness, sadness, etc, the physiological changes we have already averted to, and typical behaviours which are associated with the feeling such as smiling, crying, frowning, etc. Ever since the publication of Darwin's *The Expression of Emotions in Man and the Animals*, psychologists have been classifying feelings from the point of view of their evolutionary purpose.

Galin says that emotions are fine tunings, which govern and direct the way we cope with our environment. He argues that feelings like anger and anxiety direct us toward individual survival. Then there are cautionary feelings such as boredom and envy which warn us of a malfunction in our relationships. A third set of feelings like joy, love and acceptance, go beyond mere survival and respond to the meanings that sustain and enhance the lives of individuals and groups.

The A. B. C. of emotion

In recent years, a psychologist called Albert Ellis has proposed what he calls a rational-emotive theory to describe the dynamics of affectivity.[4] I find it convincing and helpful. Ellis talks about the A. B. C. of emotion. A, refers to an *Activating event*, either external (e. g. watching the news on TV) or internal (e. g. remembering a loving embrace the previous evening). Our conscious lives are made up of a succession of these kind of events. Ellis says that we experience events indirectly. We interpret them in terms of our previous knowledge, values and beliefs, conditioned as they are by our culture, personal history and experiences. In this sense, no two people ever see the world in exactly the same way. So Ellis says that our sense of outer or inner reality is mediated to us by our *Beliefs*, hence the letter B in his threefold schema. The letter C stands for the feelings that are evoked, not by reality itself, but as a *Consequence* of our unique perception of things.

We can illustrate Ellis's theory with a concrete example. We begin by looking at a simple activating event. I call to see a relative. When I sit on the sofa, the family dog sits up beside me and begins to lick my face and hands. There are a number of ways in which I can perceive this incident. I may believe that dogs are dirty and germ-ridden, that as wild animals they could bite me for no reason at all, or I might believe that, as man's best friend they are loyal and true. Beliefs like these are the product of one's conditioning and experience. Although my dad was a vet, we had neither a dog nor any other animal at home. As a result I have tended to see dogs as unpredictable, dirty creatures. That belief was reinforced when I had to get a tetanus injection as a result of being bitten on the leg by a terrier at the age of nine. So when I'm licked by my cousin's pet, I become physically tense and feel a sense of aversion, disgust and fear. These feelings are evoked, not by the dog, but by my questionable but understandable beliefs about him. For her part, my cousin believes that Toby is a wonderful pet, who can be relied upon to ward off unwelcome intruders. As a result of these beliefs, she loves and trusts her dog.

Feelings are revelatory

I believe that feelings are the fingerprints of subjectivity, at once similar to those of other people and nevertheless unique. They are the point of conscious interaction, where our capacity for inwardness and relatedness meet. They put us in touch with two realities, the perceived world of external reality, and our own inner world. The latter is conditioned by personal memories and by such things as familial, national and ecclesial influences. Our feelings appraise outward reality – this includes inward fantasies, memories and images, which are internalised forms of external things – and respond to them from two related points of view. Firstly, our feelings tell us inwardly whether the objects of our perception are agreeable or disagreeable, satisfying or dissatisfying. Secondly, at a deeper level, our feelings tell us about the value of things, the essential spiritual value of people, and qualitative values of people and things, such as beauty, goodness, truth, virtue, nobility and the like.[5] As we consciously respond at an emotional level, not only do our feelings put us in touch with external values, they reveal and actualise our inner capacity for such appreciation.

When awareness of this kind of transcendental meaning is informed by a desire to know God, it will sometimes become a religious experience. Feelings such as awe, peace and joy will be evoked, not by the immediate focus of our attention, e.g. a lovely sunset, but by the perception of a Presence that is revealed in and through created things. We will come back to this subject in section three of the book. At the moment, suffice it to say that all this will be particularly true when we move from an egocentric point of view, to see things with the kind of wonder that emanates from the self. In this way something of our self-worth or inner value is simultaneously published and made known.

Feelings are evoked, not willed

If we reflect on our own emotional responses, we will notice that our feelings are not under the direct control of the will. For example, while I do decide to pay attention to the dog on the couch, I don't decide to feel disgust and fear when he licks me. My feelings are spontaneously evoked by the perceived experience. So if I get in touch with what I feel, I can ask myself the question: What does my sense of disgust and fear tell me about my attitude to dogs? Surely, it tells me that, in spite of my notional conviction that everything God created is good, deep down I don't really believe it. In this sense feelings are revelatory, because they put one in touch with what one really perceives, believes, thinks and values, as opposed to what one imagines one perceives, believes, thinks and values. This being the case, it could be said, that feelings never lie. If there is anything 'wrong' with them, it's only because the way we look at life is defective and unrealistic.

To have a healthy affective life, therefore, we need to have a healthy outlook. So, for example, my negative feelings about dogs will only change if I first revise my prejudiced beliefs about them. Usually, this will happen when I learn to look at dogs in a new way, not from the perspective of understandable fear, but with the kind of sustained attention that is open and receptive to the manifestation of the 'truth of doginess' so to speak. If and when such a disclosure takes place, it will automatically evoke more positive feelings.

Now let's look at a concrete example which will help to illustrate the main points in the previous paragraph. Patricia was a student at a College of Art in Dublin. In her spare time she worked as a waitress in a downtown bar-cum-restauraunt. One Wednesday night, a barman drew her attention to the fact that two young women were sitting at a nearby table holding hands. Patricia replied, 'If that's their thing it's O. K. by me.' Some of the other customers commented on the women's behaviour when they started kissing one another. Patricia heard one young woman saying, 'Isn't that just sickening? ' to which her male companion replied, 'Get me another whiskey, I need it.' All the while Patricia was thinking, 'Wouldn't you think that people would be more tolerant in this day and age?' After an hour or so, the two women got up to leave. Patricia wasn't facing them at the time, but she did spot them leaving out of the corner of her eye. As one of them passed her, she gently pinched Patricia's bottom. Immediately she felt a wave of anger and rage welling up inside her. She swung around, wanting to slap the offender on the face. But she and her companion were already going through the door. Fighting back tears of frustration, she said to the barman, 'If those two ever come in here again, you had better call an ambulance, for fear of what I'll do to them.' Well, about fifteen minutes later they did return. One of them went to the bar, hit an empty glass with a coin and appealed for silence. 'We are psychology students at Trinity College,' she explained, 'we are doing a project on the nature of prejudice, and would appreciate your comments on our behaviour, when we were in here a short while ago.' Patricia felt ashamed. Like most of the other people present, she said nothing about her reactions, but she did question whether it was ethical to manipulate people's feelings like that.

However, when she got back to her flat later that night, she reflected on her experience in the bar. Very quickly she realised that her statement, 'If that's their thing its O.K. with me,' came from her head and not from her heart. It was only when she recalled her aggressive anger that she got in touch with her deep down attitudes. She hated these two young women for breaking a social taboo. For some reason or other, their behaviour had made her feel uneasy as a woman. She said what she did in order to appear more broadminded and liberal than other people in the bar. But her strong reaction revealed the truth: she was intolerant, conceited and lacking in self-awareness. She could see that her negative feelings were rooted in a sense of insecurity, a need for clearly defined codes of behaviour, and a desire to impress the barman. By reflecting on her reactions in this way, what was innermost in Patricia's heart was revealed. It was a moment of self-intimacy, one that enabled her to recognise, and perhaps to modify, some of her hitherto unconscious attitudes, beliefs and values.

EMOTIONAL SELF-AWARENESS

To grow in emotional self-awareness, five things are needed, namely: to notice, name, own, understand and express our feelings. We will look at each of these points in turn. In the bar Patricia was only aware of her anger. When she reflected on her experience some time later, she noticed that her indignation was rooted in feelings of threat, insecurity, humiliation, etc. But it's not always that easy. In the last chapter, we noted why many people neglect their feelings. Of course they react emotionally to everything they experience – that's part of being human, but they aren't always consciously aware of those reactions. Take anger for example. Patricia had no problem in sensing and expressing her ire. But unlike her, many people find it very hard to either feel or to express their indignation. There can be a number of reasons for this.

Some children grow up in homes where the father, for example, is inclined to lose his temper in an irrational and frightening way. As a result, the kids have to adopt a submissive attitude. They suppress their own negative feelings in order to appease their unpredictable father. Other children are brought up in families where any display of anger is discouraged in the belief that it is not only disruptive and antisocial, but also immoral and sinful. So they learn to suppress their anger in order to retain the affection and approval of their parents. As this kind of denial is repeated, it becomes second nature. By the time they reach adulthood, some of these people find it very hard to acknowledge any anger. They will have the emotion in their bodies, e.g. it will cause headaches and stress, without necessarily experiencing any feeling of anger. It is pushed down unceremoniously into the unconscious. From there it attacks the person. At first it may turn to feelings of anxiety and low self-esteem. If it remains unresolved for a long time, it may turn to depression.

Step one: Recovering and noticing feelings

To recover lost feelings of any kind, a number of steps can be taken. To begin with, we need quiet times on our own. An incident in the life of Jung illustrates this point. Apparently a wealthy, society lady phoned him to request an urgent consultation the following day at three in the afternoon. Jung said it wouldn't be possible because he was already committed to an important appointment at that time. Well, the next day, the lady in question happened to be sailing past Jung's garden which ran down to the shore of Lake Zurich. There was the famous doctor sitting on a small wall, his shoes and socks off, with his feet dangling idly in the water. As soon as she got home, the irate woman rang Jung to demand an explanation. 'You told me,' she exclaimed, 'that you couldn't see me because you had an important appointment. Nevertheless I saw you at that very hour, whiling away the time at the bottom of your garden.' 'I told you no lie,' Jung replied. 'I had an appointment, the most important appointment of the week, an appointment with myself.'

When we make a deliberate decision to spend time on our own in quite reflection, we will often find that we are up-tight as a result of the pace and pressure of everyday living. This kind of stress usually has a numbing effect on our feelings. Consequently, it can be helpful to spend some time doing simple relaxation exercises. Many books and tapes offer tried and tested suggestions in this regard.[6] Here are three simple exercises that I have found helpful:

1. Deep breathing

Sit or lie quietly. Close your eyes. Imagine a tranquil scene, e.g. lake water lapping with low sounds on the shore, or the gentle rustling of leaves in the trees. Breathe slowly and deeply, through your nose. Make each out-breath long and soft and steady. Sense the tension leave your body as you exhale.

2. Physical exercises

Sit or lie quietly. Close your eyes. Clench both your fists for about fifteen seconds. Then relax them and feel the tension draining away from your arms and muscles. Repeat this twice. Then hunch your shoulders for fifteen seconds, and relax, feeling the tension draining away. Repeat twice. Continue the same method with jaw-clenching and relaxing. And finally, screw your eyes up tightly and relax them, feeling the tension disappear.

3. Meditation

Sit or lie quietly. Close your eyes. Repeat over and over again a simple sound, word, or phrase, e.g. 'The peace I want is within.' Just concentrate on the repetition so that it fills your mind and banishes anxious thoughts. Let yourself relax into this steady rhythm for five to ten minutes.

Body and mind will usually become more relaxed as a result of exercises like these. Then we can tune into our physical sensations: is my mouth dry? are there butterflies in my stomach? have I dull headache? am I sweating? is there a lump in my throat? etc.7 Just as energy is stored in a battery, so my feelings are locked up in my physiology causing symptoms like these. By paying attention to them, I can dialogue with my body asking it to reveal what I am feeling. It does this via the unconscious, in the form of images. As pictures float into my mind, they may symbolise what I feel, e.g. spontaneously recalling an embarrassing incident on a TV show might be an indication that I feel guilty or ashamed about something. I have also noticed that when I find myself singing a song under my breath, the words often indicate what I feel, e.g. words from the Beatles tune, 'All the *lonely* people, where do they come from?

Another way of getting in touch with what we feel is to take our dreams seriously. So often these letters from the unconscious are neglected. In fact they are psychodramas which are symbolic representations of our deepest feelings. Usually the main feeling in the dream is one that was evoked during the previous day or two, but went unnoticed. For example, you might dream of being attacked by a man with a knife. Obviously, the principal feeling in the dream would be one of extreme fear. But the man with the knife could be a symbol of your own aggressive anger. Someone may have enraged you in the past day or two. But you suppressed your feelings of antagonism for one reason or another. The dream may be drawing your attention to the fact that you are afraid of your own anger and what it might lead you to do.

Frequently, feelings like these will also be related to emotionally charged memories from one's earlier life. The person who dreams of the man with the dagger, may have had to suppress her anger against a relative who harassed her sexually as a child. Her unresolved feelings about that situation may have merged with the fury she felt about another incident – not necessarily a sexual one – that occured recently. There are many helpful books on the subject of dreams. I will make only a few brief suggestions. Remember that everyone and everything in a dream is a symbol of some aspect of your own personality. Then ask yourself the following four questions:

1. Title: If your dream were a video, what would you call it?
2. Theme: What is the main gist of your dream? If it were a video, what would you say it was about?
3. Feeling: What is the main emotion in the dream, fear, joy, relief, guilt, love, etc. ? Obviously this is the vital question as far as this chapter is concerned.
4. Issue: What issue is the dream trying to bring to the attention of your conscious mind?

Step two: Naming feelings

Many of us tend to be emotionally illiterate, in the sense that we find it hard to distinguish one feeling from another. Many men and women when asked what they feel, will tell you what they think or believe. For example, a man is insulted at a committee meeting. The look on his face makes it clear that he feels hurt, humiliated and angry. But when a female colleague asks him afterwards, 'What did you feel when James spoke about your proposal?' he responds, 'What he said was very unfair and uncalled for.' That's a judgement, not a description of how he felt.

Other people may not go much further than saying, 'I felt good,' or 'I felt bad.' Others will be able to get the general feeling category correct, e.g. 'I felt afraid,' without being able to nuance what it was that they felt precisely, e.g. anxious, terrified, apprehensive, nervous, helpless, embarrassed, etc. It usually takes years before a person becomes adept at recognising the subtle shades that separate one subjective feeling from another.

Step three: Owning feelings

With their ability for coining new and refreshing phrases, Americans talk about owning feelings. It has two related meanings. A man could look at his fear, recognise that it is there inside him, without being in touch with it. He keeps it at arm's length, so to speak, without allowing himself to experience it directly. During a counselling session the same man might describe the fear he used to feel, when his unhappy father would shout at his mother. But he tells his story in a dispassionate way, with a smile on his face. He would begin to own his fear, if he allowed himself to feel it again, to the point that it would be manifest in his eyes, tone of voice and general body language.

Some people identify and experience their emotions, only to disown them in another way. They blame other people for the way they feel, saying things like: 'you made me angry, nervous and sad,' or, 'It's all my parents' fault; they made me insecure and resentful,' etc. To disown feelings in this way, overlooks an important principle. While other people can stimulate our feelings, the causes lie within. In an example we looked at earlier, the Trinity students in the bar stimulated Patricia's indignation, but they didn't cause it. It was due to her own attitudes and the circumstances that may have moulded them in the past. To own our feelings, means that we accept responsibility for them. They are our own feelings now. We are the only ones who can deal with them. Our ability to do so does not depend on what other people may do, or not do.

Step four: Understanding feelings

As we grow in emotional self-awareness we will begin to appreciate the fact that our affective lives are like an onion. As soon as you peel away one layer of feeling, another, more important one can be revealed. The further inwards we go, the more we will find that our feelings are tied in with images and memories from the past. In that sense our surface emotions are like a keyhole through which we catch a glimpse of our entire autobiography. An example will illustrate what I mean.

Dave meets Susan one of his closest friends. They go in to a cafe for a cup of coffee and a chat. In the course of conversation Susan begins to talk in a lighthearted way about the attention she has been receiving from a male admirer. It turns out that he is one of many colleagues in the office where she works. Although she likes this man, it is obvious that she doesn't take him seriously. Nevertheless, Dave feels distinctly uneasy and ill at ease. He doesn't say much and tries to change the subject as soon as he can. As he touches in to what he is feeling, he has to admit, that he is experiencing pangs of jealousy. He feels ashamed of feeling this way because he knows that Susan has always been a loyal friend. In any case she is entitled to be friendly with anyone she likes. Yet, Dave still feels jealous and insecure. He begins to realise that he is always a bit afraid that Susan will desert him. He recogises that this is an irrational fear, one that he has experienced many times before.

He has come to see that it has something to do with the relationship he had with his deceased mother. He always found it hard to please her and to live up to her expectations. He had been haunted by the possibility that she might withdraw her affection and approval from him as a result of some kind of failure or inadequacy. In fact she never did, but Dave knows that he tends to project this fear of being abandoned on to any woman that cares about him. As he comes to terms with this in his own heart, he resolves to trust Susan as a friend by telling her about his reaction and its inward cause.

Whenever we want to understand a feeling we can ask ourselves three important questions. What perception, belief or value evoked my feeling? What in my earlier life may have conditioned the way I perceive things? Is my way of looking at reality realistic and Christian?

Step five: Expressing feelings

We can appropriate our affective lives by expressing our feelings verbally. We will examine the dynamics and effects of this kind of self-disclosure in part two of the book. But self-awareness can also grow by means of journaling, i.e. not only recording external events in a diary, but also one's subjective reactions to them. For example, Dave could register the fact that, 'I realised that I felt jealous and insecure when Susan told me how much Des liked her. As I thought about it, I suddenly recognised that she means more to me than I had been prepared to admit. The truth is, I'm both afraid of losing her and of getting too involved! It's another case of the separation anxiety I have felt since childhood.'

As one layer of feeling is recognised and expressed in this way, another is likely to float into consciousness and so on. Not only that, previously unrecognised affective patterns can come to light as one re-reads the journal every now and then.

RELIGIOUS DESIRES

In the last chapter we noted how Jung believed that the spiritual dimension of the human psyche is an empirical fact. At its deepest level the self is oriented toward transcendence. As a psychologist, Jung couldn't go beyond the limitations of the scientific method to say whether God existed or not. What he was able to affirm, was the fact that even if God didn't exist, the psyche acts as if He does. Viktor Frankl's view was much the same. He said that what primarily motivates the human heart is a search for meaning. As a psychologist he couldn't prove the existence of God, but it was clear to him that the human will desires what he calls 'supra-meaning,' i. e. the divine. Men like Jung and Frankl have described the psycho-spiritual dynamics of the religious instinct mentioned by saints and theologians down the ages. Perhaps the most famous expression of this yearning was enunciated by St Augustine when he wrote: 'O Lord; You have created us for yourself, and our hearts are restless until they rest in Thee.' [7]

When we try to get in touch with our feelings, we'll become aware of all kinds of physical and psychological needs and desires. If we are really listening to our hearts we may become aware of yearnings which cannot be satisfied by the enjoyment of created things. They originate in the spiritual depths of the self. When they have no clear focus, we may find ourselves saying, 'I know that I need something, but I'm not sure what it is.' Occasionally we may be able to pinpoint what it is we want, e.g. 'There's a part of me,' we say, 'which will never be satisfied until it experiences the power and presence of God.' There are a number of memorable expressions of this kind of 'holy desire'. St Paul wrote: 'All I want is to know Christ and to experience his resurrection.'(Phil 3:10) These moving words found an echo in the well known prayer of St Richard of Chichester: 'Day by day, O Lord, three things I pray: To see thee more clearly, to love thee more dearly, and to follow thee more nearly, day by day.'

On one occasion Jesus declared: 'No one can come to me, unless drawn by the Father who sent me.'(Jn 5:24) So, when we tune into our transcendental desires, we are actually tuning into the activity of the Holy Spirit at work within us. No wonder the saints have stressed the importance of these God-prompted desires for God. For example, St Augustine wrote: 'The entire life of a good Christian is an exercise in Holy Desire.'[8] Believing this to be true, St Ignatius Loyola, emphasied the central importance of getting in touch with our religious desires.

In his *Spiritual Exercises*, he says that directors and directees alike should focus their attention on answering this crucial religious question: 'What do you want?' He suggested that religious desires manifest themselves in two predictable stages. In the first, people have an inner directed desire to experience the presence, love and consolations of God. In the second, people's desires move outward from their personal needs to reach a point where they say: 'Lord I want to be like you, and to want only what you want.'

In spite of the central human and spiritual significance of religious desires, many people are unaware of them. It seems to me that there are three main reasons for this. In our culture many men and women are so preoccupied with the satisfaction of their physical and emotional needs that they become deaf to the deeper things of their hearts. In other words they desire self-fulfilment rather than self-transcendence. As Jesus said, 'There are those who hear the message but the worries about this life, the love of riches, and all kinds of other desires crowd in to choke the message.'(Lk 8:14) Another reason for some people's inability to get in touch with their desire for God, is the fact that it is blocked by unresolved feelings such as guilt, resentment, anger and depression. Until they are dealt with, the deeper desires of the heart may lie buried beneath the rubble of negative emotions like these. Finally, we have already noted how many Christians live by a sense of moral obligation. When they are asked about their religious desires, they respond in terms of what they 'ought' to desire, as distinct from what they actually want. In psycho-spiritual terms, people like these are prisoners of their egos. The extent to which they lose touch with their deeper selves, is the extent to which they inevitably lose touch with the action of the Holy Spirit within their personalities. Often trials and tribulations have to challenge the preoccupations and control of the ego, before the voice of the religious self is released. That's one of the subjects we will look at in the next chapter.

Notes

1. *Feelings*, Ballentine, N.Y., 1979, 1.
2. cf. Gross, *Psychology: The Science of Mind and Behaviour*, Hodder & Stoughton, London, 1987, 430.
3. *ibid*, 430.
4. *Reason and Emotion in Psychotherapy*, Lyle & Stuart, N.Y., 1971, and *A new Guide to Rational Living,,* Prentice Hall, N.J., 1975.
5. B. Lonergan, *Method in Theology*, DLT, London, 1972, 31-32.
6. Nathan & Charlesworth, *Stress Management*, Ballentine, N.Y., 1985.
7. *Confessions*, Bk 1, 1-2.
8. 'Treatise on the 1st letter of St John', *Divine Office*, Vol 3, Readings, Friday.

CHAPTER 4

The pain of self-discovery

Suffering comes to all of us, either directly in our own personal lives, or indirectly because of the compassion we feel for suffering relatives, friends and neighbours. Down the ages the question has been asked, 'Why do human beings, especially the innocent, have to suffer so much?' Because suffering is a mystery in which we are all personally involved, rather than a problem that stands apart from us, the question about the why's and wherefore's of universal pain cannot be answered in a convincing way by either philosophy or theology. But there is another question that can be addressed, namely, 'Is there any meaning in suffering?'

In recent years Viktor Frankl, a psychiatrist who survived the horrors of Auschwitz, has thrown a great deal of light on this crucial issue. When he was facing the prospect of imminent death his comrades asked, 'Will we survive the camp? For if not, all this suffering has no meaning.' He tells us that he had a different question to ask, 'Has all this suffering, this dying around us, a meaning? For if not, then ultimately there is no meaning to survival; for a life whose meaning depends upon such a happenstance – whether one escapes or not – ultimately would not be worth living at all.'[1]

In this chapter I want to suggest that instead of making people bitter, suffering can make them better, if they use it as a means of growing in self-awareness and Christian virtue. As Jung has so rightly observed: 'There is no growth in consciousness without pain.'[2]

TO LIVE IS TO CHANGE

The Greeks and Romans looked at history as a cyclical phenomenon where everyday changes were viewed against the unchanging background of being. Modern thought looks at history as a dynamic, unrepeatable process of becoming, where change is viewed from an evolutionary perspective. It sees the whole of nature as being in a state of permanent flux. The earth spins on its axis while orbiting the sun, which is but one of a thousand million stars within our galaxy, which is itself moving through the impenetrable reaches of outer space. On earth the seasons change, the winds blow, the rains fall, the rivers run, the tides ebb and flow. Our bodies too are part of this process of becoming. In the space of every seven years or so, all the cells within us are replaced! We also undergo psychological and spiritual transformations, especially during times of crisis. They are *the* turning points for better or for worse, for growth or decline, in our lives. While they can be looked at from many points of view, we will focus our attention on the way in which they can help a person to grow in self-intimacy.

Life: A series of stages

The great writers like Dante and Shakespeare have been aware that our lives unfold through a series of stages. In recent years developmental psychologists have confirmed the accuracy of this artistic intuition. Jung suggested that life was divided into two periods. He pointed out that in the first half, up to the age of about forty, most people, males especially, are concerned with the development of their egos and getting established in life. Not surprisingly, their characteristic attitude tends to be extroverted. In the second half of life the same people will be more inclined to pay attention to the reality and promptings of their inner selves. He maintained that adults move from one stage to another by means of a mid-life crisis, when their egos have to endure a time of painful disillusionment, as a prelude to the emergence of their true selves.

Since then, other researchers have produced more elaborate typologies which look at human development from different but overlapping points of view.[3] Jean Piaget, a Swiss psychologist, has studied cognitive development.[4] He has shown how, in the first fifteen years of a person's life, one evolves through a sequence of four successive stages. Erik Erickson has outlined an eight stage profile of psycho-social development. He has suggested that each one is characterised by a specific developmental task. In early childhood, for example, a baby has to learn to either trust or mistrust its parents and other significant people who take care of it. In adult life men and women face three main tasks, the ability to be loving, caring and wise. We will look at these in further detail in section two.

More recently, Daniel Levinson has published an influential book which has shown how men develop through a series of six life stages.[5] He plans to publish a sequel on the distinctive characteristics of female development. For his part, Lawrence Kohlberg has indicated that people's ability to make moral decisions, develops through a sucession of six possible stages, each one more sophisticated than the one that preceded it.[6] Carol Gilligan has modified his findings to take account of the unique aspects of women's experience.[7] More recently, James Fowler has focused his attention on the act of faith, as distinct from its content, whether secular or religious.[8] He has indicated that people's ability to invest trust in centres of power and meaning beyond themselves, such as a political ideology, evolves through a series of six stages. They bear a striking similarity to those mentioned by Kohlberg.

While one could quibble with some of the perspectives and findings of these researchers, all of them are agreed that people move from one developmental stage to another, by means of crises. These are the privileged but painful moments of 'breakdown' which lead to developmental breakthroughs. Typically, people face a dilemma of some kind, either cognitive, psychosocial, moral or religious which can neither be understood or surmounted in terms of their current way of looking at themselves or reality. As a result they may go through a sort of painful conversion experience when they let go of cherished outlooks in order to embrace new ones. Without exception, advances from one developmental stage to another involve a more subtle and comprehensive understanding of the external world on the one hand, and deeper forms of self-awareness on the other.

A Biblical perspective

These findings of modern psychology confirm the teaching of the scripture. In the Old Testament, the psalmist prays, 'Search me, O God, and know my heart; test me and know my thoughts.'(Ps 139:23) We find, over and over again, that this prayer is answered when the people are purified by means of painful events. In Deut 8:2-3, we are told why the chosen people had to endure forty years in the wilderness: 'The Lord has led you ... in the wilderness, in order to humble you, testing you to know what was in your heart ... he humbled you by letting you experience hunger.' The same dynamic of purification by means of trials and tribulations is evident in the lives of individuals mentioned in the prophetic books, e.g. Jonah's sojourn in the belly of the whale, (Jon 2:1-10); the depression and suicidal feelings experienced by Elijah after his triumphant encounter with the prophets of Baal, (1 Kgs 19:1-21); and the ordeal of the three young men in the fiery furnace. (Dan 3:1-30)

In the New Testament we are told that suffering can school a person in virtue. For example, speaking of the events of holy week, Heb 5:7-8 says: 'In the days of his flesh, Jesus offered up prayers and supplications, with loud cries and tears, to the one who was able to save him from death, and he was heard because of his reverent submission. Although he was a Son, he learned obedience through the things he suffered.' In 2 Cor 11:24-32 St Paul talks about the many trials and tribulations he had to endure in the course of his ministry. In 2 Cor 12:10 he testifies: 'I am content with weaknesses, insults, hardship, persecutions, and calamities for the sake of Christ; for whenever I am weak, then I am strong.' In Rom 5:3-5 he tells us: 'Suffering produces endurance, and endurance produces character, and character produces hope.' Implicit in what the New Testament teaches is the belief that suffering is revelatory in two senses. Firstly, it enables us to see what is in our own hearts and, secondly, it opens us up, at the same time, to the presence and the power of God.

A theological perspective

Not surprisingly, the saints have always stressed the importance of self-knowledge. St Teresa of Avila wrote: 'No matter how exalted the soul may be, nothing is more necessary than self-knowledge ... Without it everything goes wrong ... Knowing ourselves is something so important that I wouldn't want any relaxation in this regard, however high you may have climbed the heavens ... Let's strive to make more progress in self-knowledge.'[9] Spiritual writers have suggested that once people embark on the Christian journey they can expect to pass through three main stages, the purgative, the illuminative and the unitive. [10]

As the word itself suggests, the purpose of the purgative stage is to purify the person's moral, religious, affective and intellectual life. Spiritual purgation is usually the outcome of two elements. Firstly, by means of acts of self-denial, e.g. fasting, people try with the help of God's grace, to overcome their sinful tendencies. Secondly, there is another form which results from the purifying effects of suffering and temptation. They enable people to experience a deeper form of dependence on God. As a result they grow in self-awareness, by coming to recognise their pride, secret idolatries, and worldly motivations and attitudes. As Margery Kempe wrote in the fifteenth century: 'Unless you have been tested by various temptations ... you can never obtain from God spiritual self-knowledge, let alone the ability to advise others.'[11]

St Ignatius of Loyola has shown how times of purgation are often associated with desolation of soul, or spiritual depression. It is experienced when the Lord withdraws his consolations. 'Desolation is the contrary to consolation,' wrote Ignatius in his *Autograph Directories,* 'contrary to peace there is conflict; contrary to joy, sadness; contrary to hope of higher things, hope in base things; contrary to heavenly love, earthly love; contrary to tears, dryness; contrary to elevation of mind, wandering of mind to contemptible things.'

In his *Spiritual Exercises,* Ignatius says that there are three forms of desolation. Although they are similar from an experiential point of view, the context and purpose of each of them is different. When people are beginners in the Christian life, they often compromise with sin and grow lax in things such as prayer, self-denial and reception of the sacraments. As a result the Lord withdraws his consolations and allows them to experience desolation of spirit. Just as the prodigal son came to his senses during a time of desolation, so the Lord hopes that people will face the fact that they have become lukewarm and so decide to return wholeheartedly to him.

When Christians are truly dedicated, they are often motivated by an unconscious desire for the consolations of God, rather than by an unconditional commitment to the God of all consolations. The Lord can purify the motivation of good people like these by withdrawing his consolations from them. He wants them to recognise whether they will remain faithful to things like prayer and spiritual reading, when they get nothing out of them from an emotional point of view. God will also allow them to experience all kinds of temptation in order to test the sincerity of their commitment. When such people fall as a result of weakness and spiritual immaturity, they learn a good deal about their true selves. They also learn, at an experiential level, about their need for the mercy, love and power of God.

The third form of desolation is what has been called 'the dark night of the soul'. In cases like these God withdraws his consolations from his faithful disciples in order to teach them how everything they are, and do, depends on the grace of God. Ignatius has written: 'God wishes to give us a true knowledge and understanding of ourselves so that we may have an intimate perception of the fact that it is not within our power to acquire and attain great devotions, intense love, tears, or any other spiritual consolation; but that all this is a gift and grace of God our Lord. God does not wish us to build on the property of another, to rise up in spirit in a certain pride and vainglory and attribute to ourselves the devotion and other effects of spiritual consolation.'[12] St Anthony of the Desert insisted that the only way that a person could grow in discernment of spirits was to undergo the kinds of spiritual experiences we have been describing. Like many another saint, he believed that they led simultaneously, to both a deeper knowledge of self and an awareness of the Lord, in whom 'we live and move and have our being.' (Acts 17:28)

CRISES AND GROWTH

Research has shown that their are two main kinds of crisis, predictable and unpredictable. We have already noted how psychologists maintain that predictable crises precede the main developmental phases in our lives, e.g. at the onset of early, middle and late adulthood. Daniel Levinson says that, typically, these transitions occur between the ages of 17 and 22, 40 and 45, and 60 and

65 approximately.[13] He also indicates that we can expect lesser transitions between the ages of 28 and 33, and again between 50 and 55 approximately. Unstable periods like these are sandwiched between the different stages in our lives. They are nature's way of urging us to grow to a new depth of maturity by facing developmental tasks appropriate to our chronological age. The so-called 'mid-life crisis' prepares people to enter middle adulthood in a number of ways. It helps them to face the fact that death is drawing nearer. It also leads to an inner willingness to forego unrealistic roles and ambitions in order to care for others in a nurturing way.

Unpredictable crises occur when the 'slings and arrows of outrageous fortune' come our way. We can suffer directly ourselves as a result of things like breast cancer, a heart attack, the loss of a job, etc. Or we can suffer indirectly when misfortunes like these afflict someone close to us. As life would have it, a predictable crisis often occurs at the same time as one or two unpredictable ones. They have a discernable structure. Their onset is associated with a sense of restlessness. The whole experience then consolidates into a long-drawn-out period of darkness and exploration. Inevitably it comes to an end, when the main issues are resolved to a greater or lesser extent. Then, once again, the person settles down to a life of relative stability. We will examine the way in which self-awareness can grow during these times of difficulty by looking at the early life of St Vincent de Paul in particular.

Vincent de Paul's transitional crisis

At the age of nineteen Vincent managed to get himself ordained in 1600 by a blind bishop.[14] Sometime later another bishop offered him a parish but there were legal problems, so he continued to live as before. He ran a small school and continued to study at the university. It was a time when, in typical male fashion, he seemed to rely on his own considerable talents to achieve success. His earnings increased, his debts grew less, and he got his degree in theology in 1604. We don't know what the priesthood meant to him. In all probability he was a good-living man who was devoted to the Lord and his Church. But we can infer from two incidents that he was probably living from his ego, identifying with the role of the priesthood, and carrying out its principal requirements in a dutiful way that lacked any depth of inner conviction. He was probably motivated by good intentions at a conscious level, while being unaware of his unconscious desire for riches, reputation, and self-sufficiency.

Early in 1605 he headed off to Bordeaux on a secret mission. It is remotely possible that he had been offered a bishopric. What we do know for certain is the fact that he thought that the visit promised to be of great advantage to him. When he returned from the South some time later, Vincent found that he had been left a bequest in a woman's will. However, there was a complication. The only way he could get the 400 crowns he had inherited, was to go to Marseilles to force a man to pay a debt he owed to the deceased. In order to finance this trip, Vincent had to borrow heavily himself. He hired a horse and set off. The future apostle of charity showed little compassion when he made contact with the man he referred to as 'a scamp'. He had him thrown in jail until he would agree to pay up. Meantime Vincent sold the hired horse. It was a bit like selling a rented car! We can see from these incidents that Vincent was a talented and well qualified priest, who despite his good points, was far from being a saint. He had shown how he could act in a callous and unscruplous way, if it served his desire for financial and ecclesiastical advancement.

Stage one: Onset and restlessness

In July 1605, Vincent embarked on another journey, part of which involved a sea voyage. He was catapulted into an unscheduled crisis when he was captured by pirates. Sometime later, he was sold as a slave in North Africa. We don't know how he reacted to this traumatic event. But it must have been a terrible shock to have his life disrupted in this frightening way. With the onset of a transitional crisis people feel that they are losing control over their lives. Confidence gives way to insecurity, idealism to disillusionment, and a sense of connection to a feeling of alienation and stress. Vincent must have felt like this. Suddenly and unexpectedly he had to come to terms with an unfamiliar country, culture, religion and language. Instead of having a position of authority in society, he was a nobody and a slave. He didn't know a soul. He was separated from his family, friends and neighbours. It must have been a very lonely experience indeed. Not surprisingly, he tells us that he used to identify with Ps 137, which says: 'By the waters of Babylon, there we sat down and there we wept when we remembered Zion (France) ... there our captors asked us for songs ... But how could we sing the Lord's song in a foreign land?' At first, he must have dreamed of escaping or being redeemed by the French government. But it didn't happen. He was well and truly trapped in this no-man's land.

Stage two: Darkness and exploration

And so his time of darkness and exploration began. It was to last for about three years. We don't know a great deal about his captivity. He said that he had three owners.[15] It has often struck me that in one way or another, each one seemed to symbolise an aspect of Vincent's shadow self. His first master was a man of the sea, 'I was sold to a fisherman,' he tells us. But the ordained fisher of men goes on to admit in ironic fashion, 'I have always been a very bad sailor; so he was obliged to get rid of me.' His second owner was an alchemist, a man who was engaged in the Faustian effort to turn base metals into gold. He seemed to represent Vincent's pride, his tendency to achieve worldly goals by his own unaided efforts. Finally, he was sold to an ex-priest who had fled to North Africia, and who had married three wives. The apostate priest seemed to be an image of Vincent's inward alienation from the spiritual significance of his calling and possibly the weakness of his commitment to celibacy.

The dynamics of worldliness

While these reflections are speculative, we have a good idea of what usually happens during times of transition. In Jer 17:9-10 we read, 'The heart is deceitful above all things and desperately corrupt, who can understand it? I the Lord search the mind and try the heart.' We have already noted how he can do this during times of crisis by withdrawing his consolations and allowing us to endure all kinds of trials and temptations. In this way he fosters the kind of mature disillusionment which helps ego-centric people to come to a conscious recognition of the unconscious nature of their worldiness and sinfulness. In his *Spiritual Exercises*, St Ignatius says that the evil spirit tries to separate people from their true selves in God, by prompting three forms of worldly desire. Firstly, he inspires them to desire riches. As Karl Rahner has pointed out,[16] this desire refers to created things that promise fulfilment such as money, a relationship, knowledge, success, qualifications, etc. Although these things are good in themselves, people may unwittingly, identify with one or more of them as having *absolute* value. There is reason to believe that Vincent de Paul had fallen prey to such an idolatrous desire for financial advancement.

The second stage in this dynamic is reached when possessing the things they desired, people find themselves seeking status and a good reputation. At an unconscious level they may be obsessed by a desire for the approval and esteem of others and a deepseated fear of losing them. A number of spiritual writers have stressed the fact that worldly attitudes are betrayed by their compulsive nature. Echoing a point made previously by Thomas Merton, Henri Nouwen has written, 'Compulsive is the best adjective for the false self. It points to the need for on-going and increased affirmation. Who am I? I am the one who is liked, praised, admired, despised ... what matters is how I am perceived by the world. If being busy is a good thing, I must be busy. If having money is a sign of real freedom, then I must claim more money. If knowing people proves my importance, I will have to make the necessary contacts. The compulsion manifests itself in a lurking fear of failing and the steady urge to prevent this by gathering more of the same.'[17] There is evidence to show that as a young man Vincent de Paul had been motivated by a worldly desire for advancement and approval. For example, when one of his relatives visited him, Vincent was so ashamed of his peasant dress and the fact that he walked with a limp that he brought him up the back stairs lest he be seen by his colleagues.

The third and final phase of this dynamic of worldiness leads to a subtle perversion of values. There is an unhealthy preoccupation with the external world and a growing insensitivity to deeper feelings, intuitions, promptings and the guidance of the Spirit. At best, people like this, out of touch with their deeper selves and God, are insensitive to the action of grace. At worst they tend to re-write the commandments to suit themselves. They rationalise their reasons for doing so, e.g. extreme nationalists trying to justify their prejudices and resentments, and unscrupulous business men trying to explain away their shady practices in the name of economic expediency. We have seen evidence of this kind of spiritual pride in the actions of St Vincent.

Mature disillusionment

During the long drawn out, middle phase of a transitional crisis, The Lord will often allow events to remove one or more of the things which have been sustaining the worldly ego. Instead of enjoying success, status and self-sufficiency, a person may have to drink the bitter wine of deprivation, failure, loss and humiliation. As the scaffolding that once supported the false self is removed, painful feelings of disorientation, insecurity, and fear begin to surface. For a time the ego fights a rear guard action, by clinging to the things that it so desperately needs. Meantime, a great deal of energy is wasted in trying to suppress negative feelings of deep-seated anxiety. As a consequence, the person suffers from a good deal of stress, and sometimes from ego-exhaustion and burn-out.

Transitional crises are often associated with spiritual desolation. Ironically, God seems to do his disappearing act just when most needed. We lose our appetite for spiritual things. At best we go through the motions where religious practices like prayer and worship are concerned; at worst they are dropped altogether, because they bring no consolation whatsoever. Instead, one is buffeted by temptations. Quite often they will be sexual in nature. The hope of erotic excitement promises to counteract the devitalising effects of on-going feelings of insecurity and depression. However, if the person engages in erotic acts or fantasies that offend against conscience, temporary relief can be followed by an anxiety, that is reinforced by guilt. Indeed this negative dynamic can be involved in any selfish or immoral forms of escapism, whether they are sexual or not.

I said earlier that the Lord allows us to experience desolation, temptations and even sin, for a purpose. That purpose becomes apparent when we take our feelings seriously. During the dark days of a transitional crisis most of them will be negative. As a result, it's hard to pay attention to them. But when we admit our anger in particular, a number of things can happen. We begin by getting in touch with the inward sense of loss and hurt that has caused it. When we ask ourselves the question, 'what is it that I'm missing so much?' we begin to see that it is things like success, status, possessions, reputation, disordered relationships, independence, self-sufficiency and the like. Up to now we may have laboured under the sincere illusion that the Lord was number one in our lives. But our anger can tell a different story. The truth is, we may have allowed created things to assume an absolute value in our lives. Perhaps we have substituted a desire for worldly fulfilment for a transcendental desire for God. Once we recognise this kind of self-denial and idolatry, and recall the weaknesses that were revealed during times of temptation, we can suffer from a strong sense of guilt.

The beginning of a new beginning

To come to terms with our negative feelings and their causes, can be a very humbling experience. As we get in touch with our inner brokenness we may discover the 'potency of disorder.' When we pour out our feelings in prayer, we begin to get in touch with a deep-down yearning for a new sense of God, self and values. Usually the Lord's response is delayed. But if ours is truly a 'holy desire,' instead of withering it will grow stronger and deeper through denial. Eventually *chronos*, i.e. secular unredeemed time, gives way to *kairos*, i.e. the sacred, redeemed time, when the Lord reveals himself and his will to the heart. For example, during a period of difficulty he could lead us to a text like Is 41:10: 'Fear not I am with you, be not dismayed, for I am your God, I will strengthen you, I will help you, I will uphold you with my victorious right hand.' Any experience like this is comforting in the sense that it gives the person the courage and energy to battle on. Consolation comes later.

It says in the Apostles Creed that, after his saving death on the cross, Jesus descended into hell, i.e. the place of the living dead, who exist in a twilight world of desolation where they are cut off from God. That's an image of the purified soul as it nears the end of a transitional crisis. One way or another the Lord reveals his presence and his love to the person. In the words of 1 Pet 3:19, Jesus, 'goes and makes a proclamation to the spirits in prison, who in former times did not obey.'

This kind of religious experience can have the effect of refocusing the personality. From a psychological point of view, egocentricity begins to yield to the voice of the self. From a religious perspective the personality begins to move away from secular preoccupations and values, to become more centred on Christ and his Gospel. In this way the words of St Paul are fulfilled: 'You must give up your old way of life, you must put aside your old self, which gets corrupted by following illusory desires. Your mind must be renewed by a spiritual revolution so that you can put on the new self that has been created in God's way.' (Eph 4:22-23)

Stage three: Resolution and restabilisation

We can only presume that Vincent de Paul experienced this purifying dynamic during the time of his captivity. His religious faith so impressed one of the wives of the ex-priest, that she persuaded him to repent of his apostasy. Eventually, both he and his slave escaped to Europe in a small boat.

Vincent was a changed man. Instead of desiring honours and riches he was content with humiliations and poverty. Two incidents bear witness to his transformation. The first concerns the way he handled a threat to his good name. He was sharing an apartment with a judge at the time. One day while he was sick in bed, a thief made off with the judge's money. Vincent describes what happened next. 'A member of the community was once accused of having robbed his companion, and that before the house where he was staying. The charge was not true. Finding himself falsely accused, although he never meant to justify himself, the thought neverthless occurred to him, "See here; you are going to justify yourself, are you not? You are being falsely accused you know!" "Oh no," he said, as he lifted his mind to God, "it is necessary that I suffer this patiently."'[18] What a change! At the age of twenty-four Vincent demanded his rights; now he was willing to renounce them even if it meant the loss of his good name.

His attitude to money had also changed. In 1611 he received a gift of 15,000 *livres* from John Latanne, master of the Paris Mint. He immediately gave it to the Charity Hospital, as he said, 'to tend and nurse the sick poor.' Gone was his earlier preoccupation with cash. In its place there was evidence of a growing sensitivity to the needs of the poor. Nevertheless, he resisted an inclination to devote his life to caring for them. He was still attached to his own ambitions. In 1610 he had written to his mother: 'I put great hope in God's grace, that he will bless my efforts, and soon give me the means of an honourable retirement so that I may spend the rest of my days near you.'[19] Retirement at the age of twenty-nine! Vincent still had mixed desires. His purification was not yet complete.

The dark night of the soul

The year 1610 inaugurated yet another transitional crisis. Vincent knew a priest theologian who was experiencing terrible temptations against faith. He was so deeply moved by the man's ordeal that the Holy Spirit prompted him to take the unusual step of offering himself to God as a substitute. He asked the Lord to restore the theologian's peace of mind while allowing him, like a scapegoat, to assume his terrible interior struggle. His prayer was answered. The afflicted priest was restored to consolation, and died a happy death soon afterwards. For his part, Vincent entered a period of desolation which was to last nearly four years. Later he was to say, 'God, often wishes to establish, upon the patience of those who undertake them, the good works that are to endure, and for that reason he allows such people to suffer many trials.' [20]

Whereas he had suffered from either of the first two kinds of desolation mentioned by St Ignatius when he was in North Africa, he endured the dark night of the soul on this occasion. During his time of interior suffering, Vincent learned to recognise and to renounce the last vestiges of his egocentric pride. Finally, in virtual desperation, he promised the Lord that he would devote the rest of his life to serving the poor. As soon as he did this, his desolation disappeared and his consolation was restored. Vincent's transformation was complete. In his youth he had tried to escape from the implications of material and spiritual poverty as from an enemy. But, as a result of two transitional crises between the ages of twenty-four and thirty-three, he learned to love his enemy, as Jesus had taught. (cf. Lk 6:27) By recognising and loving Christ in the poor of his day, Vincent was able to recognise and love Jesus in the depths of his own interior poverty and *vice versa*.

O happy fault

On two occasions St Paul tells us to thank God in all circumstances, good and bad alike. In 1 Thess 5:18 he writes: 'Pray constantly and for all things give thanks to the Lord,' and again in Eph 5:19 he writes: 'Always give thanks for everything, to God the Father.' Obviously we should thank God for the good things in our lives, but why should we thank him for the bad things like pain, suffering, desolation of spirit, temptation, and even for our sins of weakness and malice? We do so, because bitter experience has taught us that the Lord can bring good out of the negative circumstances of our lives.

In this chapter we have seen how affliction has the ability to purify the personality. It can shatter our egocentric illusions, reveal our worldly values and preoccupations, put us in touch with our shadow selves, the subject of the next chapter, and uncover our deep seated need to experience transcendent meaning. In this way suffering has a unique ability to foster both self-intimacy and intimacy with the Lord of merciful love.

So we can thank God in all circumstances, and rejoice in our sufferings (cf. Rom 5:3), because, where suffering and sin abounded, now the grace of God more abounds. (cf. Rom 5:20) Hence the notion of the *felix culpa*. It comes from the Easter liturgy where, despite its disastrous consequences, the sin of Adam and Eve is referred to as a 'happy fault.' And why is this the case? Because it 'gained for us such a great redeemer!' St Paul echoed this insight when he wrote: 'By turning everything to their good, God co-operates with those who love him.' (Rom 8:28)

Notes
1. *Man's Search for Meaning*, Pocket Books, N.Y., 1963, 183.
2. *Contributions to Analytical Psychology*, 1928, 193.
3. cf. Fowler, *Becoming Adult, Becoming Christian: Adult Development & Christian Faith*, Harper & Row, San Francisco, 1984, 20-30.
4. cf. K Lovell, *Educational Psychology and Children*, University of London Press, London, 1971, 108-115.
5. *The Seasons of a Man's Life*, Ballentine, N.Y., 1978.
6   cf. Power & Kohlberg, 'Religion, Morality, and Ego Development' in *Toward Moral and Religious Maturity*, Silver Burdett, N.J. 1980, 344-372.
7. *In a Different Voice: Psychological Theory and Women's Development*, Harvard University Press, Cambridge, 1982.
8. *Stages of Faith: The Psychology of Human Development and the Quest for Meaning*, Harper & Row, San Francisco, 1981.
9. *Interior Castle*, 1, chap. 2, Nos 8, 9.
10. cf, B. J. Groeschel, *Spiritual Passages:The Psychology of Spiritual Development*, Crossroads, N.Y., 1986, 101-189.
11. Quotation taken from *New Crossroads Review*, re: The Cell of Self-Knowledge: Seven Early English Mystical Treatises, Crossroads, N.Y., 1981.
12. *Spiritual Exercises*, [322].
13. *Op. cit.*, 57.
14. P. Coste, *The Life & Works of St Vincent de Paul*, Vol 1, New City Press, N.Y., 1987, 1-72.
15. J. Calvet, *St Vincent de Paul*, Burns Oates, London, 1952, 22-27.
16. *Meditations on Priestly Life*, Sheed & Ward, London, 1973, 175-177.
17. *The Way of the Heart: Desert Spirituality and Contemporary Ministry*, DLT, London, 1981, 22-23.
18. Coste, *Collected Works*, XI, 337.
19. Coste, *The Life and Works of St Vincent de Paul*, *op. cit.*, 44-45.
20. Coste, *Collected Works*, IV, 289.

CHAPTER 5

Me and my shadow

For years British author Robert Louis Stevenson looked for a story that would convey his 'strong sense of men's double being'. Eventually the plot of Dr Jekyll and Mr Hyde was revealed to him in a dream. In 1885 his chilling novel was published in the U.S. It examined the mystery of evil by exploring a man's schizophrenic identity, one half good, the other evil. It was a brilliant illustration of the adage that at the heart of the human problem, is the problem of the human heart.

At the conscious level of the ego, many of us try, like Dr Jekyll to have a good self-image. It is based on our ability to conform to the expectations of our society, family, church, etc. We have already seen how we tend to repress any inner feeling, desire or awareness that might threaten or undermine our arbitary sense of identity. We can do this by equating our sense of self with an aggregation of different roles. For example, a woman could lose touch with her real identity by seeing herself merely as a daughter, wife, mother, school teacher, Catholic, etc. We 'Hyde' behind roles like these rather than face the truth about ourselves. In his book, *Modern Man in Search of a Soul*, Carl Jung wrote these relevant words: 'The acceptance of self is the essence of the human problem and the epitome of a whole outlook on life. That I feed the hungry, that I forgive an insult, that I love an enemy in the name of Christ – all these are undoubtedly great virtues. What I do unto the least of my brethren, that I do unto Christ. But what if I should discover that the least amongst them all, the poorest of all the beggars, the most impudent of all the offenders, the very enemy himself – that these are within me, and that I myself am the enemy who must be loved – what then? Neurosis,' he concludes, 'is the state of being at war with oneself.'[1]

The civil war with the heart is a 'diabolical' one from a psychological, as distinct from a religious point of view. In Greek *dia-bollein* from which our English word is derived, literally means to become inwardly alienated or 'torn apart'. So when a person lacking self-acceptance is the victim of alienation and irrational inner conflicts, it is a diabolical experience from an emotional point of view. This is particularly true when passions such as rage, resentment or lust, threaten to take possesion of the person.

From a spiritual perspective, people like this, lacking inner peace, are more susceptible to temptation. The devil can exploit their vulnerability to lead them into sin. When they indulge their negative impulses and desires they can suffer from a sense of failure, anxiety and morbid guilt. Then Satan – his name means 'the accuser' – exploits this awareness of inner weakness. He can fill the person with a deep down feeling of self-condemnation. This only goes to intensify the civil war of the heart, by widening and deepening the split between what is acceptable and unacceptable within.

JUNG ON THE SHADOW

Jung called the dark, feared and unwanted side of the human personality, the shadow. He wrote: 'Unfortunately there can be no doubt that man is, on the whole, less than he imagines himself or wants to be. Everyone carries a shadow. The less it is embodied in the individual's conscious life, the blacker and denser it is.'[2] In 1945 he gave his most succinct description of this elusive concept: 'The shadow is the thing a person has no wish to be.'[3] It can be noted in passing that Freud's notion of the 'id' is similar. It can be thought of as the primitive, unconscious part of the personality, the storehouse of the fundamental drives. It operates in an irrational way seeking selfish gratification regardless of any moral code. For example, the incest taboo is normally a powerful antidote to sexual attraction between parents and children, brothers and sisters. But the possibility of such attraction is part of the 'id'. It can manifest itself in consciousness in the form of erotic dreams or daytime fantasies about members of the family. So the 'id' or the shadow personality can be thought of as the unlived life.

One image of the shadow is that of the retarded relative. Years ago families who were ashamed of a mentally handicapped son or daughter might occasionally lock the unfortunate child in a back room, out of sight. While this inhuman practice seems to be a thing of the past, we still do it to ourselves. Whenever the darker, weaker side of our nature, with its primitive urges and feelings, threatens our ego ideal, i.e. the way we like to think of ourselves at a conscious level, we reject it. It is buried in the wells of the unconscious. From there it can poison consciousness with negative moods, attitudes and urges.

Jung believed that, just as an individual can have a personal shadow, so a society can have a collective one. For example, before the Second World War, the people of Germany, like those of most nations, had an idealised image of themselves. They sincerely believed that they were civilised, and progressive. They had espoused values such as liberty, equality and democracy. But just as an individual may be 'less than he imagines or wants to be,' so too with a nation or a group of any kind. It will carry a shadow, and the less the shadow is acknowledged at a conscious level, the more dangerous and sinister it will be. One has only to recall the rise of Hitler and the Nazi party to see how the shadow can burst through the veneer of civilisation, in a nightmarish splurge of violence, murder and destruction. So perhaps Jesus was implicitly referring to the shadow side of the human psyche when he said: 'Evil words come from an evil heart, and defile the one who says them, for from the heart come evil thoughts, murder, adultery, fornication, theft, lying and slander.' (Mt 15:19)

Projection

People and societies who are out of touch with their shadows, suffer from what psychologists call, 'pseudo-innocence'. Because of a lack of self-awareness, they think they are better than they really are. When inner darkness remains unacknowledged, it exercises a malevolent influence on conscious attitudes and feelings. The principal way in which this occurs, is by projection. Just as photographic slides can be projected on to a screen, so a person can project the contents of his or her shadow on to someone else. It could be a member of the family, a colleague, or a stranger. As a result, one sees and condemns in the person who carries the shadow, the very weaknesses and tendencies one fails to acknowledge or accept in oneself.

This dynamic explains a lot of conflict, in marriage, family life and the workplace. For example, a mother may be troubled by the fact that she is harder on one of her children than she is on the others. Even her husband comments on it, while encouraging her to be more even-handed. But while the mother may feel guilty, she will be unable to change her behaviour until she accepts the weakness that she is projecting on to her daughter. She may dislike the way in which her child draws attention to herself by histrionic bouts of bad temper, while failing to see that she uses her own recurring migraines to serve the same emotional purpose. So despite the fact that most people desire to relate in a reasonable way, the shadow can break through in irrational outbursts of moodiness, bad temper and verbal abuse. Sadly, as we know, this kind of thing can lead to emotional hurt and even physical violence.

Social groups can project the contents of their collective shadow on to some minority in their midst. For example, the Nazis believed in Aryan superiority, so they made the Jews the carriers of their collective shadow. Hitler once said, 'The Jews eat like poisonous abscesses into the nation... We will not pause until the last trace of this poison is removed from the body of our people.'[4] Tragically, the gas chambers were the logical outcome of this kind of warped outlook. In the United States the shadow seems to be carried principally by the blacks. In the Republic of Ireland the travelling people are the carriers of our unconscious sense of inferiority. Not surprisingly, therefore, we force them to live as outcasts at the edge of our towns. We treat then as badly as we treat the darker side of our own natures.

The troubles in Northern Ireland can also be understood in terms of projection. The Unionist majority consciously sees itself as superior because of its Britishness and freedom from papal authority. However at the unconscious level of the shadow, many Unionists may feel a secret sense of inferiority, on account of being a misunderstood and much criticised minority both within the context of the United Kingdom and the island of Ireland. As a result, they can project the contents of their collective shadow on to the Nationalist community. This is borne out by the fact that when some Unionists travel through a Fenian housing estate they refer to it as a 'black area,' implying that the people who live there are anonymous sub-humans. Is it any surprise that they can sometimes go on to treat them as second class citizens when it comes to the allocation of jobs and housing?

For their part, northern Nationalists are part of a majority on the island of Ireland. At a conscious level, they tend to see themselves as superior to the Unionist 'planters'. They belong to the largest Christian denomination and have a distinctive Celtic culture of their own. But as a minority within Northern Ireland, they can suffer from unconscious feelings of inferiority. This is the almost inevitable outcome of hundreds of years of colonial history. As a result, Nationalists can project their collective shadow on to their Unionist neighbours in an unreasonable way. Ironically, when some of them travel through Orange estates, they too can refer to them as 'black'!

It is easy to mistrust and even to hate those who carry the collective shadow. The warlike activities of the IRA and the UVF alike are an extreme expression of this kind of prejudice. Jung was correct, when he wrote in 1928: 'The psychology of war is a matter of unconscious projection. Everything our own nation does is good, everything which the other nation does is wicked. The centre of all that is mean and vile is always to be found several miles behind the enemy's lines.'

RECOGNISING THE SHADOW

Jesus once said: 'Why do you observe the splinter in your brother's eye and never notice the great log in your own? And how dare you say to your brother, "Let me take that splinter out of your eye," when, look, there is a great log in your own? Hypocrite! Take the log out of your own eye first, and then you will see clearly enough to take the splinter out of your brother's eye.' (Mt 7:1-4) One of the ways of putting this teaching into practice, is to come to terms with the personal and collective shadow. It is not easy. We tend to resist any kind of self-awareness that might evoke a sense of guilt, undermine our idealistic self-image, or call for painful change. Jung wrote: 'The shadow is a moral problem that challenges the whole ego-personality, for no one can become conscious of the shadow without considerable moral effort. To become conscious of it involves recognising the dark aspect of the personality as present and real. This act is the essential condition for self-knowledge, and it therefore as a rule meets with considerable resistance.'

While a person can come to terms with his or her shadow at any age, it is more likely to happen from mid-life onwards. Before the age of forty, many people seem to be preoccupied with the demands of life and getting established in society. In doing so, they develop the more extroverted side of their personalities while neglecting many aspects of their inner experience, as we have seen. But from middle age, i.e. from thirty-five onwards, many people are willing to embark on a journey inwards. At this point we will look at some of the ways in which this might be done.

The shadow is revealed in dreams

It is hard to get in touch with the shadow because it is part of the unknown self. But, as I said in the context of self-intimacy, when the rational mind is off guard during sleep, and our psychological defences are down, the contents of the unconscious, can be manifested in dreams. Occasionally these night-time videos of the mind will be about the shadow side of our personalities. It will be symbolised by a figure of the same sex as ourselves whom we fear, dislike or react to as an inferior person. Sometimes the carrier of the shadow will be someone we know in real life. Other times it will be a stranger. For example, I once dreamt that after midnight I returned to the college where I was living. It was dark and frosty. As I came up the drive, I noticed a beggar, dressed in rags. He was stretched out on a bench, fast asleep. The sight of him filled me with pity. 'All the priests and students are warm and comfortable in their beds,' I thought to myself, 'and here is this poor man, literally left out in the cold.' Suddenly, I felt angry, and thought to myself, 'I must bring him inside and give him a bed for the night.' Then it occurred to me that some of my fellow priests might be displeased to discover what I'd done without consulting them. A feeling of determination welled up inside me. 'No matter what they say, I'm bringing the stranger inside, I'll defend my desision in the morning.'

Jung described the dream as the theatre of the mind,

'where the dreamer is at once scene, actor, prompter, stage manager, author, audience and critic.'[5] So everyone and everything in the dream is a personification of conflicting aspects of the personality. The beggar in rags seemed to represent my shadow self. He was a failure, inept, irresponsible, weak and a social misfit. How could anyone love a man like that? To my surprise, I realised that I loved him. I wanted to bring him in from the cold to share my accommodation. The college would represent my personality. So symbolically, my dream might have been the expression of a deep seated desire both to acknowledge, accept and integrate my shadow self into conscious awareness, no matter what other people might think. In other words, the dream seemed to be inviting me to forego hypocrisy, the tendency to hide my real self behind socially acceptable masks and roles.

Other people can recognise one's shadow

A second way of coming to terms with the shadow is to rely on the help of others. As one Shakespearian character so rightly observes: 'Since you cannot see yourself so well as by reflection, I your glass (mirror) will modestly discover to yourself that of yourself which you know not of.'[6] There is a good example of this in the Old Testament. King David was consumed with sexual desire for Bathsheba, a married woman. So he arranged to have her husband exposed to mortal danger during a battle. It was a successful ploy because Uriah was killed. Sometime later, following his marriage and the birth of a son, David was skilfully confronted by Nathan. The prophet began by appealing to his conscious ideal of justice. Perhaps he suspected that a more direct approach might evoke a defensive, unreceptive response from the king. So he told him a powerful story about a rich man who had exploited a poor farmer in an outrageous way. Unaware of his shadow, David reacted instantly and passionately. He 'flew into a great rage with the man.''As Yahweh lives,' he said to Nathan, 'the man who did this deserved to die.' This encounter reached its high point when Nathan said bluntly and directly to David, 'You are that man!' The scales of blindness fell from the king's eyes. He recognised the awful truth about himself, and humbly declared, 'I have sinned against Yahweh.' (2 Sam 12:1-12)

We do well to listen to people who know us well and

have our best interests at heart, such as friends, colleagues and relatives. They are often aware of our blind spots and will try to alert us to the truth about ourselves. If we immediately begin to justify ourselves in an agitated, bad tempered way, it is usually a sign that we are anxiously resisting any encounter with our personal shadow. It is a good thing, therefore, to reflect later on such an incident in a less threatening atmosphere. As we acknowledge our deeper feelings, we can ask ourselves questions like these: 'Why did I react so negatively? Where was my fear and resistance coming from? What is it about myself that I am afraid to face? Why?' If we stay with questions like these, we may get behind our defence mechanisms to become inwardly aware of the shadow self. By and large such efforts achieve only limited success. We are too biased in our own favour and see only the things we want to see. That's why the assistance of a counsellor, therapist or director can be very helpful. Professionals like these are trained to recognise our evasions and have the skill to reveal and out-maneuvre them in a painful but liberating way.

Other ways of recognising the shadow

Psychology draws attention to further ways in which the shadow self can be manifested. It may be detected in Freudian slips of the tongue, e.g. a priest saying to a lay person, 'I joined the cemetery (seminary) when I was eighteen years of age.' Similar mistakes can be made in the course of writing. We also tend to forget names and appointments. It could be that we don't want to remember them because of things like unconscious anger, fear or resentment.

The shadow may be apparent in our fantasies and day dreams, especially when they are concerned with sex, money or power. So, although we condemn the activities of criminals, we are often fascinated by these men and women who embody the shadow in their lives. Nowadays the imagination can also find a focus for its hidden contents in the form of 'trashy novels', the 'gutter press' and all kinds of videos which depict the darker side of the unconscious. They can emphasise things like extreme violence and uninhibited lust. Often these kinds of fantasy offend against social convention and a conscious sense of right or wrong. As a result, many people suppress morbid interests like these.

Recognising this, good comedians and satirists tap into other people's personal and collective shadows. They tread the delicate dividing line between what is acceptable and unacceptable in polite society. They crack jokes about things like death, religion and bodily functions, often in an irreverent, vulgar way. Jung said, by way of explanation, it is the shadow that laughs. This being so, humour serves an important social and therapeutic function. Not only does it release some of the repressed energy of the shadow, it gives people a chance to recognise something of their unacknowledged selves.

We have already seen how we tend to project the contents of our shadow on to individuals and groups. This point was made in a charming Irish folktale about a jealous wife. There was once a village where no one had ever seen a mirror. Then a farmer found one as he ploughed his field. When he cleaned it, he was amazed to see his late father looking at him. When he told his wife about his discovery she asked for a look. Her reaction was quite different. 'Who is this ugly old shrew?' she exclaimed, 'Have you betrayed me for another woman?' A terrible argument followed. They decided to go together to the local parish priest. Each of them told their story and handed the mirror to their pastor. He took one look and said, 'What on earth have you been fighting about? This is a picture of my saintly predecessor, Fr Murphy. Leave his portrait with me and go home in peace.'

The woman's reaction in this story illustrates the fact that the shadow personifies itself. So when we take a particularly strong and unreasonable aversion to someone, we can suspect that we are disliking a projected aspect of our shadow. These kinds of prejudice can be given free reign when we are watching TV. We can say what we like about the characters on the screen because they cannot hear us, e.g. 'I can't bear that politician. He's a smug, self-satisfied hypocrite.' Other times we will switch channels because a particular comedian or interviewer annoys us so much. We can reflect on intolerant reactions like these by asking ourselves, 'What is it that I so dislike in that person or group?

82

What do my emotional reactions such as anger, disgust or boredom, tell me about my perceptions, and attitudes?' We may well discover that they tell us more about ourselves than they do about the people we criticise.

Psychological tests and the shadow

In recent years many people have used the *Enneagram Personality Typology* [7] in order to grow in self-knowledge. It combines ancient Sufi wisdom with the insights of modern psychology and suggests that there are nine personality types. Besides their respective strengths, each one is characterised by a distinctive ego-preoccupation and an unconscious obsession. The ones are perfectionists; they like to think of themselves as right and good most of the time and are unconsciously motivated by a desire to suppress their anger. The twos are the givers, at the conscious level they want to be helpful to as many people as possible, at an unconscious level they are motivated by a desire to avoid their own sense of need. The threes are the performers, consciously motivated by a desire to be efficient and successful, while at an unconscious level they are obsessed by a fear of failure. The fours are the tragic romantics. Consciously they are motivated by a desire to be thought of as refined, sensitive and a cut above the ordinary. At an unconscious level they are preoccupied by a fear of a humdrum life style, similar to that of other people. The fives are the observers of life. At a conscious level they like to think of themselves as being wise and perceptive. At and unconscious level they are afraid of a nagging inner sense of emptiness. The sixes like the role of devil's advocate. Consciously they espouse the worthwhileness of faithfulness, and loyalty, while at an unconscious level they are afraid of non-conformity, or deviance from accepted norms. The sevens are hedonists who look at the bright side of things and are unconsciously motivated by a fear of pain. The eights are leaders, they like to be seen as powerful, effective people who get things done. At an unconscious level they avoid a sense of weakness, vulnerability and tenderness. Lastly, the nines are the mediators, who like to create the impression that they are laid back and settled. At an unconscious level they are motivated by a fear of conflict and a desire for peace at any price. The obsessions associated with each personality type are part of the person's shadow. However, by answering an elaborate questionnaire, people can come to recognise at a conscious level, what their principal blind spot might be. As a result, they will be able to curb its worst excesses. If they are aware of the personality types of the people they live and work with, they are more likely to be understanding and tolerant of their weaknesses and foibles.

In chapter two, I mentioned how the Myers Briggs personality indicator described sixteen personality types. Each of them has an opposite. So, for example a man is married to a woman who represents his shadow self. His basic attitude could be that of an extrovert, i.e. someone who is energised by means of interaction with the world of people and things. His wife, on the other hand, is an introvert, someone who gets her energy by relating to her own inner world of ideas and concepts. His basic mode of perception is intuitive, a propensity to see the possibilities and potentials implicit in any situation. For her part, his wife is a sensing type, she perceives things in a more literal, factual, down to earth way. The husband's primary way of dealing with his perceptions is that of thinking, i.e. arranging the data of his experience in an objective way according to a logical pattern. On the other hand, his wife is a feeling type, who is interested in putting the data of her experience into a pattern that is governed by her subjective values and her relationships to others. The extent to which this couple get to know, understand and appreciate one another's distinctive approaches to life, is the extent to which they will get in touch with the potentials which lie in a relatively underdeveloped state, on the shadow side of their personalities. These potentials can come to fruition as a result of being consciously appropriated during times of quiet reflection.

BEFRIENDING THE SHADOW

So far we have examined how to recognise the negative aspects of the shadow. We can befriend it in two ways, which we will examine in greater detail later: Firstly, we can reveal the darker side of our nature to a trusted friend or confidant. Secondly, we can tell the Lord about these things in prayer. As we find that we are understood and loved as we are, and not as we have pretended to be, we can begin to understand and to love ourselves in the same way. Through the grace of God, experienced in this manner, the dividing wall of division between the acceptable and unacceptable, the conscious ego and the unconscious self is breached. (cf. Eph 2:14) Having learned to love the beggar, the offender and the enemy within, we learn to love them in the community also. As this healing process takes place, we begin to withdraw our negative projections from other people and groups. In this way the causes of a lot of misunderstanding and conflict are overcome. They give way to mercy, compassion and a spirit of reconciliation. So, the extent to which we are unaware of our shadow, is the extent to which it will exert an unconscious and negative influence on our perceptions and choices. Conversely, the extent to which we acknowledge and befriend our shadow, is the extent to which we are free to make choices in the light of our conscious values and beliefs. Jung believed that, when this was done, the shadow turned out to be ninety per cent gold, by providing the personality with awareness and energy which enable a person to be more alive, realistic and compassionate.

Conclusion

As we come to the end of this chapter, we are in a position to make some observations which will enable us to conclude section one of the book, and to introduce section two. We live in the *culture of experience*. What kind of experience that will be, depends on the degree of *inwardness* and *relatedness* we can attain. We have noted that there is an important paradox involved here. Our capacity for inwardness, i.e. self-intimacy, is activated by relatedness, i.e. intimate contact with the external world of people and things and *vice versa*. Through the congruence of these intimacies, in a transcendental desire for ultimate meaning, we can experience an interior sense of relationship with God. But the quality of our relationship with the created world and its Creator, is determined by the degree of self-intimacy we have achieved. The extent to which we remain captives of our egos, is the extent to which we will be prisoners of 'I-ness' and therefore of alienation, from our real selves, the world of nature, people, and ultimately from God. This can lead to disastrous results for the individual

85

and the culture. However the converse is also true. The extent to which the ego opens up to the reality of the self, in the ways we have described, is the extent to which a person will get in touch with his or her capacity for 'we-ness' and therefore a sense of intimate connection with created reality and ultimately the Reality of God. As that sense of relationship increases, so one's potential for inwardness is deepened and activated. In this way a redemptive and healing dynamic, of a reciprocal and mutually enriching nature, is energised by the Spirit at work within the self and its intimate contact with the external world.

Notes

1. *Modern Man in Search of a Soul,* Harcourt Brace Jovanovich Inc., N.Y., 1943, 234.
2. *CW* 11, par. 131.
3. *CW* 16, par. 470.
4. R. Wait, *The Psychopathetic God: Adolf Hitler,* Mentor, N.Y., 1977, 439.
5. *CW* 8, par. 58.
6. *Julius Caesar,* Act 1, Sc 2.
7. cf. Riso, *Personality Types,* The Aquarian Press, 1988, and Palmer, *The Enneagram,* Harper & Row, N.Y., 1988.

interpersonal intimacy

'The tendency today to talk not about God,
but about one's neighbour,
to preach not about the love of God,
but about the love of neighbour,
and to use not the term "God",
but "world" and responsibility for the world
– we can see that this tendency
has an absolutely solid foundation.'

(Karl Rahner, *Foundations of Christian Faith*, p. 64)

CHAPTER 6

The intimate connection

We concentrated on the experience of *inwardness* in the first five chapters. Now we will move on to the notion of *relatedness* which finds its highest expression in interpersonal intimacy. We can begin by situating our reflections within a wider cultural and historical perspective. While I'm aware that the following observations will be extremely selective and impressionistic, nevertheless I hope that they will be helpful.

From the Greeks onwards, there seem to have been two complementary ways of looking at the material world. One was static in nature and stressed the primacy of *being*. Parmenides and Aristotle advocated this point of view. The other was dynamic in nature and stressed the primacy of *becoming*. Heraclitus was the outstanding advocate of this perspective. It tended to see everything that existed as interconnected parts of an integrated world which was governed by God-given affinities. The Pythagoreans talked of 'The harmony of the spheres,' and the Hippocratics maintained that, 'there is one common flow, one common breathing, all things are in sympathy.'

These two points of view remained in tandem in Christian Europe within the context of the medieval synthesis of philosophy, science and theology. Surely they found their most moving and poetic expression in the life of St Francis of Assisi who reverenced creation by acknowledging his kinship with animate and inanimate things, e.g. by referring to 'brother sun and sister moon,' etc. As late as 1550 AD, Pico della Mirandola could write, 'Firstly there is the unity in things whereby each thing is at one with itself, consists of itself, and coheres with itself. Secondly, there is the unity whereby one creature is united with others and all parts of the world constitute one world.'[1] This quotation holds together the notion of inwardness and relatedness. Every creature asserts its own separate identity, and transcends itself by means of its integrative tendencies.

The unitary notion of the world was shattered by the rise

of modern science. It began with the approach adopted by Galileo. He focussed on the nature of the world, from an atomistic point of view. He said that science should study the essential properties of material things such as shapes, numbers and movement, in an objective, dispassionate way. Some time later, science came of age with Newton's discovery of the universal law of gravity. From the seventeenth century onwards, scientists saw the world as a huge mechanical system, like a clock, operating according to exact mathematical laws. The notion that the world is one, was destroyed by this scientific revolution and later by the Enlightenment. The sense of a divine purpose, permeating and guiding all things to their proper fulfilment, was lost. This was particularly true of Darwin's theory of evolution. It replaced a static view of the world with a dynamic one. In doing so, it forced scientists to abandon the Newtonian idea that the world, like a machine, came ready-made from the hands of the Creator.

However, Darwin maintained that instead of adapting to their environments, as Lamarck had suggested, the different species were the product of random mutations and blind chance. Jacques Monod, a modern biologist, has given clear expression to this nihilistic point of view: 'Chance alone is at the source of every innovation, of all creation in the biosphere. Pure chance, absolutely free but blind, lies at the root of the stupendous edifice of evolution.'[2] As a result of abandoning a holistic view of nature, scientific reductionism has denied the 'sympathy of all things'.

As the scientific method and its conclusions have permeated modern culture, they have tended to alienate men and women from the natural world and from one another. As the intimate connection has withered in Western countries, people's will to meaning has, in many cases, been frustrated. So instead of seeing the world in kinship terms like St Francis, a contemporary writer like Sartre has said that 'hell is other people' and that the absurdity of nature nauseated him. Not surprisingly, spirituality and religion have declined within this cultural environment.

INTIMATE CONNECTIONS IN THE NEW PHYSICS

Although most people don't realise it, many contemporary physicists have abandoned this distorted, scientific world-view. They favour a more holistic perspective, one that rehabilitates the notion of inter-connectedness and the affinities which relate everything that exists to the whole of creation. In the wake of Einstein's theory of relativity, early in the twentieth century, quantum theorists, notably Heisenberg, studied the nature and activity of subatomic particles. As far as I can see, they discovered four things that are well worth mentioning.

Firstly, electrons, protons and neutrons are nothing like the solid objects postulated by classical physics. As one professor has written: 'An elementary particle is not an independently existing un-analysable entity. It is in essence, *a set of relationships* (my italics) that reach outward to other things.' 3

Secondly, classical laws of causality do not apply at the sub-atomic level. Solid objects dissolve into wave-like patterns of probabilities. These patterns, which can be mathematically expressed, do not describe the probabilities of *things*, but rather probabilities of interconnections. Neils Bohr has written, 'Isolated material particles are abstractions, their properties being definable and observable only through their interaction with other systems.'4

Thirdly, many physicists believe that quantum theory rehabilitates the unitary world view. It had predicted that particles could respond to one another at a distance without being influenced by classical causality. In other words, there would have to be some unity in creation which could account for Hippocratic affinities like these. On February twentieth, 1983, the science section of *The Sunday Times* reported that experimental verification of this prediction had taken place. Commenting on the implications of this momentous breakthrough, David Bohm has written: 'It may seem that everything in the universe is in a kind of total rapport, so that whatever happens is related to everything else.' 5

Fourthly, in classical Newtonian physics, the subject, i.e. a scientist, observes the objective world in a completely detached way. With the advent of quantum physics this approach is changing. As Fritjof Capra has written: 'The crucial feature of quantum theory is that the observer is not only necessary to observe the properties of an atomic phenomenon, but is necessary even to bring about those properties. My conscious decision about how to observe, say an electron, will determine the electron's properties to some extent.'[6] In other words, instead of seeing the world as a problem to be observed, modern physics is more inclined to see it as an indivisible mystery, one in which the scientist is intimately involved.

Some implications of the new science

These momentous changes in the scientific community have enormous implications. They haven't yet had much impact at the level of popular culture. It will take another fifty years or so for that to happen. But what is clear is that a new cultural paradigm is about to emerge, one that will be much more sympathetic to the religious outlook. Modern physics has exposed the limitations of a soul-destroying, mechanistic world view. It is replacing it with an organic, ecological perspective which seems to have an affinity with the views of mysticism, which stresses inwardness and transcendental relatedness. As the scientific materialism of the last two or three centuries gives way to this holistic perspective, attention will shift to the importance of interconnections which are governed by a universal blueprint and purpose. In other words, intimacy of ever-increasing degrees of intensity, is a characteristic of the relationships that should pervade the whole of creation, from the realm of sub-atomic particles to the experience of genuine human love.

Human beings the ambassadors of creation

Ironically, while the non-human world manages to maintain levels of physical relatedness, and in the case of animals conscious relatedness, proportionate to their levels of inwardness, humans often fail to do so. Instead of becoming the bearers of nature's capacity to attain greater levels of intimacy, creation is often frustrated because of human alienation. Instead of helping the natural world to reach its fulfilment through them, people often attack and destroy it. As a result it can kick back in the form of things like the greenhouse effect.

At this point I'd like to state a number of personal convictions which inform my Christian outlook. I believe that God is Love. Specifically, I believe that God is a trinity of persons, The Father loving his divine Son, and *vice versa*. The Spirit that searches their inner depths, reveals those depths to one another and is equal to them in divinity. *The Spirit, then, is the intimacy of God.* Because God created the world, I believe that everything that exists bears the imprint of God's loving nature in two senses. Proportionate to its level of being/becoming, everything that exists finds its immediate fulfilment through relationship. Not only is there affinity and interconnection between everything that exists, there is also a blueprint implicit in the whole of creation. Natural laws, whether those described by Newton, Einstein or Heisenberg, are the expression of that plan. Like the banks of a river, they guide the development and evolution of everything that exists in the way that is appropriate to its status in creation. Like the genes and chromosomes that guide the development of the entire body and its individual organs, the blueprint of creation governs the unfolding of its God-given potential and purpose. While implicit in the rest of nature, it can become conscious and explicit in human beings. We carry the baton of possibility on behalf of the natural world in which we are immersed. The propensity of all things to seek for mutual interconnection and transcendental connection with God, reaches its highest form of intensity in the human soul, which animates the human personality.

Extrasensory perception and mysticism

The body of a man or woman is rooted in the rest of the material world. So the world can articulate itself through the body. Jung has suggested that our physical nature can articulate itself through the unconscious mind. This notion would help to explain what is sometimes called 'the sixth sense,' i.e. an ability to acquire knowledge about a person or an event without the use of the ordinary means of perception. It seems to imply some kind of underlying unity in creation, whereby particular items of information can occasionally be deciphered by people with the right kind of psychic sensitivity. Psychologists refer to it as clairvoyance, ascetical theology talks of infused knowledge[7] and Hinduism refers to subtle consciousness.[8] Writing about this faculty, Alexis Carrel, a Nobel winner for medicine, has observed: 'Clairvoyance is exceptional. It develops in only a small number of human beings. But many possess it in a rudimentary state. They use it without effort and in a spontaneous fashion. Clairvoyance appears quite commonplace to those having it. It brings them a knowledge that is more certain than that gained through the sense organs. The clairvoyant does not observe. He does not think. He knows.'[9]

Jung believed that experiences of clairvoyance could only be accounted for if one abandoned the classical laws of causality in favour of an 'acausal connecting principle.' The world is like a giant telephone exchange, whereby everybody and everything is linked via its overall unity. By means of their intuitive powers, clairvoyants are sometimes enabled to have intimations about reality which seem to transcend the usual limitations of time and space. Just as such a unity has to be invoked to explain the acausal behaviour of particles that act in tandem at a distance in quantum physics, the same sort of phenomenon may be involved in the spiritual workings of the human mind.

It seems to me that it is this overall unity which is sensed by the mystics. For example, in his well-known study, Bucke referred to it as 'cosmic consciousness,'[10] Jaspers referred to it as 'the Comprehensive,'[11] and Fowler as 'Universalising Faith.'[12] Priest scientist, Teilhard de Chardin, wrote: 'The mystic only gradually becomes aware of the faculty he has been given of perceiving the infinite fringe of reality surrounding the totality of all created things, with more intensity than the precise, individual core of their being.'[13] No less a person than Einstein bore witness to this intuitive rapport with the unity of all things, when he wrote, 'The most beautiful and most profound emotion we can experience is the sensation of the mystical. It is the sower of all true science. He to whom this emotion is a stranger, who can no longer wonder and stand wrapt in awe, is as good as dead. To know that which is impenetrable to us really exists, manifesting itself as the highest wisdom and most radiant beauty which our dull faculties can comprehend only in their most primitive form – this knowledge, this feeling, is at the centre of true religiousness.' [14]

Reflections like these about the nature of extrasensory perception, and what Jung called 'synchronicity,'[15] are tentative. Suffice it to say, that like mysticism, they could have found no place in classical physics, but they can be accomodated within the new scientific paradigm which is emerging.

What we can say with greater certainty is that the self,

with its capacity for intimacy with the realities of this world and with the mystery of God, is obviously a focal point for God's presence to the world, and *vice versa*. Jung believed that the capacities of the self included, among other things, the collective unconscious which related us to the collective memory of the human race, and the God-archetype which enables us to relate, by means of the God-image, to the Divine. While some psychologists would question whether Jung was correct about these two concepts, it seems to me that the general gist of his thinking is accurate.

The results of either lacking or experiencing intimacy

The extent to which the conscious ego ignores the true self, is the extent to which it becomes incapable of the intimacies we have mentioned. At best it settles for closeness, at worst it can become the anxious victim of estrangement and what Mother Teresa calls, in a graphic phrase, 'the famine of love.' The unhealthy ego, starved of intimacy, may manifest itself in the following neuroses and personaltiy disorders: hysterically, e.g. 'I need to be loved'; compulsively, e.g. 'I have to do it'; dependently, e.g. 'I need to be taken care of'; obsessively, e.g. 'I'll think of something else'; or psychopathetically, e.g. 'I'll neither think nor feel.'

The extent to which we consciously recognise and realise the potential of the self for intimacy with nature, other people, and, through them, with God, is the extent to which creation, through us, grows to fulfilment. This would tie in with what we said, near the end of chapter one, about the relationship that exists between the activity of the Holy Spirit, both in creation and in the human personality. This notion seems to be implicit in the words of St Paul in Rom 8:22-26: 'We know that the whole creation has been groaning in labour pains until now; and not only the creation, but we ourselves, who have the first fruits, groan inwardly while we wait for adoption, the redemption of our bodies. For in hope we were saved. Now hope that is seen is not hope. For who hopes for what is seen? But if we hope for what we do not see, we wait for it with patience.'

ASPECTS OF INTERPERSONAL INTIMACY

Before going any further, we can clarify and refine what the word *intimacy* connotes. We have already noted that, in a dictionary sense, it means, 'to publish or make known that which is inmost.' I have been suggesting that everything that exists in the natural world is bound to everything else by what we have called an intimate connection. While everything that exists in the non-human world enjoys a degree of inwardness proportionate to its material complexity, that inwardness is not expressed in subjectivity or self-awareness. As a result, we can only speak analogously of a latent capacity for intimate relationship in the non-human world, because things like rocks and plants are incapable of revealing that which is inmost in their identities to one another. But in a holistic view of creation, men and women are an integral part of the non-human realm of nature.

As people capable of self-awareness, humans can reveal their inner selves to one another. In moments of revelation, even that which is innermost in nature can be revealed to those people who know how to attend to it with a contemplative attitude. In that sense, the inwardness of animate and inanimate forms of non-human reality can enjoy a sort of unilateral intimacy with human beings. In that way, their inward natures come to conscious awareness, in and through men and women. Through this kind of intimate knowing, people not only come to understand something of the mystery of the world in which they themselves participate, they simultaneously grow in self-intimacy. The degree to which the created world is opened to the same intimacy, albeit indirectly and unknowingly, is the degree to which it reaches its fulfilment. Understood in this sense, I believe that intimacy has a healing and redemptive power that ushers in the new heaven and the new earth mentioned in Rev 21:1.

THE NATURE AND DYNAMICS OF INTERPERSONAL INTIMACY

We will look at some of the ways in which a person can establish an intimate relationship with nature in the third part of this book. But in the next few chapters we will focus exclusively on the nature and dynamics of intimacy between people.

Developmental psychology on intimacy

We begin with Erik Erickson's 'life stages' approach to psychology. It was mentioned briefly in chapter four. Having developed a sense of personal identity in adolescence, Erickson maintains that a young adult, between the ages of twenty and forty, is ready to engage in the risky business of relating deeply with another human being/s. Young adults feel a spontaneous inner prompting which urges them to develop intimate relationships. Erickson uses the word 'intimacy' in a technical and restricted sense of his own, to refer to people's ability to *commit* themselves to on-going relationships and partnerships. Strengths of character have to be developed in order to sustain such commitments, especially when they require sacrifices and compromises. He says that a prime example of the kind of intimacy he has in mind would be the full genital union of a man and woman, within the context of mutual commitment. However, he is at pains to point out that intimacy doesn't require sexual expression. It can be present in a closely-knit religious community, in friendships, in the comradeship of soldiers during a war, and in numinous moments of contemplative intuition. Erickson believes that intimacies like these enable people to develop what he calls the ego-strength, and the virtue of love.

Erickson's psychology suggests that, for one reason or another, such as a lack of trust or low self-esteem, a person may be either unable or unwilling to develop bonds of intimacy in early adulthood. He or she can avoid this developmental task in three different ways. Instead of getting close to people, a person could lead a rather private, withdrawn kind of life, where a lot of time is devoted to solitary pursuits such as reading or walking. Another way of avoiding intimacy is to cultivate a lot of superficial relationships and inconsequential chat. Such a person may be friendly with lots of people while being friends with no one. A third way of avoiding any depth of contact is to become sexually permissive. In this form of pseudo-intimacy, the emphasis is placed on romantic infatuation and sexual contact, without any committed giving of oneself to the other person. As soon as the relationship begins to become threatening or demanding, the person abandons it in favour of a new erotic liaison.

Erickson says that a lack of intimacy inevitably leads to a sense of isolation. Even married people can suffer from this kind of loneliness, if their fear and insecurity prevent them giving themselves fully to their partners. He also believes that this sad inability to love could lead to the kind of self-absorption and excessive self-reference that reverses the sentiments in the prayer of St Francis. As a result, when they reach middle and perhaps late adulthood, people like this are in a poor position to face the twin developmental challenges of becoming *caring* and *wise*. However, Erickson does offer a word of encouragement. Even when people fail to develop real intimacies in their early adulthood, they can do so, albeit belatedly, later in their lives.

Five degrees of intimacy

Priest-psychologist, Henri Nouwen, has indicated[16] that there are five degrees or circles of intimacy. They move from the outer circles, where intimacy is weak, to the inner ones, where it is stronger. *Acquaintances* are situated on the outermost circle. They are people we know in a superficial way. We may have the habit, for example, of going daily to the local newsagent to get the paper. While in the shop, we talk to the proprietor about the weather, the political situation, and the like. There is familiarity, yes, but without any depth of communication. Next on the list are our *colleagues*. These are the people we work with. When I was a teacher, I was one of a staff of twenty-five men and women. Some of us were quite friendly – we tended to have our meals together and to sit and chat with one another in the staffroom. We would discuss how pupils were getting on and other impersonal things like sport, union business, holidays, etc. Then there are our *relatives*, grandparents, uncles and aunts, cousins and assorted in-laws. Although we may only meet occasionally, at funerals, weddings and christenings, we actually know a lot about one another. Often this information is confidential, known by family members and relatives, but not by the general public. For example, we know that uncle Tom was involved in a shady business deal that nearly landed him in court, and that cousin Maura had a brief but passionate affair with a married man. The next circle of intimacy involves our *family and friends*. These are the people we spend a great deal of time with. They know us well and we talk to them about a lot of things. There is affection, mutual support and a great deal of trust. Nouwen believes that this is as far as most people are prepared to go as far as intimacy is concerned. Finally, the innermost circle includes *intimate* friends. A person is lucky to have two or three of them in a lifetime.

How do we distinguish one degree of intimacy from another? By the degree of self-disclosure involved, replies Nouwen. Intimate friendship is different from friendship because those involved are willing to tell the whole uncensored truth about themselves, their experiences, memories, feelings, desires, etc.

Intimacy as self-disclosure

Like Nouwen, many writers equate intimacy with self-disclosure. It seems to me that in some instances self-disclosure may have very little to do with intimacy. For one thing, the motive for sharing is important. When I was younger and greener, I used to tell one of my friends a lot about myself. Although I was slow to admit it, I had an ulterior motive in doing so. I had an idealised notion of friendship which said that friends *should* share openly and fully with one another. So I'd try to share my thoughts and feelings in order to get my friend to do the same. Not surprisingly, she was slow to respond because, in actual fact, she felt she was being 'got at' in a manipulative sort of way. Sharing of this kind isn't true intimacy. Over the years I have also noticed that some people are only too ready to pour out their story to any person who is willing to listen. They are motivated, not by a desire to communicate with another human being, but rather by a need to experience a sort of therapeutic release. I know that this kind of ventilation of problems and painful memories, can help troubled people to find some relief, but normally it doesn't bring them deeper insight or healing, and it isn't a form of intimacy.

In the course of counselling people, I have noticed something else about self-disclosure. Despite the fact that I might be in good spirits myself, an hour of listening can sometimes leave me drained of energy. On other occasions, the reverse is true. Even though the counselee may talk about difficult and emotionally demanding issues, I can feel energised by the experience. I have come to recognise the reason for the difference. If a person lacking self-intimacy, shares from the ego, he or she remains a prisoner of 'I-ness', taking rather than giving, and so the listener's energy is drained. But if the same person shares from the self, the ensuing sense of 'we-ness' enables the speaker to give, as well as to receive, thereby energising the self of the person who listens. Communication is intimate, therefore, when it is *self*-disclosure as distinct from *ego*-disclosure.

Closeness and intimacy contrasted

A distinction that is often overlooked is the difference between *closeness* and *intimacy*. It can be illustrated by looking at different kinds of marriage relationship. During the first half of this century, the emphasis was on authority, specifically the authority of clearly delineated roles, rather then on a mutual sharing of personal experience. Although the husband was usually the patriarchal head of the house, both he and his wife were expected to conform to the higher authority of the social and religious expectations of the day. She would be the homemaker, he would provide for it. She would bear the children and raise them, he would support and discipline them. She would subordinate her life to his, and make every effort she could to further his career. He would take this for granted and hardly notice the sacrifices she had made. He would try to achieve status and success outside the home; she would try to do so vicariously through her children.

Couples like this were often very close, in the sense that they felt affection, tenderness and love for one another. They would recognise their respective virtues, foibles, blind spots, strengths and weaknesses. But not infrequently there was very little depth of personal sharing. This was particularly true when husbands were a good deal older than their wives. Not surprisingly, if he was in his forties and she in her early twenties, they might have very little in common. She would have had the freshness, enthusiasm and energy of a young woman on the threshold of life, while he would have moved on to face the more disillusioning issues of middle age. But in a way, the communications gap didn't matter all that much. Regardless of any age difference, many, if not most, marriages were formal roles rather than deeply personal relationships. Conformity to the duties of their state gave husband and wife a sense of security, status and standing in the community. If the wife felt lonely, she could usually talk to a female friend or a member of the extended family. If he needed company, he could meet his male friends in the pub or go to a sporting event. So in spite of their emotional closeness, many of these couples were in many ways intimate strangers, sharing their lives and their beds but not their hearts.

Research has shown that the emotional repression involved in some of these kinds of marriages could have a particularly negative emotional effect on women. As a result, they sometimes reacted by becoming depressed or moody or inclined to nag a lot at home. I need hardly mention that, in spite of the more formal and dutiful attitudes of a bygone era, many couples did enjoy real intimacy within the context of a traditional marriage. We will look at the possibility of loving communication without a great deal of verbal self-disclosure in chapter eight.

Modern marriages

While many role-marriages still exist today, they are becoming the exception as a result of the enormous changes that have affected family life in recent years. The centre of gravity is shifting, as we noted earlier, from the expectations associated with authoritative marital roles, to the experience of satisfying psycho-sexual marital relationships. Many factors have contributed to this change.

In the first chapter we noted the reasons for the growth of the women's movement. Nowadays, wives and mothers are well educated, they go out to work and have incomes of their own. Now that they are no longer economically dependent on their husbands, women expect to be treated as equals by their spouses. They see marriage in terms of partnership, where the traditional roles are abandoned in favour of shared decision-making, housework, child-rearing, etc. As the extended family gives way to the nuclear model, couples have only their own relationship to depend on for emotional satisfaction. Not only that, because they are living much longer than their forebearers, they can look forward to many years together after the children have left home. In circumstances like these, the quality of their relationship becomes very important.

I suspect that a new type of closeness is emerging within modern marriages. The notion of love by implication, which was a characteristic of many marriages in the past, is being replaced by a lot of *ego*-disclosure. An increasing number of couples can talk a lot to one another about their thoughts, emotions, experiences, needs and desires. They try to tune in to one another's conscious awareness. But they do so in such a way that awareness of the other doesn't, at the same time, bring about an increase in self-awareness, i.e. being in touch with one's real self, which is the characteristic of genuine intimacy.

The effects of close and intimate relationships

Two American psychiatrists, Tom and Pat Malone, maintain that this distinction between closeness and intimacy is rarely understood. They believe that most of the available 'how to' books, which deal with relationships and communication, foster an ego-centred closeness rather than intimacy. 'The essence of intimacy,' they write, 'is feeling closer to myself while I am in relationship to something other than me. I can more easily experience this with a flower, a river, music, or a poem, than I can with a person ... *intimate knowledge is knowledge of connection.*'(My italics)[17] In another place they explain: 'When I am close, I know you; when I am intimate, I know myself. When I am close, I know you in your presence; when I am intimate, I know myself in your presence. Intimacy is a remarkable experience.'[18] They go on to argue persuasively that without closeness, stability is impossible - it affirms and sustains a relationship. But only intimacy can change such a relationship and foster the personal growth of those involved in it. Needless to say, a good relationship, marital or otherwise, includes a mixture of closeness and intimacy. But if the oxygen of true intimacy is lacking, the sense of closeness will, in time, become stale and boring. Perhaps that is one of the reasons why so many apparently 'good marriages' eventually break down and finally split up.

Infatuation and intimacy

Another pointer about what intimacy is not: it cannot be equated with the experience of infatuation or falling in love. By and large, such experiences serve a useful purpose in so far as they can inaugurate an emotional awakening, increase mutual trust and foster a sense of closeness. But they tend to be unrealistic and less altruistic than they appear.

After its birth, a child has no separate sense of identity. It sees itself as an extension of the mother, with whom it totally identifies and upon whom it totally depends for the satisfaction of all its physical and emotional needs. It begins its life with a sort of Garden of Eden experience, where it enjoys the bliss of perfect union with a loving human being. But after a while, the child is banished from this paradise as it develops a sense of identity separate from that of the mother. But from that time onwards, the growing child carries the memory, the possibility, the hope of recovering that initial sense of total union.

That's what happens when we fall in love. We try to escape from the anxiety that accompanies responsible personhood, to recover the secure sense of symbiotic union which we enjoyed in the first days of our lives. We can't, of course, because no matter how much we allow our ego boundaries to melt and merge with those of the loved one, we still have a separate identity of our own. No doubt romantic infatuation increases a sense of closeness. Ironically, however, adult intimacy is only possible when our sense of self is enhanced rather than lost in relationships.

Psychologists are also of the opinion that each of us carries around an unconscious image of an idealised partner. It is a composite which contains elements of the ideal mother/father, heroine/hero, and lover. Jung believed that because men, in particular, have lost touch with their latent femininity, they are inclined to project it on to particular women. They, in turn, become the carriers of their own projected feminine selves. By falling in love with them, such men actually love their partners, not as individuals, but as carriers of their own unconscious ideals. Much the same dynamic is at work when women fall in love with men. It may be an ecstatic experience, but it isn't necessarily intimacy. That kind of relationship is only possible when projections are recognised, withdrawn and owned internally. Then, and only then, can a couple attend to one another in a realistic way that allows that which is innermost to be revealed and loved, as a result of mutual self-disclosure.

Notes
1. *Opera Omnia*, Basle, 1557, 40.
2. *Chance and Necessity*, Knopf, N.Y., 1971, 122.
3. Quoted by Capra, *The Turning Point: Science, Society & the Rising Culture*, Flamingo, London, 1983, 70.
4. *Ibid.*, 69.
5. Quoted in Samuels, *Jung and the Post Jungians*, RKP, London, 1985, 30
6. *The Turning Point, op. cit . 77.*
7. cf. D. Lewis, Appendix D, 'Signs and Wonders in Sheffield: A Social Anthropologist's Analysis of Words of Knowledge, in J. Wimber, *Power Healing*, Hodder and Stoughton, London, 1986, 252-273.
8. B. Griffiths, *A New Vision of Reality: Western Science, Eastern Mysticism and Christian Faith*, Collins, London, 1989, 49.
9. *Man the Unknown*, Hamish Hamilton, London, 1935, 124.
10. *Cosmic Consciousness: A Study of the Evolution of the Human Mind*, Dutton, N.Y., 1923.
11. *Way to Wisdom*, Yale, New Haven, 1954, chap. 3.
12. *Stages of Faith: The Psychology of Human Development & the Quest for Meaning*, Harper & Row, San Francisco, 1981, chap. 21.
13. *Hymn of the Universe*, Collins, London, 1965, 85.
14. Quoted by Barnett, *The Universe and Dr Einstein*, Bantam, N.Y., 1968, 108.
15. cf. Samuels, Shorter & Plaut, *A Critical Dictionary of Jungian Analysis*, PKP, London, 1986, 146-147, and Koestler, *The Roots of Coincidence*, Picador, London, 1974, 91-101.
16. *Intimacy: Pastoral Psychological Essays*, Fides/Claretian, Notre Dame, p.118.
17. *The Art of Intimacy*, Simon & Schuster, London, 1987, 49.
18. *Ibid.*, 29.

CHAPTER 7

Intimacy as self-disclosure

Some time ago I asked myself the question, 'Do you believe anything with absolute certainty?' Then I went through a list of the
most important beliefs that sustain my life, such as the existence
of God, the divinity of Christ, the real presence of the Lord in the
eucharist, the resurrection of the dead, the promise of eternal life,
etc. While I can give notional assent to these doctrines, I'd have to
admit that I can't always give them the unquestioning assent of
my heart. At times, when doubts assail me, I have to say, 'Lord I
believe, help my unbelief.'

As I was meditating along these lines, I discovered that I
had one constant conviction. As a result of experiencing many
kinds of love, I have come to believe unreservedly in love itself. I
believe that that it is the ultimate justification and explanation of
all things, while being beyond all explanation and justification
itself.

I recalled that in her autobiography,[1] Thérèse of Lisieux
seems to describe how she came to a similar conclusion when she
was undergoing temptations to atheism. Some time after her untimely death in her twenties, one of her companions recalled the
following conversation: 'Sister Thérèse admitted something to me
which surprised me and struck me as strange: "If only you know
the darkness into which I have been flung! I don't believe in eternal life; I think, after this life there will be nothing more. Everything has vanished from me." But she added afterwards - and this
is the point – "All I have left is love."' [2]

There was nothing sentimental about Thérèse's unshake-
able belief in the primacy of love. As she endured the dark night
of the soul and the final purification of her will, surely all her
Christian beliefs were implicit in her unreserved adherance to the
reality and demands of charity, for, as St John has assured us,
'God is love and those that abide in love abide in God and God
abides in them.'(1 Jn 4:16)

I have a growing conviction that it is only through our loving interpersonal relationships, especially those of an intimate kind, that we receive the experiential key which unlocks something of the meaning of the universe and of its Mysterious Creator. If ultimate reality is love, then all of creation must bear the imprint of that love. Dame Julian of Norwich bore witness to this awareness. She says that, as she contemplated a little thing like a hazel nut, it was revealed to her that 'it represented all that is made. I was in awe at the fact that it continued to exist, rather than falling back into nothingness. But I was given to understand that *it exists and ever shall exist because God loves it,* and so all things owe their existence to the love of God.' [3]

St Aelred saw the reflection of that love in a more nuanced way. 'Even in inanimate nature,' he wrote, 'a certain love of companionship, so to speak, is apparent, since none of these exists alone but everything is created and thrives in a certain society with its own kind.' A little later, speaking of the animals, he says, 'How they run after one another, to play with one another, thereby expressing and betraying their love by sound and movement. So eagerly and happily do they enjoy their mutual company that they seem to prize nothing more than those things that pertain to friendship.' [4]

In this century, Teilhard de Chardin integrated intuitions like these within a scientific perspective. Not only does creation emanate from love, its inward nature impels it, in an evolutionary way, toward ever greater degrees of consciousness, subjectivity and intimacy. The longings of creation are vested in the capacity of human beings to love. 'Love,' said de Chardin, 'is the higher form of human energy, the higher and purified form of an inner universal attraction.' Love alone is capable of 'carrying the personalisation of the cosmos to its term,' when God will be 'all in all.' [5]

It seems to me that intimate human relationships, especially those of a loving nature, need to be understood within the wider context we have been describing. We will look at them in the following chapters from three inter-related points of view. We will begin by exploring the dynamics of honest self-disclosure. That will be followed by a description of loving attention to other people and things. Finally, we will examine the various forms of healing that can result from experiences like these.

TWO KINDS OF SELF-DISCLOSURE

Because there are two kinds of interpersonal intimacy, there are two kinds of self-disclosure. The first of these is unilateral or one way self-revelation. This form of communication is common in our culture. For example, over the years, I have noticed that in many marriages there is a surprising lack of mutual self-disclosure. One partner, usually the wife, pours out her heart to her spouse, but for one reason or another, he is unable to reciprocate. Not surprisingly, many women get so discouraged by this lack of response that they stop trying to reveal their deepest thoughts and feelings to their husbands. They talk instead to a female friend, if they are lucky enough to have one.

Dependency relationships are a slightly different version of unilateral communication. Instead of needing a person because of loving him or her, a dependent person says implicitly, 'I love you because I *need* you.' Relationships of this kind are often characterised by unilateral self-disclosure. Mary is an unmarried woman of thirty-five. Two years ago she became friendly with Dorothy, a married woman of forty-seven, who works at the same school as herself. Mary likes Dorothy, trusts her and finds her easy to talk to. She tells her things about herself that she would never mention to anyone alse. Mary tells other people that Dorothy is her best friend. Strictly speaking, this isn't really correct. Although Dorothy likes Mary, she has good friends of her own, and doesn't feel inclined to tell her very much about herself. Indeed, she suspects that if she did, Mary wouldn't be really interested. Like many insecure people, she has a need to be understood, rather than to understand. Strictly speaking, therefore, Dorothy is a confidant rather than a friend. The fact that the younger woman can reveal aspects of her experience to Dorothy could help to increase her self-esteem, trust and openness.

Unilateral self-disclosure is a characteristic of the relationship between those engaged in the various helping professions and their clients, such as counsellors, therapists, analysts, spiritual directors, confessors, etc. While the aim of each is different, one way self-disclosure is a common characteristic. The effectiveness of the helping relationships involved depends, to a considerable extent, upon the ability of clients to tell the unedited truth about their experiences. As for the helpers, they are trained to say little or nothing about themselves. Although they abstain from verbal self-disclosure, they do reveal something of their inner selves in a non-verbal way. They do this by the quality of their attention and empathy, together with the sensitivity, understanding and appropriateness of their responses. When clients sense these caring attitudes, they find it easier to tune into their experiences and to express them with honesty.

Friendship in Jewish and Greek literature

When self-disclosure is mutual and on-going, friendships are often the outcome. It is my belief that relationships of this kind are the epitome of true intimacy. They can transform and fulfill relationships, between brothers and sisters, children and parents and especially between husbands and wives. Because of their importance we will look at them more closely.

Friendships were highly regarded in the Bible and classical literature. They are mentioned throughout the Old Testament, especially in the Wisdom Books. Perhaps the most striking verses are to be found in Sir 6:14-18: 'Faithful friends are a sturdy shelter: whoever finds one has found a treasure. Faithful friends are beyond price; no amount can balance their worth. Faithful friends are life-saving medicine; and those who fear the Lord will find them. Those who fear the Lord direct their friendship aright, for as they are, so are their neighbours also.' The friendship between David and Jonathan embodied these sentiments. It is recounted in 1 Sam 18-20. We are told: 'Jonathan became one spirit with David and loved him as himself ... He swore eternal friendship with David because of his deep friendship for him. He took off the robe he was wearing and gave it to David, together with his armour and also his sword, bow and belt.' This ideal of sharing goods was symbolic of the deeper sharing of the heart by means of mutual self-disclosure. It would come to fruition in the life of Jesus and of the early Church.

The Greeks believed that friendships were the noblest form of interpersonal intimacy. For example, in the fifth century B.C., a holy man called Pythagoras founded a community of friends. It had four guidelines: [6]

Friends share the perfect communion of a single spirit.
Friends share everything in common.
Friends are equals, and friendship is an indication of equality.
A friend is a second self.

These ideals were developed by later Greek writers, notably Plato in his *Lysis* and Aristotle in his *Ethics*. It has been said that when Aristotle was asked to define friendship, he replied: 'One soul dwelling in two bodies.'

I mention these points because, when the author of the Acts of the Apostles came to describe the early Christian community, he saw it as a fulfilment of these ancient ideals. United by the Holy Spirit and their faith in Jesus, the first believers 'were one in heart and soul, and no one said that any of the things he possessed was his own, but they had everything in common.' (Acts 4:32) In other words, the first Christians were bound together by a network of overlapping friendships. By sharing their love and their goods like Jonathan and David, they also fulfilled the first two guidelines of Pythagoras. In doing so, they also carried out the Lord's command that they love one another as he had loved them, i.e. as friends who were willing to disclose that which was deepest in their hearts to one another.(cf. Jn 15:15)

Friendship in Christian literature

Later Christian writers such as Augustine,[7] Thomas Aquinas,[8] Aelred of Rievaulx[9] and Francis de Sales,[10] agreed that genuine friendships had to be based on equality, good-will, and mutual self-disclosure. We will take a brief look at each point in turn.

We have already seen how Pythagoras said that friends are equals. That explains why there are so few examples of male-female friendships in the Old Testament or in classical literature. The reason for this was not so much a fear of sexual complications – the Greeks had no such inhibitions – as a widely held assumption that women were not equal to men. As a result, a man could befriend another man, but not a woman, and *vice versa*. Happily, this prejudice is now being challenged, both in theory and in practice, by an increasing number of men and women. Genuine heterosexual friendships assert the radical equality of men and women in an effective but non-ideological way.

False friendships

Writers from Aristotle onwards have pointed out that there are two types of false friendship. They are based on a self-centred desire for either advantage or pleasure. Friendships based on *advantage* are particularly common in our market-oriented economies. A dependency relationship, like the one between Mary and Dorothy, is a typical example. One person can make friends with another because, consciously or unconsciously, there is some advantage to be derived from the relationship. It could be an enhanced reputation, improved prospects, or greater material or emotional security, an escape from loneliness, etc. These can be furthered through association with a person with good qualifications, status, power, money, influence, property, contacts, etc. For example, many marriages are a sort of exchange. A young woman has her figure, beauty and charm to exchange for the wealth and social standing of a powerful man. They may talk a lot about love, but, deep down, their relationship may be a question of mutual need-satisfaction. She escapes from her humble social background, and he can affirm his success, where other males are concerned, by the fact that he could win over such a desirable woman. As Erich Fromm has wryly observed, often such 'egoism-a-deux is mistaken for love and intimacy.' [11]

Friendships based on *pleasure* are also common in our relatively hedonistic culture, especially when they are motivated by erotic attraction and romantic infatuation. Despite repeated declarations of undying affection, such relationships may be founded on the fact that the friends satisfy one another's emotional and sensual desires. False friendships are exposed when the advantages or pleasures that motivated them in the first place are removed. More often than not, they come to an end. As the scriptures say, 'One kind of friend is only so when it suits him, but will not stand by you in your day of trouble.'(Sir 6:8) There is also some truth in an adage ascribed to St Ambrose: 'The friendship that ends, never was.'

True friendships

Unlike false friendships, genuine ones are based on *good-will*. Rightly it has been said that love begins when a person feels that another person's needs are as important as his or her own. We will have more to say about this in the next chapter. Suffice it to say, at the moment, that whenever good-will is the primary dynamic in a friendship, advantages and pleasures may be the results, as distinct from the motives, of the relationship.

Both classical and Christian writers are agreed that the good-will characteristic of genuine friendships is best expressed in the form of mutual self-disclosure. St Francis de Sales wrote: 'Friends love one another. They know that they love one another. And they have communication, intimacy and familiarity with one another ... *for this is the basis of friendship.*'[12](my italics) What should be communicated? Cicero gave a general answer: 'You can speak as freely as to your own self about any and every subject upon earth.'[13] St Aelred of Rievaulx was more specific: 'A friend shares all the secrets of your innermost heart. You are so closely united to him as to become almost one. To him you confide *everything* as if he were your other self.'[14] The phrase, 'as if he were your other self,' is an important one. It means that the distinction between the public and private self is done away with. In an intimate relationship, as distinct from a friendly or a close one, masks and uniforms are put aside. One's true self is revealed. The principle motive for doing this is not a sense of obligation or dependent need, but a loving desire to give the other person the greatest gift of all: that of one's true self.

MUTUAL SELF-DISCLOSURE

Surely the need to be understood, accepted and loved is one of the deepest in the human heart. It energises our conscious desire to publish and make known that which is innermost, to trusted confidants and friends. Although the intention of communicating in this way may be present, just as we have seen in the case of self-intimacy, we often discover that there are inner barriers to self-disclosure. A common one is a lack of self-awareness.

Over the years I have had the privilege of hearing the confessions of thousands of people. It is *the* sacrament of self-disclosure, where one human being tells another about his or her greatest shortcomings and sorrows. I have discovered that, despite their obvious good intentions, the confessions of some people are surprisingly lacking in content. For example, a man might come in and say, 'Bless me, father, I have sinned. It has been two years since my last confession. I cursed once and I took the Holy Name in vain once or twice. That's all, father.' Sometimes I might respond by saying something like this to the penitent: 'I noticed that you mentioned nothing about your relationships with other people. How are you getting on with them?' He might reply, 'O.K., father, no problems there.' 'You never say a hurtful word in anger, or act selfishly?' 'No, father, I get on well with everybody.' Sometimes I wish one could ask family members, friends, colleagues and neighbours if this is really true. Because if he only committed a couple of venial sins over a period of two years, we could get such a man canonised after his death!

Sadly, the extent to which people seem unable to disclose the truth about themselves, to either confessors, confidants or friends, is the extent to which intimacy will evade them. We will only be known and loved as we really are, insofar as we are willing to reveal our true selves to others. We can only do this to the extent that we are in touch with the deeper things in our own hearts. That is why the different forms of self-awareness, that we explored in the opening chapters, are so important. If we don't know what is innermost in our own experience, how can we publish and make it known to other people by means of self-disclosure?

Intimacy requires trust

One author, who has worked in the area of human development for many years, has concluded that a loss of trust is one of the greatest barriers to intimacy in modern culture.[15] Erickson believes that it begins during the first few years of life, as a result of experiencing conditional love from parents and carers such as nurses and relatives. We have noted this before, while talking about barriers to self-intimacy. The child gets the impression, sometimes a false one, that it will be accepted and loved to the extent that it can conform to the expectations of those upon whom it depends. As an adult, that same person will tend to conceal weaknesses, failures and vulnerabilities, because of a fear of being judged and rejected. The mistrust inherited from childhood can be reinforced by traumatic adult experiences. An engaged woman may pour out some of her deepest and most personal secrets to her fiancé. Then he breaks off the relationship and marries someone else. It is not hard to understand why his former girlfriend might feel that, in leaving her, he has taken part of her inner life with him. She will always have the fear that he will reveal something personal about her, to his wife.

Mistrust is also reinforced when secrets we have revealed to a spouse or friend are used against us during a heated argument. Perhaps worst of all is the betrayal of a confidence. We tell a trusted person some intimate detail about our own lives, only to find that our secret has been revealed to a third party.

Experiences like these tend to reinforce the mistrust that began in childhood and to make self-disclosure less likely. However the extent to which we fail to disclose our innermost secrets to anyone else, is the extent to which the deepest part of us is unavailable for relationship. It leaves pain unresolved, leads to loneliness, and means that, at best, we have to substitute closeness for real intimacy in our lives.

Intimacy and the problem of anger

Another block to genuine self-disclosure is an inability to cope, in a reasonable and skilful way, with our negative emotions, especially anger. We all get hurt in life. Usually it begins in our infancy and continues down the years. Invariably hurt leads to anger. If it remains unresolved, a feeling like this can turn to resentment. With the passage of time, these memories, with their associated feelings, slip into the pre-conscious and then into the unconscious mind. Although we are no longer aware of them, they can exercise a negative influence on our current relationships. For example, the anger we may feel against a parent can be projected on to somebody with whom we have a good relationship. Furthermore, because nobody is perfect, even the best-intentioned spouse or friend will upset us occasionally. It could be an insensitive remark, a broken promise, a selfish deed, a judgemental attitude, etc. The list of possibilities is nearly endless. One way or another, we get hurt. Sometimes that sense of grievance will trigger the unconscious memory of some unresolved issue from the past, so that the two incidents merge and express themselves in negative feelings such as annoyance, frustration, disappointment, mistrust, etc. When our emotional reactions are out of proportion to the incidents that evoked them, we can be pretty sure that this dynamic is at work.

As I said earlier, many people are reared in homes where anger is neither displayed nor accepted. So, as children, they learn to suppress their negative feelings in order to retain the affection and approval of their parents. As this kind of denial is repeated, it becomes second nature. When they reach adulthood, many of these people find it hard to acknowledge any anger. They instinctively push it down into their unconscious minds where it attacks them. It lowers self-esteem, increases anxiety, and, in some instances, turns to either a mild or a serious form of depression. The extent to which anger like this, with its associated feelings, is put into cold storage, is the extent to which one's whole affective life, negative and positive, is, by definition, unavailable for intimate self-disclosure. Until such a person can recover, name, own, understand and express his or her anger, and its causes, in an appropriate way, it will remain a block to intimacy.

Many other people can feel their anger all right. It is not supressed. Instead, it is expressed in an aggressive way in the form of criticism, sarcasm, cruel jokes, judgemental comments, silences, refusal to make love, etc. Aggressive reactions like these hurt the other person, evoke his or her anger, and so a vicious circle is formed, one that can lead to a progressive alienation of affection and the eclipse of intimacy. In instances like these, angry people often renounce responsibility for their resentful feelings. In effect they say to one another: 'It's all your fault. You made me feel like this!' thereby implying that unless the 'offender' admits wrongdoing and changes, there will be no reconciliation. John Powell has made the helpful observation that, 'While other people can *stimulate* my anger, the *causes* lie within.'[16] So instead of *suppressing* feelings of anger in an unhealthy way, or expressing them in a reactive and *aggressive* way, we have to learn to *assert* them in a constructive way. Instead of reacting negatively to the other person, we can *report* our negative feelings in a way that implicitly asserts our dignity and worth.

Take the simple example of a friend who shows up for an appointment some twenty minutes after the time arranged. Instead of saying in an aggressive way, 'You are always late, you don't give a damn, you are so self-centred that you don't mind taking people like myself for granted!' the person can disclose what he or she feels, and why. For example, 'I felt hurt and angry when you didn't keep to the arrangement that we agreed to last night. I really feel cheesed off, let-down and taken for granted.' By and large, the kind of communication that begins with the pronoun *you* tends to be judgemental and makes a bad position worse. However, when it begins with the pronoun *I*, the ensuing *self*-disclosure serves to increase a sense of intimacy because it allows the other person to see what is innermost in the heart. It also affords him or her the opportunity of responding in a less threatening emotional atmosphere.

In this context, it is worth mentioning that a willingness to admit wrong-doing and to ask for forgiveness is nearly as important as a willingness to forgive those who have hurt us. As Thomas Fuller once wrote: 'He that cannot forgive others, breaks the bridge over which he must pass himself; for everyone has need to be forgiven.' Forgiveness, therefore, is the guardian of intimacy.

SELF-DISCLOSURE IN THE LIVES OF MEN AND WOMEN

In recent years, research has confirmed the common-sense impression that women find it easier than men to disclose what is innermost in their hearts. Lillian Rubin has studied friendships in the lives of single men and women.[17] She discovered that women have more friendships than men and that the difference in the content and quality of their friendships is marked and unmistakable. Over two-thirds of the single men interviewed couldn't name a best friend. Of those who could, it was much more likely to be a woman than a man. In contrast, over three-quarters of the single women had no problem in identifying a best friend. In the majority of cases it was another woman.

Daniel Levinson has confirmed these findings where single and married men are concerned. 'As a tentative generalisation,' he writes, 'we could say that close friendship with a man or woman is rarely experienced by men ... Most men do not have an intimate friend ... and most men have not had an intimate non-sexual friendship with a woman.'[18] Recently I noticed that another piece of research reported that, when the nature of intimacy as self-disclosure was explained to men, eighty seven per cent of them had to admit that they had never experienced such intimacy with anyone, male or female.[19] While the research underpinning these statistics was conducted in the United States, I have no reason to think that the situation is any different in other English-speaking countries. It indicates that women are the experts at intimacy as self-disclosure, especially in their relationships with one another.

The research also shows that, at best, most men are friendly rather than intimate in their relationships, especially with one another. They share activities and engage in abstract discussion rather than personal dialogue. They talk about impersonal things like sport, politics, women, etc. However, deeper feelings and personal problems are not usually revealed. Because of their reluctance to share their real selves, many married men disappoint their wives, who end up feeling lonely and frustrated.

The influence of childhood experience

Why is it that, generally speaking, women find it easier both to get in touch with their inner experience and to express it honestly in conversation? In recent years, two researchers, Nancy Chodorow and Dorothy Dinnerstein, have suggested a very helpful interpretation of the available evidence.[20] When boys and girls leave the biological wombs of their mothers, they enter psychological ones. They feel that they are part of their mothers, with no separate sense of identity or 'I-ness'. In our culture, most children depend upon their mothers, as the principal carers in their lives, to satisfy all their physical and emotional needs. So, at the beginning of their lives, before their ego identities have formed, babies relate to their mothers from the self. They disclose their inner lives in an involuntary way by means of body language. By paying attention to their children's actions, expressions, and sounds, mothers can tune into their feelings, and through them, to their perceptions, reactions, and needs.

In this Garden of Eden experience, babies have a sense of

'we-ness', of being in perfect union with their mothers and, through them, with the whole of reality. It is similar to the ecstatic feeling that couples try to recapture when they fall in love, and analogous to the 'oceanic feeling' that mystics enjoy as a result of their intimate connection with the unity of all being in God. As time passes, however, boys and girls have to separate from their mothers in order to form identities of their own. It is a particularly difficult time for boys, one that has knock-on emotional effects for the rest of their lives.

A boy's experience of being nurtured

Mothers relate differently to their sons and daughters. If she has a boy, a mother says, albeit at an unconscious level, 'I love my child, but he is not the same sex as me.' He will have to develop a male identity, and so, for good reasons, she distances herself - in a qualified sense - from her son, in the belief that it is only by doing so that he will discover and develop his maleness. This is a traumatic experience for the boy. In spite of the fact that he wants to remain in the paradise of perfect union with a loving woman, he is cast out like Adam and Eve. This is a painful experience of rejection, one which evokes a good deal of separation anxiety. So the boy has to repress his feelings for two reasons. Firstly, he has to reduce empathy for his female mother in order to develop a sense of his male identity. Secondly, because the trauma of separation from the mother is so painful, he tends to deny it. Chodorow and Dinnerstein argue that, from that time onwards, men find it harder to either touch into, or express their feelings, especially feelings of vulnerability.

Rubin also points out that words are not at the centre of men's notion of intimacy.[21] Because boys had to suppress their identification with their mothers before they had developed the verbal ability to express their complex emotions, a split between language and feeling took place. It continues into adult life. That dynamic is reinforced by 'macho-stereotypes' which stress the importance of independence, strength, control and manly stoicism, from boyhood onwards. As a result, feelings of vulnerability, dependency, tenderness and need, are either denied altogether or remain unexpressed in words. Almost inevitably, men who bottle up their feelings displace their intimacy needs in the form of un-healthy attitudes and behaviours, such as over-eating, alcohol abuse, workaholism, cynicism, hypochondria, rationalism, etc. Is it any surprise that many men who are emotionally repressed suffer from psychosomatic disorders which are stress-related, like high-blood pressure and heart disease? Perhaps a lack of self-disclosure is one of the reasons why, on average, men have a shorter life expectancy than women.

The sexual development of boys

However, the baby boy can have 'erotic' feelings for his mother precisely because she is a member of the opposite sex. In other words, his genital sexuality is affirmed while, at the same time, his empathic feelings are suppressed. This division of genital sex and interpersonal feeling, which begins in childhood, tends to become established as a permanent characteristic in the lives of most males. However, a man's sense of gender-identity will tend to be more insecure than that of a woman. He has to *become* a male, firstly by a process of physiological change in the womb, and later by a process of psychological separation from his mother. One effect of this process is the fact that a man's sense of identity is at once more rigid and more closely tied to genital potency and performance than that of a woman, who is conceived female, and *remains* so, physically and psychologically, ever afterwards. It also means that men tend to make love in order to get in touch with what they feel, whereas most women prefer to be in touch with their feelings before wanting to make love.

Because so many men find it hard to share their deepest selves with anyone, it is not surprising that they often experience feelings such as anxiety, self-doubt and loneliness. Instead of acknowledging and expressing them to a trusted person, they often ignore emotions like these by resorting to the false promises of impersonal sex. Although it may counteract the devitalising effect of negative feelings for a short time, it actually reinforces them, by substituting fleeting pleasure for the life-enhancing effects of on-going self-disclosure.

To my fellow males I'd want to say: Instead of judging yourself harshly on account of your sexual weakness, try to understand it. What does the symbolism in your fantasies tell you about your deeper self? As one author has written, 'If a man is able to examine the content of his fantasies objectively, he may reach a new understanding of himself.'[22] What does your obsessive pursuit of sexual stimulation disclose about your deeper emotional needs? What do you really desire? A sense of life, potency, closeness, tenderness, excitement? What is it you are avoiding? A feeling of worthlessness, powerlessness, failure, nagging insecurity, isolation? Why are you afraid of revealing yourself to anyone? Because you may be rejected, misunderstood, overwhelmed, emasculated?

A girl's experience of being nurtured

When a girl is born, her mother says, either at a conscious or an unconscious level, 'This child is the same sex as myself. She will grow up to be a woman like me.' As a result of this sense of identification, a baby girl is not banished in the same way as her brothers from the idyllic world of union with her mother. She can develop a sense of female identity by empathising with her. This has a number of important effects. Firstly, a woman associates her awareness of personhood with a sense of relationship. By and large, this will remain true for the rest of her life. Whereas a man's sense of identity can be threatened by the vulnerability involved in intimacy, a woman's identity is affirmed by such relationships. Secondly, she finds it easier to tune into her feelings, including painful ones, and to express them openly and honestly. Unlike a man, a woman is not saddled with a social stereotype which discourages any admission of needing tenderness. Aware of her own feelings, a woman is better equipped to attend to the feelings of other people in an empathetic way. That is why Nancy Chodorow could write: 'The basic feminine sense of self is connected to others in the world.'[23]

It is that sense of connection that will be so important within the new cultural paradigms that are forming. It is contemplative, holistic, experiential in orientation, and open to the mystery of a personal God who is revealed in and through such a felt sense of interrelationship. This female characteristic may explain why women far outnumber men at religious events. As modern

Christianity slowly rediscovers the essentially personal and relational nature of its central doctrines, worship, and community life, women will become increasingly critical of the male bias of much of its institutional expression. I suspect that many men would be more comfortable with the didactic, ritualistic and dutiful characteristics of pre-Vatican II Catholicism. It is ironic, therefore, that leadership in the Church remains almost entirely in male hands. It is my belief that institutional forms of Catholicism will continue to decline until we switch from an overly male perspective, one that stresses separateness rather than intimacy, detached reason rather than felt thought, objective truth rather than subjective authenticity, action rather than being, the masculine characteristics of the God-image rather than the feminine ones. This will present a challenge of major proportions for male Christians. Unless they are willing to get involved in their own human development, and the challenge of relating to God through more intimate contact with people and nature, they will become increasingly alienated from the new forms of Christianity that are about to emerge.

The sexual development of girls

Because her mother is the same sex as herself, a girl's erotic feelings are not directed toward her. Ever afterwards, therefore, she will tend to experience her sexuality primarily in terms of felt relationship, and only secondarily as a genital activity. This would explain why unlike men, women are less interested in pornography and less inclined to masturbate, or to have multiple sexual partners.

To women in general, I'd make this appeal: through your understanding, compassion and love, help the men in your life to get in touch with their inner vulnerability and to express it. As they learn to reveal that which is innermost in their hearts, they will escape from their loneliness, and learn to integrate their sexuality in a healing way, within the life-enhancing dynamics of inter-personal intimacy.

Relationships between men

In the light of what I have been saying, it is easier to see why men find self-disclosure so difficult. I have lived in all-male communities for a quarter of a century now. It is clear to me that, with few exceptions, my colleagues have a great deal of affection for one another. The more perceptive members have a great deal of insight into the personalities and foibles of the men they live with. There is a lot of mutual tolerance and respect for each one's privacy and independence. Men can form a team in order to accomplish some agreed task. It can be informed by an obvious sense of emotional bonding, where there is a feeling of 'all for one, one for all.' But this sense of closeness isn't intimacy, although men often think that it is.

Because they affirm their male identity by means of competitive pursuits, men find it extremely difficult to let go of their macho *personas* in order to reveal their vulnerability to one another. Of course men can become intimate if they want to, and if they work at it. If their desire to communicate is strong, and their courage outweighs their fears, they can learn that the power of real Christian love is made perfect in their shared vulnerability. However, it is my belief that most men first learn the arts of self-revelation by relating to women in an intimate way. This can prepare them, so to speak, to engage in honest self-disclosure with male friends. St Gregory Nazianzen described such a friendship between himself and St Basil in these words: 'We seemed to have a single soul animating two bodies. And, while those who claim that all things are in all things are not equally to be believed, we at least, had to believe that we were in and with each other. The sole ambition of both of us was virtue and a life so led in view of future hopes, as to sever our attachment to this life before we had to depart it.'[24]

The ambiguity of male-female relationships

Most men find it easier to reveal their true selves to women. There are a number of reasons for this. For one thing, they don't have to compete with women in the way they do with other males. As a result, there isn't as much need to appear macho and self-sufficient. Added to this is the fact that men are haunted by the memory of a time when they enjoyed the bliss of perfect union with a loving mother. So, deep within their psyches, there is a desire to return to that sense of loving connection. The arms, breasts and warmth of women's bodies are a reminder of a time of mainly non-sexual and reassuring tenderness that enveloped and nourished them in the first months of their lives. So, not surprisingly, a man not only wants to be close to a woman, he wants to forego his normal separateness and to open up his heart to her. This he tries to do in a hesitating, inarticulate way. But when he makes a start, the woman will often want to know a little more about what he is thinking, feeling, desiring. As he senses this, a long-standing fear may be evoked in the man's heart, the fear of being caught up in a powerful sense of union with a woman, who, like his mother, may then go on to push him away from her.

So, for a man, the prospect of self-disclosure touches into a world of ambiguous pre-rational desires and fears, a desire for union and happiness and a fear of losing his male identity and the prospect of painful rejection. And so he draws back. He may find that the implications of self-disclosure are so threatening that he settles for emotional closeness and sexual union. When he makes love, he feels affirmed in his male identity, he gets in touch with what he really feels, without having to name or express it in words. As a result, the woman feels cheated and shut out from his inner life. Although she opens up her heart to him, she may discover that he isn't really interested. He may say that she is too emotional, goes into too many details, fails to get to the point, etc. Again she feels shut out. What she really wants is that he would want her to disclose her true self to him. Research shows that, if a woman persists in honest self-disclosure of her deepest thoughts and feelings, with no ulterior motive, or secret agenda, the man will tend to reciprocate in his own way and in his own good time. So women need the patience of real love.

As Lilian Rubin says: 'There is one important definition of intimacy among adults – the wish to know another's inner life, along with the ability to share one's own.'[25] We will look at the dynamics of this kind of loving attention in the next chapter.

Notes
1.   *Story of a Soul*, ICS Publications, Washington D.C., 1976, 212-214.
2.   Bernard Bro OP, *The Little Way*, DLT, London, 1979, 53.

3. *Revelations of Divine Love*, Penguin, London, chpt 5.
4. *Spiritual Friendship*, Cistercian Publications, Kalamazoo, 1974, 62-63.
5. *The Religion of Teilhard de Chardin*, de Lubac, Desclee, N.Y., 1967, 159.
6. Rosemary Radar, *Breaking Boundaries: Male/Female Friendships in Early Christian Communities*, Paulist Press, N.Y., 1983, 24.
7. Mc Erlane, 'Friendship According to Augustine,' *Review for Religious*, July-Aug 1982, 596-604.
8. *St Thomas Aquinas: Theological Texts*, ed. Gilby, Oxford, London, 1955, 208-211.
9. *Spiritual Friendship*, Cistercian Publications, Kalamazoo, 1977.
10. *Introduction to the Devout Life*, Harper, N.Y., 1966, Pt 3, chaps 17-22. Wright, *Bond of Perfection: Francis de Sales & Jane de Chantal*, Paulist Press, N.Y., 1985.
11. *The Art of Loving*, Unwin, London, 1969, 65.
12. *Treatise on the Love of God*, Tan, 1975, Bk 1, chap. 13, #3.
13. 'Laelius: on Friendship' in *On the Good Life*, Penguin Classics, 188.
14. *Spiritual Friendship*, Cistercian Pubs., Kalamazoo, 1977, 112-113.
15. *Lift Your Sails*, Dwyer, Image, N.Y., 1987, 91; 149.
16. *The Secret of Staying in Love*, Argus, 1974, 96.
17. *Intimate Strangers*, Fontana, Glasgow, 1985, 129.
18. *The Seasons of a Man's Life*, Ballantine, N.Y., 1978, 335.
19. *Lift Your sails, op. cit.*, 57.
20. *Intimate Strangers, op. cit.*, 48ff.
21. *Just Friends: The Role of Friendship in our Lives*, Harper & Row, N.Y., 1986, 97.
22. *What Men are Like*, Sanford & Lough, Paulist Press, N.J., 1988, 219.
23. *Intimate Strangers, op. cit.*, 169.
24. *Divine Office*, Vol 1., Office of Readings, 2 January.
25. *Intimate Strangers, op. cit.*, 79.

CHAPTER 8

Intimacy as loving attention

At school many of us had to study Grey's Elegy. It was the very first poem that impressed me deeply. Some thirty years later, I'm still moved by the beautiful and poignant words:

Full many a gem of purest ray serene,
The dark unfathomed caves of ocean bear:
Full many a flower is born to blush unseen,
And waste its sweetness on the desert air.

These lines describe the anonymity of animate and inanimate things before the advent of human beings on planet earth. As we have already noted in previous chapters, they enjoyed ascending degrees of inwardness and connectedness proportionate to their level of material complexity. They had a God-prompted propensity to publish and to make known that which was innermost in their natures. Speaking of the heavenly bodies, the psalmist said: 'There is no speech, nor are there words; their voice is not heard; yet their voice goes out through all the earth, and their words to the end of the world.'(Ps 19:1-4) Of course the Creator did behold all things in love, but nature was unaware of the fact, because there was no one in the world to consciously mediate that appreciation on God's behalf. As a result, there was something frustrated and incomplete about the world. In Rom 8:20-21 St Paul writes: 'For the creation was subjected to futility, not of its own will but by the will of the one who subjected it, in hope that the creation might be set free from its bondage to decay and will obtain the freedom of the glory of the children of God.'

It is my belief that the self-disclosure of the non-human world can only reach its fulfilment when we humans consciously reconcile creation, of which we are an integral part, with its Creator. We begin to do this, when, by means of contemplative wonder, we perceive and appreciate what the world of nature is 'saying' to us. This self-declaration can lead to three levels of inter-related awareness.

Firstly, there is the wonder that something rather than nothing exists. I can recall the occasion when I was first graced with this intuition. I was studying for an exam at the time. I dozed off to sleep at my desk. As I woke up, there was a fleeting moment when I was conscious, but not of anything in particular, there was no idea or image in my mind. Instead I had a vivid awareness of my sheer *existence* and by extension the existence of all things. It was accompanied by an inner conviction that being, which included my own, was *good* and *meaningful* in itself, but that it wasn't the adequate explanation of its own existence or qualities. In that moment of awareness, I was sure that God existed as the One who sustains in being all the good and meaningful things that exist, including myself. [1]

Ever since having that gratuitous, spiritual experience, my perception of particular objects, whether human or non-human, has often been tinged by this background awareness. It has enabled me to see that Wittgenstein was correct when he said: 'It is not how things are in the world that is mystical, but that it exists.'[2]

Secondly, when anything is contemplated as a mystery in which we participate, rather than as a problem which we observe from the point of view of detached reason, we can intuitively grasp its intrinsic beauty, goodness, truth and meaning.

Thirdly, this process reaches its high point when, by means of a religious experience we consciously acknowledge that God's 'eternal power and divine nature, invisible though they are, have been understood and seen through the things he has made.' (Rom 1:20) By coming to know what creation manifests in these ways, we humans can act as ambassadors in a process, whereby we enable the non-human realm to reach beyond itself to attain conscious intimacy with the One in whom all things, including ourselves, live and move and have their being.(cf. Acts 17:28)

The spiritualisation of matter

I believe that when we receive the self-disclosure of nature in the light of our conscious relationship with God – a relationship which, paradoxically, can itself be manifested through nature – a number of things happen. Non-human creation reaches toward its completion through us. Animate and inanimate matter is spiritualised, in a qualified sense, through its relationship with human beings. By the power of the Spirit which searches *everything*, even the depths of God, (cf. 1 Cor 2:10) we enjoy simultaneous intimacy with nature and with the God who made it.

Surely Jesus was such a bridge person when as the Son of God he spanned the gulf between the world of matter and the Spirit. His way of contemplating the world was the keystone in this process of transformation. His parables, such as the one about the weeds and the wheat,(Mt 13:24-31) and his charming reference to the lilies of the field and the birds of the air, (Lk 12:22-32) show that he was a keen observer of creation. What are sometimes referred to as his 'nature miracles,' like the calming of the storm at sea,(Lk 8:22-26) and his walking on the waters,(Mt 14:22-34) seem to imply, however one interprets them, that once the material world is in relationship with Spirit, the natural laws familiar to science are transcended. The 'spiritual' potential hidden in matter is actualised as it is elevated to a higher realm and therefore to different 'laws'. Because he had a material body, Jesus, like all of us, was a child of the earth. This mystery was symbolised by the evangelists when they maintained that Jesus was born in a cave, i.e. in the depths of the earth, and that he was buried in another one.(cf. Eph 4:9)

As the Christ, the anointed Son of God, his personality became the point of intersection between the world of matter and the realm of eternal Spirit. This relationship was manifested and actualised by the healings of Jesus. In each of them, broken minds and bodies were recreated and transformed by the power of the Spirit at work in and through his earthly humanity. When Jesus reached out his hands in compassionate prayer, 'power went out from him'(cf. Mk 5:30) and flowed into the spirit of the afflicted person. Because of the intimate union of the human spirit with mind and body, the Holy Spirit was able to override the defects of nature by releasing healing power within, thereby restoring the person's harmony and peace. These so called *preternatural* or *supernatural* events were, in fact, natural in the sense that they were revelations of the potential of matter when it is elevated, through intimacy with the incarnate Son of God, to a new level of spiritual potential.

Surely this vision of reality underpins the remarkable character of the following promises Jesus made to his disciples as the adopted sons and daughters of God. In Mk 11:22-23 he said: 'Have faith in God. Truly I tell you, if you say to this mountain, "Be taken up and thrown into the sea" and you do not doubt in your heart, but believe that what you say will come to pass, it will be done for you.' Again in Jn 14:12-15 he said: 'Very truly, I tell you, the one who believes in me will also do the works that I do and, in fact, will do greater works than these, because I am going to the Father. I will do whatever you ask in my name, so that the Father may be glorified in the Son. If in my name you ask me for anything, I will do it.' Finally, in Mk 16:2 Jesus said: 'These signs will accompany those who believe ... they will lay their hands on the sick, and they will recover.' When the Spirit enables us to be in intimate contact with the mind and heart of God, we can share in a Christ-like authority over the limitations of unredeemed nature, even to the point of healings and miracles.

This point of view would also help to make sense of those rare and strange occurances in Christian history such as levitation,[3] bilocation,[4] and the incorruptability of the bodies of some saints. Like all signs and wonders they are intimations of the inauguration of the new creation mentioned in 2 Pt 3:13. I suspect that the final coming of the heavenly kingdom will occur when the world of matter finally sheds its limitations. Then it will be transfigured by the intimate reconciliation of nature, through human beings, with God. This will be made possible by the transforming experience of Divine Love as it is mediated to creation through the co-operation of the Spirit-filled children of God.

THE IMPORTANCE OF ATTENTION

I will have more say about the religious dimensions and implications of contemplative forms of knowing in the third section of the book. Meantime we will focus our attention on important but more mundane realities, where all the points we have been making can be involved. We will examine the way in which interpersonal intimacy as self-disclosure can only reach fulfilment when someone else pays attention to it, in such a way that it is known and accepted in a non-judgemental way. I believe that this kind of intimate knowing is the key that unlocks the meaning of *all* genuine forms of human loving.

Perhaps no other subject has been as celebrated as love in song, paint and the printed word. However, Jules Toner has maintained that, over the centuries, only a handful of significant books have ever been published on the subject.[5] All the others could be seen as so many footnotes on the thinking of authors like Plato, Aristotle, Augustine, Aquinas, Freud and Scheler. For a number of years now, I have been asking myself the question: 'What is love? Is it good-will, service of others, romantic infatuation, warmth of feeling, union of wills, etc.?' I have come to the conclusion that essentially it probably isn't any of these things.

The nature of love, as intimate knowing, will be examined from an experiential rather than a theoretical perspective. It seems to me that the dynamic of loving can be looked at from three interrelated and overlapping points of view. We will begin with the necessary *antecedents of love*, i.e. a desire to know the other. This desire expresses itself in respectful and empathetic attention to his or her inner life. Then we will suggest that the *essence of love* consists in a recognition, appreciation and reverential approval of the perceived and potential inner value of the person. We will conclude by looking at some of the principal *effects of love*, such as the kind of affirmation that helps to uncover and to actualise the person's hidden potential. It seems to me that this dynamic is not only common to all forms of loving, it can be used to discern true love from its many counterfeits.

THE ANTECEDENTS OF LOVE

The impetus that prompts us to become interested in the inner life of other people is energised, first and foremost, by a *desire* to know them as they really are. A number of points can be made about such desire. It is evoked by some form of attractiveness in an other person. Even if her child is handicapped, a mother can be intensely interested in her baby. Besides being bone of her bone and flesh of her flesh, she is motivated by its utter dependence on her for everything and by lovable aspects of its personality which no one else even notices. A young man may desire to know his girlfriend because he has fallen in love with her and thinks she is beautiful, sexy and charming. As wounded healers, people in the helping professions, who desire to know their clients, are often motivated by a certain liking and compassion. Friends desire to know one another because they experience a sense of mutual affinity and attraction.

In my experience, all these forms of desire can be influenced in a fundamental way by a personal experience of the unconditional love of God, the height and breadth, the length and depth of it which, as St Paul says, surpasses understanding. (cf. Eph 3:18) Like the intuition about the goodness and meaning of all existence, this personal awareness of God's unconditional love can illumine the value of someone who seems to be devoid of any perceptible attraction, e.g. an enemy, or underpin the forms of attractiveness already mentioned above.

Transcendental desire

When one person wants to know another, the motive for doing so can be rooted in a deep-seated desire for meaning, which can only be satisfied by a conscious sense of relationship with the mystery of God. This sense of meaning can be disclosed in and through the meaning of another person's inner life. It is worth noting in passing that desires of this kind originate not in the ego but in the self. As we saw at the end of chapter three, theologians rightly believe that yearnings and longings of this kind originate in the human spirit, and are promped by the Holy Spirit. Trancendental or God-prompted desires can only be satisfied when the Lord chooses to reveal himself. This he promises to do in a number of places in the scripture, for example in Jer 33:3: 'Call to me and I will answer you, and will tell you great and hidden things that you have not known.'

The Lord can fulfil promises like these by revealing himself through his two great bibles of creation and the holy scriptures. Indeed, in the New Testament we are told on a number of occasions that the Lord can be revealed in a special way in and through our loving relationships with people, e.g. 'Whoever welcomes this child in my name welcomes me, and whoever welcomes me welcomes the one who sent me,'(Lk 9:48) and 'For where two or three are gathered in my name, I am there among them,'(Mt 18:20) and 'Truly I tell you, just as you did it to one of the least of these who are members of my family, you did it to me.'(Mt 25:40) So like the intuition of existence and the experiences of God's unconditional love, a person's desire to know God can inform in a pre-conscious way the attention he or she pays to the self-disclosure of another individual.

Desire as the primordial act of will

The desire to know another human being is all important. It alone will motivate and energise the decision, the act of will a person needs to make, in order to pay attention to the inner life of someone else. Without it, there will be no real intimacy or love. While acts of will that originate in the ego lead to *wilfulness*, i.e. a tendency to understand people in terms of preconceived ideas, those that originate in the self lead to a *willingness* to be open to the uniqueness of each person. Gerald May describes the difference between the two in this way: '*Willingness* implies a surrendering of one's self-separateness, an entering-into, an immersion in the deepest processes of life itself,' e.g. another person's inner life. 'It is the realisation that one already is a part of some ultimate cosmic process. In contrast, *wilfulness* is the setting of oneself apart from the fundamental essence of life in an attempt to master, direct, control, or otherwise manipulate existence.' [6]

I believe that grace operates first and foremost in and through our trancendental desire to know other people and, through them, to get in touch with the mystery of God. I also suspect that the choice to go beyond egocentric concerns in this way, by focusing attention on the inner experience of another person, is not only the primordial act of will, it is arguably the prerequisite for all other derivative acts of decision making. This is so because it is only as the self is energised inwardly by growing relationship to other people, nature and to God, that one has both the *desire* and the *power* to make the kind of responsible choices that promote inner freedom and growth, e.g. to give up an addictive habit, or to make personal sacrifices in order to help another person. Without the kind of contact with created and uncreated reality, which is the graced result of self-forgetful attention, one remains a prisoner of the ego's wish to do the right thing, but without the willpower do so. St Paul described the inevitable effect of egocentric attention and wilfulness in these words: 'For I do not do the good I want, but the evil I do not want is what I do.'(Rom 7:19) I will come back to this important point later.

The contemplative outlook

The kind of attention that leads to intimate knowing has a contemplative dimension. The word *contemplate* in English is derived from Latin, and according to the Shorter Oxford Dictionary, it means 'to look at, or gaze upon something, with continual and sustained attention.' The contemplative attitude has been variously described as 'a long, loving look at the real,'[7] 'a gaze of the mind accompanied by admiration,'[8] 'the alertness of the understanding which finding everything plain, grasps it clearly with entire apprehension,'[9] and finally in one of his poems, D. H. Lawrence described it as, 'A man in his wholeness, wholly attending.'

In order to pay attention to another person in this way, one has to bracket out one's ideas, theories, memories, and projections. As far as I can discover, the late Simone Weil was one of the few philosophers who has appreciated the importance of the contemplative attitude. Writing about the kind of attention involved, she said: 'Attention is an effort, the greatest of all efforts perhaps, but it is a negative effort.' A little later she explains why: 'Attention consists of suspending our thought, leaving it detached, empty and ready to be penetrated by the object. It means holding in our minds, within reach of this thought, but on a lower level and not in contact with it, the diverse knowledge we have acquired which we are forced to make use of.' [10]

Attention as passive concentration

A few years ago, I had reason to discover just how difficult it is to pay simple, sustained attention to any one thing or person. I was investigating natural ways of reducing stress and nervous tension.[11] I discovered that Benson's 'Relaxation Response' and Schultz's 'Autogenic Training' were similar in approach and could influence the autonomic system, which automatically controls many body functions, to such an extent that high blood pressure would return to normal without the use of drugs. Both of these therapies emphasise the importance of focused attention.

Having analysed the dynamics of transcendental meditation, Dr Benson of Harvard Medical School discovered that its effectiveness depended on concentration. During stressful times the mind flits restlessly from one thing to another. It cannot focus on anyone or anything for long. So he devised a secularised version of TM which inculcates a sense of tranquility by concentrating attention, for about twenty minutes, on a word or a phrase of seven syllables.

Dr Schultz and his disciple Dr Luthe discovered that people could learn to relax, and thereby reduce hypertension by concentrating on physical sensations, specifically the warmth of different parts of the body. By sensing the warmth in their feet, for example, and affirming that they were getting warmer, they could feel their skin temperature increasing. Because of the intimate union of mind and matter, this form of focused attention induces capillaries to dilate. It increases the blood supply, eases tension and lowers blood pressure.

Although these seem to be simple exercises in concentration, I have found that they are hard to practice. If I'm using Benson's method, I often find that, instead of concentrating on my chosen word or phrase, I'm either *thinking* about concentrating on them, or distracted by remembering things that have happened in the past, or anticipating things that might happen in the future. When I'm trying to concentrate on the physical sensation of warmth in my feet, I find that I'm focusing on the autogenic method itself and the *idea* of warmth. However, I have found that, with practice and the passage of time, not only has my ability to concentrate on words, phrases or sensations improved, it has had the knock-on effect of helping me to pay more sustained attention to other people and to nature.

Respectful attention

In interpersonal relationships, attention of a contemplative kind finds expression by means of respectful listening. In a culture where one's image is so important, and where there is a tendency to label and pigeon-hole everyone, there is a great need for respectful attention. The word *respect* is derived from two Latin

131

ones, literally meaning 'to look back,' i.e. to give someone a second look by going beyond appearances to see what lies innermost in the heart. We show respect by the way in which we listen, whether it is active or passive in nature. In the former, people listen with their total selves, more or less - including their special senses, attitudes, beliefs, feelings and intuitions. In the latter, the listener becomes mainly an organ for the passive reception of sound, with little self-perception, personal involvement, or active curiosity.

Interestingly, in both the Greek and Latin languages, the words *to listen* and *to obey* are closely related. We can only listen in an active way to another person when our minds and hearts are willing to submit to the reality of his or her inner life. One reason why we fail to do this, why we prefer an egocentric and wilful form of passive listening, is the fact that the reality of another person's life can be so threatening. To perceive it as it is might undermine our pre-conceived ideas and attitudes. A man who grows in intimate knowledge of his wife, might have to forego his stereotypical view, not only of his wife but of women in general. I know that I have been simultaneously impressed and scared by the ability of women friends to reveal themselves with heart-rendering vulnerability. By doing so, they have challenged me to forego my male propensity to be in control in relationships by avoiding the kind of in-depth sharing that calls for greater sincerity, tenderness and commitment. In other words, attentive listening usually involves a sort of intellectual, affective and attitudinal dying to the egocentric self. So it is not surprising to find that in Greek the word *epistrophe* can mean either 'attention' or 'conversion.' So, intimacy as loving attention involves a cognitive crucifixion; one that disrupts the system of meanings that, up until then, had secured the identity of the ego.

Empathetic attention

If it is to be truly intimate, one's attention needs to focus on the feelings of other people. This is what the caring professions call *empathetic* listening. Apparently the word itself was derived from the German *Einfuhlung*, meaning to 'feel-into' somebody else's experience. Etymologically however, the words *empathy*, *sympathy* and *apathy* in English can be traced back to the Greek *pathos* meaning a deep and strong feeling akin to suffering. People pay attention in an apathetic way when they listen 'without' any such feeling. Their approach is rational, detached and objective. They focus on ideas and facts, and usually respond by giving good advice. For example, a latent alcoholic admits to being depressed, guilty and worried by his excessive drinking. A man who listens in an apathetic way asks the question, 'How many pints do you drink each day?' When he is told the number, he replies, 'You are drinking too much. You will have to do something about it, or else things will get much worse.' It is likely that a trite response of this kind, lacking in understanding, will re-inforce the drinker's depression and his need to seek comfort by drinking again.

Attention is *sympathetic* when people 'feel with' the sufferings of men or women they are listening to. Objectivity is abandoned altogether in order to share in the other person's feelings. For example, a sympathetic listener could get so depressed by the drinker's tale of woe, that he might join him in a nearby pub, there to drown their sorrows together! To literally share in a person's feelings in this way usually isn't helpful. One is in danger of becoming part of the problem, instead of being part of a possible solution.

In contrast, we pay attention with *empathy* when we 'feel into' what other people experience, and respond to their feelings in a loving and compassionate way, without necessarily having to share them. If a person with empathy heard the drinker's story, he might respond, 'My heart went out to you when I sensed how much the drinking is getting you down. I can understand why you feel so dejected and worried.' This is an intimate response in so far as it shows that the listener has tuned in to what lies innermost in the other person's experience.

Focusing on feelings

In chapter three, we saw how the awareness and understanding of one's feelings is a key to self-intimacy. Not only are they conditioned by our past experiences, they disclose what we really perceive, value, believe and desire, as we react to our environment. The same is true in interpersonal relationships. We have to focus on other people's feelings because they are the key which can unlock the door that so often shuts off the public from the private and the unknown self. By sensing what other people feel, we can enter into the private world of their subjectivity. In this way, that which is innermost in their hearts begins to manifest itself. People's feelings are revealed through their body language and their words. It is obvious that subjective states and secrets can be revealed in words. But it is equally true that, in spite of talking a lot, many people's words serve only to conceal that which is innermost in their experience. As Paul Simon put it in his song, *The Sounds of Silence*, it is a case of 'people talking without speaking.' There are many possible reasons for this, e.g. lack of self-awareness, mistrust, a poor self-image, or an overweening desire to please, etc.

Non-verbal communication

Over the years, I have come to appeciate the importance of non-verbal forms of communication. Just as foreign language movies have sub-titles, so the things people say are accompanied by a number of different non-verbal sub-titles which help to convey what they really feel. Researchers talk about diverse types.[12] Firstly, there is the study of *bodily movements* such as posture, gestures and facial expressions. For example, the pupils in people's eyes automatically dilate when they like the men or women they are with. Secondly, there is the area of *tactile communication*, the mediation of feeling through touch, embraces and kisses, etc. A third form of study shows how people can convey their feelings by the way in which they *use spaces*, e.g. leaning toward someone they like. Apparently when we feel really close to someone, we tend to stand about eighteen inches apart, whereas we 'keep our distance' where people we fear or dislike are concerned. Fourthly, there is the study of *non-oral communication*. It shows that no matter what people might say or not say about themselves, their true feelings will often be apparent from the way they speak, e.g. in the pitch, rate, inflection, volume, and tone of their speech. Finally, there is what is sometimes referred to as *object language*. It shows how things like dress, hair styles, jewellery, cosmetics and possessions can be a form of communication which may indicate what the person's self-concept is like. With practice, a person can acquire the skill of interpreting the subtle and sometimes ambiguous messages that other people convey in these non-verbal ways.

I know a nurse who has grown to be an expert in this form of empathy. She cares for mentally and physically handicapped children who are incapable of expressing themselves in words. On the face of it, one would think that while a doctor, nurse or relative could feel close to such a child, intimacy would be ruled out on account of its inability to disclose its inner self in a verbal way. However, the nurse I mentioned has told me that her desire to know each of her children, at a deeper level, was satisfied by means of patient, persistent and respectful observation. Because a handicapped child fails to form a strong ego or *persona*, it tends to relate to others from its true self, without a hint of hypocrisy. When a nurse, who is in touch with her own self, pays sustained attention to the child's body language, she can sense what it feels, e.g. fear, discomfort, joy, affection, etc. As she empathises with the child in this way, she finds that its feelings disclose the rich world of its subjectivity. Despite the fact that it cannot reason or talk, it becomes apparent that the child has much the same needs, reactions, values and beliefs as the rest of us.

Some time ago, my nursing contact decided to show her patients a video of the tenors Carreras, Domingo and Pavarotti in concert in Rome. One would think that a sequence of seventeen operatic arias would mean little or nothing to children with very low I.Q's. In the event, the opposite was the case. The nurses and doctors who watched the video with the kids were moved to tears when they saw how they reacted. They were obviously enraptured by the music. Their joy was evident in their eyes, faces, and gestures. Children who couldn't even talk tried to hum along with the tunes. Clearly, they appreciated the beauty and the high emotion of the music. The nurses and doctors say that they enjoyed a 'peak experience' of the kind that Maslow describes.[13] This occurred when they recognised not only what the children felt but also the aesthetic sense that accounted for their reactions.

The same children relate to other people, their companions and carers in terms of empathy rather than reason. In doing so, they display a capacity for considerable compassion and love.

In other words, they have rich interior lives. Their Christian faith finds a mysterious focus in the eucharist. Despite the fact that they have received no religious instruction, their reactions during Mass, e.g. uncharacteristic calm and silence, seem to indicate that they have a spiritual awareness of a mysterious Presence. As Jesus said, 'I thank you, Father, Lord of heaven and earth, because you have hidden these things from the wise and the intelligent and have revealed them to infants; yes, Father, for such was your gracious will.'(Lk 10:21)

Together, these considerations have led me to wonder whether it wouldn't be more accurate to say that the primary way in which we reveal our feelings is through the body. It is what we say that provides the sub-titles, which may or may not reflect and clarify what is being disclosed. Indeed I saw one piece of research which suggested that the content of the things we say accounts for only 7% of the impact of our communication; the other 93% can be accounted for in non-verbal ways.[14]

Things that impede empathic attention

It isn't easy to focus with empathy on the experience of another person. There are a number of common impediments. The extent to which people suffer from the pain of low self-esteem, is the extent to which they will be inclined to be insecure, mistrustful and defensive. Just as a physical toothache prevents one from paying attention to external things, such as a TV pro-gramme, so the toothache of unresolved emotional pain can pre-vent one from paying self-forgetful attention to the feelings of other people. A lack of inner healing and love inclines people to be self-absorbed. Instead of projecting themselves into the experi-ence of their neighbours, they tend to use it as a mirror in which to see the reflection of their own thoughts, pre-occupations, feelings and memories. In the months following my mother's death, many people asked, 'How do you feel?' Although I wasn't sure what I felt, I did try to describe what I was going through. I discovered, however, that very few people wanted to tune into my sense of loss, and grief. 'I know exactly what you feel,' they would com-monly respond, 'I went through the same thing when my father … or uncle … or grandmother died, a few years ago.' Then they would go on to tell me all the gruesome details. I realise that they meant well, but I didn't find their responses very helpful. For one thing, I had enough troubles of my own. I needed to feel listened to and understood. But I ended up trying to listen to my would-be comforters as they talked on and on about themselves. When I shared with people whose fathers and mothers were still alive, I found that my sense of bereavement tended to trigger their fears rather than their empathy. The prospect of their parents' inevitable demise, would often induce them to move away from my feelings. They would do this by either focusing on facts, changing the subject, theorising about death, giving good advice, or resorting to pious clichés.

Lack of compassion

It takes considerable reserves of compassion and self-discipline to tune into the painful feelings of other people. As Simone Weil has written: 'Those who are unhappy have no need for anything in this world but people capable of giving them their attention. The capacity to give one's attention to a sufferer is a very rare and difficult thing; it is almost a miracle; it is a miracle. Nearly all those who think they have this capacity do not possess it. Warmth of heart, impulsiveness, pity are not enough.' Weil goes on to say: 'The love of our neighbour in all its fullness means being able to say: "What are you going through?" ... It is enough, but it is indispensable, to know how to look at a person in a certain way. This way of looking is first of all attentive. The soul empties itself of all its own contents in order to receive into itself the being it is looking at, just as he or she is, in all truth. Only the person who is capable of attention can do this.'[15] A common hindrance where compassionate attention is concerned, is a judgemental cast of mind. Instead of accepting the experience and feelings of other people, some of us tend to hear them in terms of moralistic 'oughts', 'shoulds' 'musts' and 'have tos.' A moralistic attitude of this kind is always conveyed in a non-verbal way, and frequently in cheap words of advice which are substitutes for the demands of real empathy.

THE ESSENCE OF LOVE

Over the years, empathic attention has enabled me to recognise what other people have been feeling. As I have learned to stay with their emotions, without theorising about them, I have begun to sense the perceptions, values and beliefs that evoked them in the first place. Intuitions have been confirmed and deepened as the subjectivity of other people, especially of close friends, has been published and made known in an on-going way. But that's not all. As I have become increasingly aware of the richness, the goodness, beauty and integrity of other people's inner lives, I have had intimations of their inalienable value as persons. As this sense of appreciation has grown, I have found that it has seduced my will, so to speak, into an effortless disposition of approval. As I said earlier, I believe that the decision to attend to another person is not only the primordial act of will, it is arguably the pre-requisite for all other acts of will. That said, I'm convinced that it is only when one person recognises and approves of the inner value of another, that he or she makes the most important act of will of all, the will to love. As a result, I'm convinced that *love is an act of will whereby one approves of the perceived and potential inner value of a person or thing.*

Human love as a reflection of divine love

By the grace of God, I have been loved in this way by a few people. Sometimes the way they have looked at me has liter-ally brought tears of joy to my eyes. As I have reflected on these precious experiences of intimacy, I have asked myself the ques-tion, if mere mortals can look at me in this way, how does God see me? There have been times when I have become inwardly aware of the Lord's gaze searching and knowing me. Without a hint of judgement or condemnation, God has recognised and approved of my inner worth and potential. Occasionally as I have sensed God's love, I have been filled with inner consolation. It was as if the eyes of friends had been used as sacraments in order to medi-ate the warmth of the Lord's look of love. So I can identify with the sentiments of Nicholas of Cusa who once wrote: 'My experi-ence proves that you love me because your eyes are so attentively upon me, your poor little servant. Lord, your glance is love. And just as your gaze beholds me so attentively that it never turns from me, even so it is with your love.'[16] Later in the same book he says: 'Your vision, Lord, is your essence.' [17]

Adequate and inadequate notions of love

Personal experiences of human and divine love have put living flesh on the dry bones of my rather abstract definition of the essential nature of love. I would take issue with Scott Peck's much quoted assertion that love is 'The will to extend one's self for the purpose of nurturing one's own or another's spiritual growth.'[18] It seems to me that the desire to nurture one's own or another's spiritual growth is a *consequence* of love: it is not part of its essence. Nor is love a state of romantic yearning or a sense of union with one's beloved. It isn't a state of good feeling, or a common sharing of interests. These may be some of the typical antecedents and effects of true love, but they do not belong to the core of its nature. However I agree with Joseph Pieper when he says: 'In every conceivable case love signifies much the same as *approval* (my italics). The approval I'm speaking of is rather an expression of the will. It signifies the opposite of aloof, purely theoretical neutrality. It testifies to being in agreement, assenting, consenting, applauding, affirming, praising, glorifying and hailing ... All of them are expressions of the will and all of them mean, I want you to exist.'[19]

SOME EFFECTS OF TRUE LOVE

The perception and loving approval of the value of another person can have a number of predictable consequences. It will automatically evoke feelings such as joy, tenderness, affection, well-being, harmony, gratitude, etc. They may be accompanied by physiological reactions such as weeping, smiling or sighing. Sometimes, these reactions will be associated with an attitude of reverence, together with feelings such as awe, fascination and peace. They may indicate that the attentive person was aware of a mysterious something or Someone over and above the immediate object of perception. In cases like these, an experience of interpersonal intimacy can have a religious dimension, one that reveals the presence of the Lord. As the poet Hopkins has written somewhere: 'Christ plays in a thousand places, lovely in limbs and lovely in eyes not his, to the Father, through the features of men's faces.' So loving intimacy can reveal what St Bernard referred to as 'inner glory,'[20] i.e. the God of another person's inner self. Psychotherapist Irene de Castillejo has written: 'For there to be a meeting, it seems as though a third, a something else, is always present. You may call it Love or the Holy Spirit. Jungians would say that it is the presence of the Self. If this 'Other' is present, there cannot have failed to be a meeting.'[21]

Being affirmed

When people sense the approval and possible reverence of a loving person, they will feel affirmed at a deep level of their personalities. This is the first and perhaps the most important consequence of the dynamic of love. The word *affirmation* comes from the Latin meaning 'to make strong.' It is etymologically similar to the words *comfort* and *comforter* which we associate with the Holy Spirit. Both are also derived from Latin, meaning 'to endow with strength.' When one person approves the inner value of another, he or she becomes an agent of the Spirit, thereby doing two important things. Firstly, one helps the loved person to recognise and to assert his or her inner value. Secondly, one helps to manifest and release the person's hidden potential. Surely Viktor Frankl is correct when he says: 'By the spiritual act of love a person is enabled to see the essential traits and features in the beloved person; and even more, *he sees that which is potential in him or her, that which is not yet actualised. Furthermore, by his love the loving person enables the beloved person to actualize these potentialities* (my italics). By making him aware of what he can be and of what he should become, he or she makes these potentialities come true.'[22]

Max Scheler, who wrote so perceptively about the subject of love, has endorsed this point of view. Love, he suggests,[23] not only responds to present values, it is always creative in the sense that it helps both to reveal and to actualise as yet unrecognised values and potentials in the other person. In effect it says, in the words of Nietzsche, 'become that which you are.' In doing so it enables interrelated powers of the spiritual and psychological self to be activated in the loved person, thereby enabling him or her to attain greater degrees of integration and wholeness. I will have more to say about the potential healing effects of intimacy in the next chapter.

Loving relationship leads to loving service

Once loving attention establishes this kind of relationship with another person or persons, the dynamic of intimate knowing invites the will to make further choices. In the light of my love for them, what could I decide to do in order to promote their welfare? Because people have differing needs, this question can be answered in disparate ways, e.g. giving gifts to friends, spending time with the lonely, giving money to the poor, seeking justice for the oppressed, counselling the disturbed, encouraging the timid, etc. True love will not only energise one's *desire* to act in a loving and appropriate way, it will also provide the *power* to do so. This means that love is primarily a way of relating to other people and only secondarily a way of serving them, so to speak. That being so, love as service should always be the expression of an intimate relationship, instead of being a dutiful substitute for it, as is sometimes the case. If a Christian serves the poor, for example, because of some ideological conviction, or unacknowledged feelings of 'ressentiment,'[24] i.e. unacknowledged feelings of envy, hostility, and anger toward the rich and the successful, his or her activities will be 'a noisy gong and a clanging symbol,'(1 Cor 13:1) signifying nothing, because they aren't the expression of a loving relationship.

Loving leads to personal growth

Quoting a saying of Jesus that isn't found in the gospels, St Paul says: 'It is more blessed to give than to receive.'(Acts 20:35) However in Lk 6: 38, Jesus assures us: 'Give and it will be given to you. A good measure, pressed down, shaken together, running over, will be put into your lap; for the measure you give will be the measure you will get back.' When I go out to another person in love, it can have many good effects in my life. By loving I fulfil a God-given and a God-prompted desire, and so I become a lover. This may be true in a romantic sense, but I'm using the word to describe anyone who loves somebody else, a member of the family, a friend, a neighbour, etc. By getting to know and to love another person in an intimate way, simultaneously enables me to relate to myself in a deeper way. By perceiving the inner value and worth of another person, my own 'inner glory' is also illuminated. By affirming and enabling the hidden potential of another person to blossom and thrive, I activate my own capacity for self-actualisation. So there is a paradox involved in loving. It is only as I break free of the magnetic pull of self-absorption, to become absorbed in the inner life of another person, that I can truly become myself. In the sometimes ecstatic activity of coming to know another person – the word *ecstasy* comes from the Greek meaning 'to stand outside' of oneself in a self-forgetful way – I can experience a unique sense of emotional and spiritual fulfilment. This is particularly true when it is a question of a mutual love, one that creates a union of minds and hearts.

This dynamic can also be involved in one way or unilateral intimacy. Speaking about this kind of relationship, St John of the Cross once said: 'Where there is no love, put love and you will receive love.' While this won't necessarily be the case on all occasions – people are free to refuse our love and its implications – many will not only receive the gift of our approval and appreciation, they will also learn to return our love.

When intimacy as self-disclosure and loving attention informs a relationship, inwardness is deepened, and connectedness is established in ever-increasing degrees of reciprocal intensity. Not only does love of this kind heal personal and interpersonal forms of alienation, it also overcomes our alienation from creation and from God.

Notes
1. The late Jacques Maritain has shown how this intuition can be used as a basis of a demonstration of the existence of God in his 'A Sixth Way' in *A Maritain Reader*, ed. D. & I. Gallagher, Image, N.Y., 1966, 92-106.
2. *Tractatus Logico-Philosophicus*, London, Routledge & Kegan Paul, 1961, 44.

3. *Christian Mysticism: The Future of a Tradition*, Egan, Pueblo, N.Y., 1984, 315-316.
4. *Spiritual Theology*, Aumann, Sheed & Ward, London, 1982, 436-437.
5. *The Experience of Love*, Washington, 1968.
6. *Will and Spirit*, Harper & Row, N.Y., 1982, 6.
7. 'Contemplation,' Walter Burghardt, in *Church*, Winter 1989, 15.
8. Quoted by G. May, *op. cit.*, 25.
9. *Selected Spiritual Writings*, Hugh of St Victor, Harper & Row, N.Y., 1962, 183.
10. *Waiting on God*, Fontana, Glasgow, 71, 72.
11. *Stress Management*, Nathan & Charlesworth, Ballantine, N.Y., 1985.
12. *Understanding and Sharing: An Introduction to Speech Communication*, J. Pearson & P. Nelson, Brown Comp. Iowa, 1979, 74-90.
13. *The Further Reaches of Human Nature*, The Viking Press, N.Y., 1972.
14. H. N. Wright, *Communication and Conflict Resolution in Marriage*, Elgin, Il, 1977, 6
15. *Op. cit.*, 75.
16. *The Vision of God*, Ungar, Pub. Co. N.Y. 1960, 15.
17. *Op. cit* , 39.
18. *The Road Less Travelled*, Rider, London, 1983, 81.
19. *About Love*, Franciscan Herald Press, Chicago, 1974.
20. *On Loving God*, Hodder & Stoughton, London.
21. *Knowing Woman: A Feminine Psychology*, Harper & Row, N.Y., 1973, 12.
22. *Man's Search for Meaning*, Pocketbooks, Simon & Schuster, N.Y., 1963, 176-177.
23. Vacek, 'Scheler's Phenomenology of Love,' *The Journal of Religion*, Vol.l 62, no. 2, April 1982, 160, 165.
24. cf. B. Lonergan, *Method in Theology*, DLT, London, 1971, 33 .

CHAPTER 9

The healing power of intimacy

The Taoist philosophy of China believes that all energy oscillates between the two poles of Yang and Yin. The word Yang refers to the masculine principle, i.e. all that is expansive, aggressive and demanding. The word Yin refers to the feminine principle, i.e. all that is contractive, responsive and conservative. These two principles exist everywhere in the created world and every feature of nature reflects one aspect or the other. For example, the north side of a river which receives the sun is Yang, while the South side which is in shadow is Yin. Yang and Yin also exist within people. They are very similar to Jung's notion of the male *animus*, or *logos* function which is oriented toward discrimination and thought and the female *anima*, or *eros* function which is oriented toward connectivity. Both exist within the human psyche. When Yang and Yin, *animus* and *anima* are harmonised within a person through right relationship with other people and nature, the Tao, or reality of God, is manifested within the self.

THE MASCULINISATION OF CULTURE

It is my belief that this ideal of universal harmony has been forfeited because of an almost exclusive concentration on the worthwhileness of the male point of view. The masculinisation of culture in recent centuries has been brought about by the Protestant Reformation, the scientific revolution and the influence of capitalist economics. We will look briefly, at each point in turn.

The influence of the Reformers

In spite of their strongly patriarchal tendencies, Catholic and Orthodox forms of Christianity offset some of the more extreme implications of a 'male' notion of God by incorporating the feminine principle in two ways. Firstly, they encouraged the cult of the Virgin Mary. Secondly, they believed that, just as God became immanent in the womb of the Blessed Mother so he is immanent in the womb of *mother* nature as well. Incidentally, the belief that God's presence could be mediated by the sky, mountains, stones, trees, lakes, rivers and every kind of animal, was a particularly striking aspect of Celtic spirituality.[1] However all that began to change with the Reformation. As H. G. Wells has pointed out,[2] communities of obedience (i.e. stable societies of the South, which stressed the virtues of contemplation) like Catholicism and Orthodoxy, were challenged by communities of will (i.e. the restless nomads of the North, who stressed the importance of dynamic action), such as Calvinism and, to a lesser extent, Lutheranism. They focused exclusively on the maleness of God and abolished Marian devotion. They maintained that revelation came solely through the word of God, while denying that mother nature could also mediate the Beyond who is in her midst. In this way, a masculine notion of revelation predominated over a more feminine version. God could only be mediated to rational consciousness by the conceptual *logos* or word. God could not be mediated in an intuitive way by means of pre-rational religious experiences such as dreams, or by sacramental symbols such as the eucharistic bread and wine. Sheldrake has indicated how the disenchanted world-view of the reformers was conducive to the emergence of the mechanistic perspectives of the so-called 'Enlightenment'.

Science sees nature as a machine

We have already noted how Bacon, Galileo and Newton replaced the medieval conviction that nature was an organism with the notion that it was an inanimate machine. At the same time, René Descartes became the father of modern philosophy by articulating the implications of the new world-view. Having adopted a methodology of universal doubt, he came to the conclusion that he could only be sure of one thing. Because he was conscious of being conscious, he must therefore exist, or as he put it, 'I think, therefore I am.' When he drew out the implications of this basic insight, Descartes began to undermine the intimate connection between mind and body. He wrote: 'I consider the human body as a machine, my thought compares a sick man to an ill-made clock and a healthy man to a well-made clock.'

He also undermined the intimate connection between

145

human beings and the world. With typically male detachment, scientists have aspired ever since to control and subdue *mother* nature with the Faustian power of objective reason. So, by the end of the seventeenth century, she had ceased to be feminine at all. Indeed, man's conquest of nature is inseparable from sexual imagery. As one feminist writer has noted: 'By re-conceptualising reality as a machine rather than a living organism, science (which was conducted by men and which reflected an exclusively male point of view) sanctioned the domination of both nature and women.'[3] Ironically, a number of male scientists have shown how this kind of detached rationalism has had negative effects in areas such as health care, psychology and economics.

Capitalism and the exploitation of nature

For their part, sociologists and historians like Weber and Tawney have shown how capitalism was able to thrive within the cultural ethos created by the Reformation and Enlightenment. By desacralising the world of nature and stressing the importance of the work ethic, both movements paved the way for capitalism. Far from feeling scrupulous about their desire to dominate nature, capitalists saw it as an ideal in a world where nothing was sacred. By applying the best insights of the new sciences, they learned to master, subdue and exploit the earth's resources. This became increasingly true with the advent of the industrial revolution. Not only has it tended to sever the intimate connection between people and nature, it has subordinated people, their relationships and rights to the abstract and uncaring demands of market forces such as profit and loss, supply and demand, etc. Now as we face into the twenty-first century, we have to cope with the consequences of this form of unfettered masculinisation. Not only are we facing an environmental crisis of major proportions, we human beings are in trouble also.

Five effects of cultural masculinisation

As culture has been defeminised in recent centuries, a sense of connectedness has been weakened with disastrous effects. I call them the five A's of absurdity, alienation, anxiety, apathy, and agnosticism. We will take a brief look at each.

146

Absurdity

Newtonian science and Cartesian philosophy have tended to set human beings adrift in an alien universe devoid of any ultimate meaning. This has given rise to the nihilistic belief that, despite all appearences to the contrary, reality is ultimately absurd. Novelist André Malraux has one of his characters say: 'In the depths of European man, where it dominates the great moments of his life, there resides an essential absurdity.'[4] As a young man in the nineteen sixties, I shared this sense of meaninglessness on a number of occasions. I found that it was reflected in works like Sartre's *Nausea*, Camus's *The Outsider*, Beckett's *Waiting for Godot*, Kafka's *The Castle*, nearly all of Bergman's films and the apparently formless and anarchic nature of a lot of modern music and pictorial art.

Alienation

Not surprisingly, the extent to which people lose touch with a sense of meaning, is the extent to which they will suffer from a sense of alienation. It is experienced, says Erich Fromm, when 'man does not experience himself as the active bearer of his own powers and richness, but as an impoverished "thing", dependent on powers outside himself, unto whom he has projected his living substance.'[5] Fromm shows how this form of estrangement can be reinforced by bureaucratisation and consumerism. However, he agrees with the Marxist view that workers lose both the product of their labour and their sense of productive activity, following the expropriation of both by capital. While he thinks that this is the fundamental cause of alienation, I believe he is mistaken. Modern estrangement can be traced back to the breaking of a feminine sense of connection with nature as a result of the threefold masculinisation of culture which we have described.

Anxiety

As more and more people lose touch with the meaning of life, they experience deep down anxiety which is not necessarily neurotic in nature. In fact this phenomenon has become so widespread that the poet W. H. Auden described the twentieth century as 'The Age of Anxiety.' As we already noted in chapter two, the word *anxiety* comes from the Latin *angustus* meaning 'to narrow'. It is etymologically related to the words *anguish* and *angina*. One would be tempted to believe that, as people lose a sense of meaning, their attitude to life becomes more narrow-minded and defensive. Their deep-down sense of anxiety, or even anguish, can lead to psychosomatic disorders such as the widespread incidence of angina and heart-disease (dis-ease). Indeed modern medicine confirms the fact that anything between sixty and eighty per cent of all illnesses are stress-related.

In an earlier chapter, we noted how psychiatrist Viktor Frankl has argued that the will to meaning is deeper and more important than either Freud's will to pleasure or Adler's will to power. 'The striving to find a meaning in one's life,' he writes, 'is the primary motivational force in man.'[6] However, the extent to which the sense of meaning has faded in our disjointed culture, is the extent to which people experience a nagging sense of emptiness. Like St Augustine before him, Frankl argues that those who fail to detect the meaning of life will try to compensate for its loss in many unhealthy and negative ways. For example, there can be an idolatrous pursuit of power, especially in the form of money, or a craving for pleasure, especially in the form of impersonal sexual activity.

Apathy

Anxious, alienated people tend to become apathetic, i.e. indifferent, lacking passion, feeling, emotion or enthusiasm in their response to life and nature. In his book, *Love and Will*, psychiatrist Rollo May has suggested that many apathetic people in our culture are 'schizoid,' i.e. out of touch with life. He uses the term, in a non-pathological sense, to describe those who avoid close relationships and suffer from an inability to feel deeply about anything. They tend to be cold, detached, aloof and superior. 'Apathy and lack of feeling,' he wrote by way of explanation, 'are defence mechanisms against anxiety. When a person continuously faces dangers he is powerless to overcome, his final line of defence is at last to avoid even feeling the dangers.'[7] It seems to me that the contemporary 'famine of love,' which seems to afflict affluent societies, is going to produce a generation of men and women who suppress their painful feelings of insecurity and deprivation by becoming apathetic.

Agnosticism

I have long believed that the crisis of belief in Western societies is due to the masculinisation of culture. By the way I'm using the

words *masculine* and *feminine* as metaphors for archetypal characteristics which are culturally conditioned. As the typical powers
of the male ego have predominated, men have lost touch with
their deeper feminine selves. In so doing, they have lost touch
with those archetypal powers of the *anima* and the spiritual self
which can only be fulfiled by an awareness of the transcendent
Other. God's presence is mediated to the soul – which in our culture is feminine to a male God – by means of intimate relationship
with women and through them with the rest of nature. Alienation
from the *anima* has been reinforced by the fact that cultural conditioning has separated many women from their own feminine
depths. Indeed Freud often said that the aim of successful psychoanalysis was a 'repudiation of femininity'[8] in the lives of men *and*
of women!

This crisis of the feminine is one of the main reasons for
the religious crisis of our times. The word *religion* comes from the
Latin *religare* meaning 'to bind'. The extent to which men and
women lose touch with the feminine archetype, is the extent to
which they lose touch with that power of the self, which alone can
bind us in an intimate way to one another, to nature and through
both to God. The decline of the feminine dimensions of the
human psyche leads almost inevitably to either agnosticism or
even atheism.

INTIMACY AND THE HEALING OF NATURE

It seems to me that the kind of intimate relationships I have been
advocating can only blossom within a unified world-view, one
which is open to the experience of transcendence. We have seen
how Newtonian science and Cartesian philosophy replaced the
holistic perspectives that had prevailed in Medieval Europe. Now
some five hundred years later, science itself is undergoing a paradigm shift of major importance. It is being pioneered by scientists
like Einstein, Heisenberg, Jung, Bohm, Wilber, Capra, de Chardin
and Sheldrake.

We can look at this transformation from two points of
view: the way in which scientists try to understand reality, and
the conclusions they come to. For example, a biographer has observed: 'Einstein revealed two aspects in his approach to science

which became keys to his work: *the search for a unity behind the disparate phenomena, and the acceptance of a reality apart from the direct visible truth.*'(my italics)[9] Clearly his desire for understanding was religious in nature. He wrote: 'My religion consists of a humble admiration of the illimitable superior spirit who reveals himself in the slight details we are able to perceive with our frail and feeble minds. That deeply emotional conviction of the presence of a superior reasoning power, which is revealed in the incomprehensible universe, forms my idea of God.' [10]

Religion and the new physics

Unlike the reductionist science of the last few centuries, the conclusions of modern science seem to be amenable to a religious point of view. They embrace both the notion of classical causality and the a-causal 'sympathy' of all things. Nowadays, physicists understand the universe as an integrated whole. Because everything that exists is interrelated, each part can only be understood in terms of the whole and *vice versa*. As Bede Griffiths has noted: 'The whole universe is in every part. That is the principle. Just as the structure of the whole human organism is present in every cell, *so the whole universe is present in each one of us.*'(my italics)[11] So the notion of observing the world in a detached and objective way has given way to the realisation that we are inescapably part of the world we observe. That being the case, not only is reality modified by the way in which we contemplate its secrets, we for our part are changed by the mundane and transcendental realities we experience as a result.

Modern science also sees men and women as an integral part of the evolutionary process. The aspiration of animate and inanimate matter for fulfilment in God, can only be realised through the conscious and loving mediation of those who know how to relate to creation in the proper way. Biologist Rupert Sheldrake interprets something akin to this dynamic in the light of trinitarian theology when he writes: 'In the context of evolutionary cosmology, the Spirit underlies the outward flow of energy and the expansive impulse of the universe; the Word is in the patterns of activity and meaning expressed through fields. God the Father is the speaker, the conscious source of both Word and

Spirit who yet transcends both. Thus the energy and fields of the evolutionary cosmos have a common source, a unity. And not just a unity, but a conscious unity.'[12] It is worth noting in passing that, in an attempt to explain what he means by energy fields, Sheldrake compares them to the concept of forms in Platonic philosophy. How times have changed when an eminent scientist interprets his findings in terms of Greek philosophy and Christian theology!

The extent of the ecological and cultural crisis we are facing at the moment is proportionate to the need we have for reconciliation with the created world. It will only come about when we learn to pay loving attention to the self-disclosure of mother nature. She will have to be respected, even reverenced as a living organism, instead of being observed, controlled and exploited as an inanimate machine. In the words of Martin Buber we will have to move from the alienation that characterises I-It relationships, to experience the healing intimacy that occurs as a result of I-Thou ones, which are open to the experience of mediated transcendence.

From I-It to I-Thou relationships

There is a memorable example of what I mean in Buber's writings. He describes how, at the age of eleven, he used to go to the stables at his grandparent's house to stroke the neck of a much-loved, dappled-grey horse. He says that his sense of relationship with the horse, mediated as it was through a sense of touch, was a profound one. 'I must say what I experienced in touch with the animal was the Other, the immense otherness of the Other.' He goes on to say that because of his sense of connection with the horse, its otherness was different from that of an ox or a ram. It allowed him to draw near and to touch it in an intimate way. As he stroked the horse's mane 'and felt the life beneath my hand, it was as though the element of vitality itself bordered on my skin, something that was not I, was certainly not akin to me, palpably the other, not just another, really the Other itself; and yet it let me approach, *confided itself to me* (my italics) placed itself elementally in the relation of Thou and Thou with me.'[13] Buber tells us that the spontaneity of his experience was lost when he became conscious of being conscious of stroking the horse and so the sense of intimacy was broken.

This reminds me of what St Augustine said about the ending of the mystical experience he shared with his mother Monica at Ostia: 'While we spoke of the eternal Wisdom, longing for it and straining for it with all the strength of our hearts, for one fleeting instant we reached out and touched it. Then with a sigh, ... we returned to the sound of our own speech, in which each word has a beginning and an ending.'[14] That kind of fall from the graced immediacy of contemplative awareness is inevitable. However, while it lasts, it not only actualises the capacity of the self for trancendental intimacy, it also helps to actualise the spiritual potential of the non-human world in two interrelated ways.

In the preceding chapter, I mentioned that intimacy, as loving attention to mysteries, is quite different from the problem-solving detachment of a scientific observer. It is not only *responsive* to the perceived being and value of an object, e.g. Buber's horse, it can be *creative* also in so far as it enables an object to attain its higher potential and value. We saw how this could be so in interpersonal relationships. It can also be true with regard to our relationship with non-human reality.

Love and the fulfilment of creation

Because I believe that everything that exists is impinged upon by the Divine Spirit of Love, I'm inclined to agree with Max Scheler who thought that love is a persistent and deep urge to develop and evolve, rather than merely to reproduce. He wrote: 'Love is the tendency, or as it may be, the act that seeks to lead everything in the direction of the perfection and value proper to it – and succeeds, when no obstacles are present ... Love ... is a dynamic becoming, a growing, a welling up of things in the direction of their archetype, which resides in God. Thus every phase in this inner growth of the value of things, a growth which love produces, is always an intermediate station on the way of the world toward God.'[15]

This belief makes even more sense when it is understood within the evolutionary context I have mentioned a number of times. Contemplative experiences, like the one described by Buber, change our relationship to ourselves as people in relationship with the Mysterious Other. God is experienced as the One who is revealed in and through our contact with nature as the 'notebook of the Master.' As *relatedness* increases in this way, so does *inwardness*. Our relationship to our real selves is modified in such a way that we become more consciously aware of the presence of the Spirit active within our spirits. It is this self that empowers our sense of intimate connection with a horse or any other object in nature. It is the point of encounter where the Spirit who searches everything in the created world, including the horse, leads us at the same time into a more intimate relationship with the life of God. As our relationship with nature is transformed by this kind of reconciling intimacy, it will inspire a radical re-evaluation of our current attitudes, e.g. to consumerism, growth economics, pollution, wastefulness, and the wilful and destructive exploitation of natural resources.

PERSONAL AND INTERPERSONAL HEALING

We have examined the healing potential of intimate relationships with the world about us. They can transform the five A's from absurdity to meaning, alienation to connectedness, anxiety to receptivity, apathy to emotional responsiveness, and agnosticism to religious faith. Now we will focus our attention on the dynamics of emotional and interpersonal healing.

In adult life most of us are aware of inner hurts. We lack a sense of integration and harmony. Instead we can be bedeviled by neurotic attitudes and behaviours. Psychologists argue convincingly that nearly all of them can be traced back to a lack of self-esteem. As Jung pointed out, 'the acceptance of self is the essence of the human problem.' Many of us can identify with the story of Dr Jekyll and Mr Hyde. Like Stevenson's character, we are divided within. As we saw in chapter five, we accept those aspects of our personalities which conform to our idealistic beliefs and values, and reject those which fail to do so as contemptible and unlovable. Because we cannot accept the inept, weak and irrational side of ourselves, we hide the Mr Hyde within. Honest self-disclosure is avoided as we put on masks and hide behind roles.

Inner healing requires intimacy

Psychologists argue convincingly that many, if not most of our emotional conflicts are due to a lack of unconditional love, especially during childhood. Some of these experts maintain that healing can only come through either psychotherapy or psychoanalysis. Both are hard to come by, time-consuming and expensive. Other experts, such as Jung, Rogers and Erickson, believe that inner healing can come about as a result of experiencing unilateral or reciprocal intimacy of a loving kind. It begins when people who, hurting inside, overcome their fear of rejection to reveal their true selves, shadow and all, to a confidant, counsellor or friend. If the trusted person understands, accepts and loves them as they are, without a hint of judgement or condemnation, they will learn to understand, accept and love themselves in the same way. Research has confirmed the subjective impression that this kind of inner healing depends to a great extent on the way in which the helper pays attention to the self-disclosure of the other person.

As we know, there are many forms of psychotherapy, each with its distinctive theoretical assumptions and methods. Yet despite their obvious differences, all of them are capable of bringing healing to their clients. It has been shown[16] that the only healing factor that all of these therapies have in common is the empathy, warmth, and genuineness of the therapist. A compassionate ability to get inside the skin of a suffering person in order to identify what he or she is going through, seems to release the healing powers of the self.

Three types of compassion

It seems to me that there are three interrelated forms of compassionate intimacy. Firstly, there is *fellow feeling*, the ability to project oneself into the sufferings of another person because one has endured something similar, e.g. alcoholism in the family, depression, etc. Secondly, there is what I call *wounded wonder*. In the previous chapter, I described how love goes beyond appearances to recognise, with approval, the unique value of another person. Such an awareness evokes a heart-felt sense of wonder. However, the extent to which the person has been wounded in any way, spiritually, emotionally or physically, is the extent to which one's sense of wonder is wounded. This is an important point. The person's woundedness is not the primary focus of attention. Rather, it is experienced in the light of an intuitive real-isation of the person's inalienable value. Thirdly, the tension im-plicit in this two-fold awareness gives rise to what has been called *indignant compassion*. In the light of a loving recognition of the innermost value of someone who is suffering, a compassionate adult resists anything that might militate against the other person's health or happiness. It is this kind of compassion that motivates him or her to heal or to help in any way possible.

There is a good example of these forms of compassion in the life of Jesus. A man with a virulent skin disease came to him and pleaded on his knees, 'If you are willing, you can cleanse me.' In our version of Mark's gospel, we are told that Jesus was moved with compassion, stretched out his hand, touched the man and said, 'Of course I want to. Be healed.' (Mk 1:40-41) Scripture schol-ars maintain that in an earlier version of his gospel the evangelist wrote: 'Jesus was angry,' and said, 'of course I want to. Be healed.' Fearing his readers might think that Jesus was displeased with the man rather than the skin disease which was afflicting him, Mark changed the wording in the final edition of his gospel. So the reply, 'Of course I want to,' was energised by the three forms of compassion we have described. Jesus could project himself into the man's feelings because he himself was ostracised on a number of occasions. (cf. Mk 3:21) While he reverenced the man's value as a child of God, his sense of wonder was wounded when he became aware of his afflictions. Sympathy for the leper was matched by an antipathy to his illness. As the Spirit assured him that he was sharing in the feelings and will of God himself, he *knew* that the same Spirit would release the healing power which was latent within the self of the diseased man to bring him healing.

Compassion releases the healer within

Like Jung, it is my belief that these forms of Spirit-filled compassion are the key to psycho-spiritual healing. He was opposed to the Freudian approach in so far as it aimed to cure people by means of detached and objective forms of analysis. He believed that this form of apathetic relationship implied that anal-ysts were superior to their clients. While they would appear to be healthy, powerful and wise, their patients, in contrast, would seem to be unhealthy, weak and dependent. As a result, the clients would be inclined to project their own *self*-healing capacities on to their analysts.[17] While analysis might lead to intellectual insight, and a *desire* for change, the fact that it increased inward alienation would rob clients of the very power they would need to bring it about. However, Jung believed that if prospective therapists realised that, like their clients, they too were wounded, i.e. *'wounded* healers', a *therapeutic relationship* could be formed. As therapists simultaneously tuned in to the inner worth of their clients and lovingly resisted all that was opposed to it, e.g. self-condemnatory attitudes, they would help to affirm and release the healing potential of the self in each of their afflicted clients. As a result, the latent self-regulatory powers of the psyche would begin to assert themselves in a therapeutic way, e.g. in the form of healing dreams.

Because grace builds on nature, it is my belief that the Holy Spirit is intimately associated with the dynamics we have been describing. The Spirit is the great Healer within and can act through therapists by releasing the healing power of the restricted self in each client. As a result, they come to have both the desire and the power to attain inner harmony and peace.

Alcoholics Anonymous on inner healing

All that I have been saying is well illustrated by steps four and five of the recovery programme of Alcoholics Anonymous. The founders of the fellowship realised that many unhappy adults drink heavily in an effort to deaden the nagging pain of self-rejection and low self-esteem. They also realised that to stop drinking, with the help of the higher Power, was only the beginning of a new beginning. The recovering alcoholic was dry, yes, but not yet sober. Sobriety would only be experienced when the psychological and emotional hurts, that led to the addictive behaviour in the first place, were progressively healed. As far as I'm aware, one of the founders of A.A. went to Switzerland and talked to Carl Jung about this problem. Presumably, the learned doctor pointed out that two vital steps would have to be taken by recovering alcoholics if they were to experience the inner healing that could lead to sobriety and spiritual growth. Firstly, they would have to make a fearless list of all the wrong-doings they were guilty of, together with a list of the shameful and hurtful things that had been inflicted on them by others. Secondly, they would have to admit those wrong-doings and hurts to themselves, to God and *to another human being*. It seems to me that the need for self-disclosure of this kind to another person is not only the hardest of the three things to do, it is also the most important as far as inner healing is concerned.

Over the years, I have had the privilege of listening to recovering alcoholics as they took the brave step of revealing their most secret and hidden selves to me. I have noticed at times like these, that two emotions predominate, those of desire and fear. They have a strong, God-prompted desire – that emanates from their deepest depths – to be known and accepted as they really are and not as they have pretended to be. They also have a fear of rejection, one that resonates with the painful echoes of let-downs in the past, e.g. by parents and friends. At an emotional level they seem to say, 'If people who were significant in my life, rejected me for my imperfections in the past, if I even rejected my own shadow personality, why should I believe that you of all people, will accept me as I am?'

To begin with, recovering alcoholics are motivated by a desire to tell me at least part of their story. It is a bit like a card game. Initially, they reveal their less important secrets. All the while, they nervously watch to see how I am reacting. Is it condemnation and disgust or acceptance and understanding? If they sense that they are evoking a compassionate response, they keep upping the anti until, finally, desire prevails over fear and they reveal the most hidden contents of their hearts. Usually they are extremely anxious and agitated at this point. They have broken the inner sound barrier of fear, to reveal the most 'hateful' things about themselves. They wait with trembling expectation to see how I will react.

Invariably my response is much the same. Their extraordinary courage evokes my admiration, their sufferings evoke my compassion, and sometimes my tears, and their honesty and good-will evoke my love. Most times I say nothing; I just give them a reassuring hug. These are wonderful moments of inner healing. As recovering alcoholics sense, for the first time, that they are accepted, understood and loved as they are, they begin to accept, understand and love themselves in the same way. The dividing wall of self-rejection begins to fall, thereby allowing a deep-seated reconciliation and healing to take place within their personalities.(cf. Eph 2:14) Freer to accept and be themselves, they are empowered to forget themselves in out-going love of others.

I have no doubt that the Spirit of God is active in the whole dynamic. As St Paul assures us: 'God did not give us a Spirit of cowardice or fear,'(2 Tim 1:7) rather, as 'the Spirit of truth,'(Jn 14:16) he prompts and empowers people's desire to disclose the inner truth about themselves. The Spirit also enables the listener to 'be compassionate as the Father is compassionate' without a trace of judgement or condemnation. (cf. Lk 6: 36) Finally, it is the Spirit that initiates the on-going process of inner healing, as Jas 5:16 reminds us, 'Confess your sins to one another, and pray for one another that you may be healed.'

Learning from alcoholics

Gerald May has written: 'I am not being flippant when I say, that *all of us suffer from addiction* (my italics)'[18] and goes on to say: 'I have come to view addiction as the sacred disease of the modern world.'[19] Just as the suffering of recovering alcoholics can lead them to experience inner healing in the way I have described, so it can be for all of us.

I had been so impressed by the honesty of recovering alcoholics, that I experienced a growing desire to imitate them by revealing my true self to at least one of my trusted friends. This I did for the first time on new year's eve 1985. I had gone to visit a family I knew. When everyone else had retired to bed, I was left alone with my friend. By the way, the word *friend* comes from the middle-English *frend* and the Anglo-Saxon *freond* which means 'loving', the present participle of *freogan* meaning 'to love'. It can also mean 'free' because in Anglo-Saxon it referred to the 'dearly beloved' members of a household as opposed to the slaves. When we experience the love of a friend we enter a zone of psychological safety, one where we are free to take off our masks and to be our true selves. That's what happened on this graced occasion.

We chatted in a relaxed way while waiting to drink a toast together at midnight. Without consciously intending to do so, I found myself talking about personal things that I had never mentioned before. At one point I thought to myself, 'It's great that you have revealed so much of yourself, but that's enough. Don't go any further. You risk being rejected and abandoned.' While my mind told me that this wasn't true, my heart was filled with fear. But it must have been the Spirit at work within, because I found the courage to continue, until I had disclosed everything I was consciously aware of at the time. It was the best general confession I had ever made. In the past, I had told different priests about my various weaknesses. However, none of them was aware of the complete picture. But now, this friend had all the pieces of the jigsaw. She knew me as I really was, sins and all. She said nothing for a quite a while. In the silence I knew that I was not only understood and accepted, I was also loved as I was. It was a precious moment of inner healing. Rightly have the scriptures said, 'A faithful friend is a healing medicine.'(Sir 6: 16)

I have often reflected on the therapeutic effects of that experience. I have never doubted the fact that by accepting me as I was, without judgement or condemnation, my friend had been used by God to mediate his mercy and love. And so I had the grace to accept that I was accepted. I had an experiential understanding of what Jesus meant when he said, 'If you forgive the sins of any, they are forgiven them, if you retain the sins of any they are retained.'(Jn 20:23) It has been said that we are no closer to God than we are to our enemy. By loving me as I was, my friend was able to love the enemy within, with all my selfishness, weakness and irrationality. As a result, I learned to accept and to love my alienated self. A biblical image comes to mind in this connection. It was as if my conscious self, like the father in the parable, was able to embrace the prodigal son of my weakness in a joyful experience of psycho-spiritual reconciliation.(cf. Lk 15:11-32)

Because of this change in attitude, I have found that I have a greater ability to love my so-called 'enemies' in the wider community, i.e. people I find hard to accept because they have hurt me in some way or other in the past.(cf. Mt 5:44)

It is clear, therefore, that inner healing of this kind leads to interpersonal healing because, as self-absorption diminishes, projections are withdrawn and, having received love from one's friend, one is more able to give it to others, whether they are friends or not. By learning to love that which is least in one another, friends are empowered to love Christ in the least of the brethren. (cf. Mt 25:40) Surely St Augustine was correct when he wrote: 'There can be no true intimacy unless those who cling to each other are welded together by God in that love which is poured into our hearts by the Holy Spirit.' Intimate relationships, whether romantic or otherwise, can reach beyond themselves through love of the neighbour to the source of all charity, namely God.

Psycho-sexual healing

Male-female intimacy brings about another kind of healing by helping each person to grow in psycho-sexual maturity. The word *sex* in English comes from the Latin *secare* which means 'to cut' or 'to divide'. The sexes are divided in two interrelated ways. Firstly, men and women are divided from one another by physical and psychological differences. Some of the latter can be attributed to nature, others to nurture, i.e. the influence of our cultural prejudices and stereotypes. We have already noted in this chapter how men and women alike are victims of a masculinisation of culture. Secondly, men and women are divided within themselves. Carl Jung has suggested that all of us are bi-sexual from a psychological point of view. As a man, I am consciously and predominately male. But at an unconscious level, there is a feminine dimension or *anima*, as Jung called it. Conversely, while women are predominately and consciously female, at an unconscious level there seems to be a masculine dimension or *animus*.

When men and women learn to go beyond the closeness that characterises ego to ego relationships, to experience the kind of intimacy that relates oneself to the self of another person, two things happen. Firstly, they are reconciled to one another in love. Secondly, they experience an inner reconciliation of the male-female sides of their natures. As one church document put it: 'Sexuality is one of the most powerful of our biological and emotional endowments. It is one of the deepest constituents of personality. Men and women are complementary to one another, not just in their physical sexuality, but also in their psychology, their sensitivity, and even, in important respects, in their spirituality. The words of Genesis have a profound meaning: The Lord said, "It is not good that the man should be alone. I will make him a help-mate like himself."(Gen 2:12)'[20] I am convinced that psycho-sexual healing is very important from a personal and a cultural point of view. Until the masculinisation of culture is offset by a recovery of the feminine dimension of experience, our alienation from one another and the natural world will continue with disastrous results.

INTIMACY AND PHYSICAL HEALING

Western medicine has come to the conclusion that the majority of physical illnesses are psychosomatic in origin. As people experience different kinds of inner healing, as a result of growing intimacy with nature and one another, many of their physical sicknesses and diseases are healed. For example, as anxiety is reduced, stress levels fall and high blood pressure returns to normal. But surely George Montague is correct when he writes: 'If the *psyche* has such an influence on the body, might not the spirit in turn have a powerful influence on the *psyche* and through the *psyche* on the body as well? If we can speak of psychosomatic diseases, might we not also speak of pneuma-psychosomatic diseases? Such diseases have psychic and somatic effects but their roots are really in the underdeveloped or constricted *pneuma* (or self).'[21] If this is so, and I'm convinced it is, then the possibility of physical healing occurs when one person relates in a compassionate way to the wounded or constricted self of another. I'll explain what I mean by reflecting on a memorable experience. It will encapsulate the content of the last few pages and introduce us at the same time to section three of the book, which deals with our intimacy with God and *vice versa*.

A memorable personal experience

During an extended stay in the United States, I lived in the chaplain's quarters of a large city hospital. During my time there, I formed a deep and lasting friendship with a member of my order, a nursing sister who was working in the children's ward. We spent many happy hours conversing together. As time passed, we learned to open our hearts to one another with complete honesty. On one of our days off we went for a drive in the countryside. At one point in the journey, Sr Catherine turned to me and said, 'There is something wrong with my health, my ankles have been swelling lately and I have been experiencing a lot of pain.' I was really taken aback. So much so indeed that I stopped the car. 'What do you think it is?' I asked anxiously. 'I don't want to alarm you,' she said, 'but there is a slight chance that I have bone cancer, the symptoms are the same as those of another member of my family who had the disease a few years ago.'

I was on tenderhooks for the next few weeks. Sr Catherine underwent a series of tests and we were both delighted when she was told that, whatever she had, it wasn't cancer. In the meantime however, the swellings increased, the pain got worse, and Catherine found it harder and harder to do her work. Finally, the on-going tests confirmed the fact that she was afflicted by rheumatoid arthritis. I was appalled by the news. While it wasn't a deadly disease, it was an incurable one. It would get progressively worse over the years, until, racked by unceasing pain, my friend would have to give up nursing and be confined to a wheelchair.

In great distress I headed straight to the chapel. I poured out my feelings. 'Lord,' I prayed, 'you know how much this woman means to me. The thought that she will be crippled by arthritis is unbearable. It just can't happen.' My whole personality was behind those words. It was as if my compassionate indignation, like an X-ray, went in an affirming and approving way to the core of my friend's inner being and adamantly resisted the disease that was threatening her health. At that very moment, I got an unforgettable sense that the Lord was saying within me, 'I love Catherine even more than you do.' Immediately I felt united to Jesus. I knew that like me, he was saying a firm 'No!' to the illness. I also had a conviction that the Lord would heal my friend at some indefinite time in the future and that I would recognise the moment of grace when it arrived.

Well, the next time I met Sr Catherine I told her about my experience in the chapel. 'You don't have to worry any more,' I said reassuringly, 'God is going to heal you completely in his own good time.' She said that she hoped my premonition was correct. As the weeks passed, however, her symptoms got worse. About two months after the experience in the chapel, the two of us visited some mutual friends in another town. When we arrived at our destination, we sat and chatted for quite a while. Then, in the midst of this united and loving atmosphere, it suddenly occurred to me, 'This is the hour of the Lord. It's time to pray for healing.' I asked Sr Catherine if she would like to receive the anointing of the sick. She said she would. So I got the oils from the glove compartment in the car and, together with the people present, began to celebrate the sacrament. During the laying on of hands we all prayed fervently. I was firmly convinced that our prayers were being heard. As Jesus promised, 'Whatever you ask for in prayer, believing you have it already, you will receive.'(Mk 11: 24) Two days later Catherine got in touch with me. 'I have great news, Pat,' she joyfully exclaimed, 'The swellings have disappeared, the pain is gone, I'm healed!'

That all happened a few years ago. Catherine has had many tests since then to see if there is any trace of the arthritis left in her joints. Thank God, they have all confirmed that there is no trace of the disease.

This wonderful experience has taught me a number of things about healing. St Aelred of Rievaulx is so correct when he writes: 'A friend praying to Christ on behalf of his friend, is the more efficacious in proportion as his prayer is lovingly sent to God, with tears, which either fear excites or affection awakens or sorrow evokes. And thus a friend praying to Christ on behalf of his friend and for his friend's sake, desiring to be heard by Christ, directs his attention with love and longing to Christ; then *it sometimes happens that quickly and imperceptibly the one love passes over into the other* (my italics), and coming, as it were, into close contact with the sweetness of Christ himself, the friend begins to taste his sweetness and to experience his charm.' [22]

This kind of Christian intimacy is an essential constituent of healing prayer. It enables one to share in the Lord's affirmation of the inner value of another person and God's resistance to any illness or injury that might disturb his or her harmony and peace. This type of relationship enables one to believe that anything alien to the compassionate will of the Lord must yield to his power as it is released in the spirit, mind and body of the suffering person. [23]

The Cartesian split between mind, body and creation is

overcome as three redemptive intimacies overlap. There is intimacy *with creation* as represented by another person, *with oneself* through the compassion of the loving self, and intimacy *with the Lord* who is present in and through the first two types of relationship. As Nicholas of Cusa wrote: 'Divinity is the enfolding and unfolding of everything that is. Divinity is in all things in such a way that all things are in divinity.'[24]

Notes

1. J. Macquarrie, *Paths in Spirituality*, SCM, London, 1972, 123. A. & B. Rees, *Celtic Heritage*, Thames & Hudson, London, 1978, 99.
2. cf. K. Clark's, *Civilization*, BBC/John Murray, London, 1971, 177.
3. C. Merchant, *The Death of Nature*, Harper & Row, N.Y., 1980, xvii.
4. *La Tentation de l'Occident*, 1926.
5. *Man Alone: Alienation in Modern Society*, ed. E. & M. Josephson, Dell, N.Y., 1962, 59
6. *Man's Search for Meaning*, Simon & Schuster, N.Y., 1963, 154.
7. *Man's Search for Himself*, Allen & Unwin, London, 1953, 25.
8. Quoted by N. Goldberg, in 'A Feminist Critique of Jung' in *Women's Spirituality*, ed. J. W. Conn, Paulist Press, N.Y., 1986, 15.
9. R. W. Clarke, *Einstein: the Life and Times*, Avon Discus, 77.
10. Quoted by L. Barnett in *The Universe and Dr Einstein*, Bantam, N.Y., 108.
11. *A New Vision of Reality*, Collins, London, 1989, 263.
12. R. Sheldrake, *The Rebirth of Nature*, Random Century, London, 1990, 167
13. *Between Man & Man*, Fontana, London, 1961, 41.
14. *Confessions*, Penguin Classics, London, 1961, Bk 9, sec 10.
15. From 'Ordo Amoris' in *Philosophical Essays*, Northwestern University Press, Ill., 1973.
16. Strupp & Hadley, quoted by R. D. Gross, *Psychology: The Science of Mind and Behaviour*, Hodder & Stoughton, London,

1987, 777.
17. cf. Samuels, Shorter & Plaut on 'Healing' in *A Critical Dictionary of Jungian Analysis*, Routledge & Kegan Paul, London, 1986, 64-65.
18. *Addiction and Grace*, Harper & Row, N.Y., 1988, 3.
19. *Will and Spirit: A Contemplative Psychology*, Harper & Row, N.Y., 1982, 41.
20. Irish bishops, *Human Life is Sacred*, Pt II, # 85.
21. *Riding the Wind*, Word of Life, Ann Arbor, Michigan, 1977, 36.
22. *Spiritual Friendship, op. cit*., 131.
23. See my 'Praying for Healing' in *Maturing in the Spirit*, Columba Press, Dublin, 1991, chap. 9.
24. Quoted by Sheldrake in *The Rebirth of Nature*, Century, London, 1990, 167.

PART III

intimacy with God

Our knowledge of God is paradoxically
a knowledge not of him as the object of our security,
but of ourselves as utterly dependent
on his saving and merciful knowledge of us.
It is in proportion as we are known to him
that we find our real being and identity in Christ.
We know him in and through ourselves
insofar as his truth is the source of our being
and his merciful love is the very heart of our life and existence.'

(Thomas Merton, *The Climate of Monastic Prayer*, pp. 113-114)

CHAPTER 10

Christian intimacy

Pope John Paul II has written: 'People today put more trust in ... experience than in doctrine.'[1] In the opening chapter, we saw that authoritative religious truths which are unrelated to subjective religious experiences are dead, while subjective religious experiences which are unrelated to authoritative religious truth are blind. Doctrines are not only symbolic statements which can mediate transcendent mystery, they enable people to discern the authenticity of their experiences of God from a Christian point of view. In this chapter, we will use experiences of self-intimacy and interpersonal intimacy to indicate how they can illuminate the meaning of some of the central Christian teachings such as those concerning the Trinity, creation, redemption, and *vice versa*.

Intimacy and the Trinity

We will begin with one of the central of these dogmas. Stated abstractly, it maintains that the One God exists in three persons and one substance. While the word *trinity* is not found in the scriptures, the concept is there implicitly. For example, in Mt 28:19 Jesus says to the apostles: 'Go therefore and make disciples of all nations, baptising them in the name of the Father and the Son and of the Holy Spirit.' That's the doctrine; how can its meaning be illuminated by experience?

It seems to me that there are at least two possible answers to this question. Firstly, there is the awareness that comes from the everyday living of the Christian life. Through our union with Jesus, we are empowered by the Spirit to relate to God as to a much-loved Father. Secondly, one can adopt St Augustine's approach by understanding the Trinity in terms of the analogical processes of self-awareness and self-love. We will examine what he says about these experiences of self-intimacy in his book *De Trinitate*.

Augustine, emphasised that the mind must rise above sensory images based on material things, in order to think truly about God.[2] He used the experience of self-intimacy as a spiritual analogy of the inner life of the Trinity. Normally, when we know anything in the external world, the subject, i.e. the knower, is very different from the object, i.e. the thing known. However, when we know ourselves, the knowing subject is the same as the object known. In Books IX and X of his treatise, St Augustine says that when a person knows his or her inner self (or mind), as it relates to transcendental meaning (or eternal truth), it gives birth to an inner 'word' which is the 'self-knowledge' which constitutes one member of the natural trinity being described by Augustine. Love is not another offspring of the mind; it is the means by which the self and its self-awareness are joined together. This trinity: the self (or mind), its knowledge of itself, and love, is an image, in the soul, of the Divine Trinity.[3]

Augustine's psychological theory is not only based on the experience of loving self-intimacy; it indicates that the Blessed Trinity is a mutual intimacy of Father and Son. By the power of the Spirit 'which searches the hidden depths of God' (cf. 1 Cor 2:10) the Father publishes and makes known that which is hidden in the mysterious and unknowable recesses of God's eternal love. This manifestation, or Word, which is equal to the Father in every way, is the Son. In like manner, the Spirit searches the hidden depths of the Son and lovingly discloses them to the Father who attends to his revelation with perfect love and approval. Finally, the Spirit, which is equal to Father and Son, and which unites them both, is the subjectivity and self-intimacy of the triune God.

In the medieval period, St Thomas Aquinas augmented Augustine's introspective approach by drawing on another human analogy, namely, the experience of interpersonal intimacy as friendship. Speaking of human relationships he says: 'There is no happiness without joy, and joy comes from friendship above all.' Then he adds that 'God's true and perfect happiness requires a trinity of persons,' because, 'The love of oneself alone is a private love, not true charity.' So he concludes: 'The perfect goodness of divine happiness and glory postulates friendship within God.'[4]

Intimacy and creation

In the superabundance of his love, God the Father created the world through his eternal Son by the power of the Holy Spirit. As Col 1:16 says: 'Through Christ, God created everything in heaven and on earth, the seen and unseen things.' To understand this truth, one could refer to the experience of human creativity. It was brilliantly described by Shakespeare: 'The poet's eye, in a fine frenzy rolling, doth glance from heaven to earth, from earth to heaven; and as imagination bodies forth the forms of things unknown, the poet's pen turns them to shapes, and gives to airy nothing a local habitation and a name.'[5] When a person has such an all-consuming and uncompromising desire to express his or her perception of goodness, beauty or truth, it mobilises the deepest psycho-spiritual resources of the self. There is an intimate dimension to all forms of creative expression in so far as they publish and make known that which is deepest in the heart of the artist. To the extent that creative acts are the expression of the transendental awareness of the self, they have a religious dimension. Describing his own experience, Beethoven wrote to his friend Schlosser: 'Every real creation of art is independent, more powerful than the artist himself and returns to the Divine through its manifestation. It is one with man in this: that it bears testimony to the mediation of the Divine in him.'

Not surprisingly, therefore, God's creative activity is likened to that of a potter at his wheel, fashioning something beautiful from a lump of clay. (cf. Jer 18:1-7) The universe is his work of art. It is an expression of divine intimacy in so far as it publishes, makes known and embodies some of the invisible qualities of the Creator. In Platonic theory, these qualities are known as the *forms*, i.e. of beauty, truth and goodness. By contemplating them, the soul can ascend to a spiritual intuition of God as the One in whom the forms coalesce. A modern hymn states a similar point of view when it says, in a poetic way: 'God has given his children the wonder of the world, in which his power and glory, like banners are unfurled.' As people come to appreciate the manifestation of God's inner nature in this way, it can evoke a prayerful response of thanksgiving, praise and worship.

Because God is love, everything that exists originates in

divine love, bears the imprint of that love and is sustained in being by the same love. The élan of divine charity is detectable in the dynamic processes of evolution which find their fulfilment in and through the transcendental capacities of loving men and women. To the extent that we exercise them, we become co-creators with God, thereby enabling creation to reach its fulfilment, in the Almighty. This occurs as people grow in conscious relationship with the Lord by means of intimate relationship with one another and the world of nature. We have seen what this might involve in earlier chapters. The ideal was realised until the sin of Adam and Eve broke the spiritual umbilical that had connected them to God, through their connection with creation and with one another. From then on, the human race and the whole of the created world was 'subjected to futility.' (Rom 8:20)

Intimacy and redemption

In the book of Genesis, we find a threefold pattern where sin is followed by punishment and a merciful promise of future deliverance. For example, the Lord punished the people of Babel for their sin of pride by confusing their language and scattering them far and wide. (cf. Gen 11:1-10) However, he showed mercy by blessing Abraham and promising that he would be the father of a great nation. (cf. Gen 12:1-4) From then onwards, the Lord manifested his saving power, firstly by means of great historical events such as the Exodus and, secondly, through the words of the prophets. For example, in Is 52:13-53:12, we read the messianic prophecy which describes the saving death of the Suffering Servant with uncanny accuracy. Revelations of this kind were intimate expressions of the Lord's saving intention of restoring and renewing the whole of creation.

INTIMACY IN THE LIFE OF JESUS

The Letter to the Hebrews begins with these profound words: 'Long ago God spoke to our ancestors in many and various ways by the prophets, but in these last days he has spoken to us by a Son, whom he appointed heir of all things, through whom he also created the world. He is the reflection of God's very being, and he sustains all things by his powerful word.' (Heb 1:1-3) The intimate self-disclosure of God reaches its climax in the life of Jesus. 'He is the image of the invisible God,' says St Paul in Col 1:15. In him God publishes and makes known, in a new and definitive way, that which is innermost in his own secret depths. As Jesus said of himself: 'Many prophets and righteous people longed to see what you see, but did not see it, to hear what you hear but did not hear it.' (Mt 13:17) He is our window on God. His words and actions are like so many panes of glass through which we can see what the Father is like. Before examining how this is so, we will look at the way in which Jesus related to himself and to his Father in an intimate way.

Jesus was intimate with his Father

At his baptism, the Father addressed Jesus as his 'beloved Son.' (cf. Mt 3:17) It seems to me that this was the primordial awareness that informed Jesus's consciousness of himself and of his Father. We have a clue as to what it might have been like in Ps 131. I suspect that Jesus could have identified with its sentiments. Having renounced pride and independence the psalmist says: 'Enough for me to keep my soul tranquil and quiet like a child in its mother's arms, as content as a child that has been weaned.'

Psychologists say that early in its life a child experiences symbiotic union with its mother, i.e. a merging of identities. While being breast-fed satisfies its biological needs, the child is also being fed spiritually and emotionally by the mother's love. The mother may speak, the baby may gurgle, but basically it is not an exchange of thoughts. Rather the child is en-wombed spiritually and psychologically, as its identity is established in the reflected light of the mother's love.

So too with Jesus. As he surrendered his inner being to the Father, he was aware that their identities were one and the same. As Jesus was drenched, soaked, and innundated in the power of the Spirit, he was progressively enabled to grasp 'the length and breadth, the height and depth of the love of God which surpasses understanding.' (cf. Eph 3:18) Ever afterwards, when he prayerfully entered the inner chamber of his heart, he encountered himself in the light of the father's love.

It would seem that the Father was not the object of Jesus'

awareness. The usual subject-object dichotomy, which structures our everyday acts of knowing, was transcended to become a subject-in-subject one. In other words, through the action of the Holy Spirit, Jesus' growing awareness of his own subjectivity seemed to become synonymous with his awareness of the subjectivity of his Father. In this communion of love, Jesus' individualism rather than his individuality was surrendered. His self-intimacy was intimacy with God and *vice versa*. That is why he could testify: 'I am in the Father and the Father is in me,' (Jn 14:10) and 'to have seen me is to have seen the Father.' (Jn 14:9) The unique intimacy which Jesus enjoyed with his Father would explain why and how he could say: 'What the Father has taught me is what I speak,' (Jn 8:28) and 'The Son can do only what he sees the Father doing; and whatever the Father does the Son does too.' (Jn 5:19) In other words, everything Jesus said and did published and made known something of the mysterious depths of God.

Jesus ministered in an intimate way

We have already seen how intimacy can be described in terms of loving and compassionate attention. Jesus displayed this capacity to a remarkable degree. Indeed St John says of him: 'There was no need for anyone to tell him about people, because he himself knew what was in their hearts.' (2:25) Jesus was acutely aware that appearances could be deceptive. Often they disguised the intimate truth about men and women. Some people honoured God with their lips but their hearts were far from him. Others appeared to be chaste, but they secretly harboured lust in their hearts. The scribes and pharisees appeared to be God-fearing but they were actually full of self-righteousness and pride. On the other hand, Jesus saw beyond the rags, smells and deficiencies of the poor, to appreciate, approve and affirm their inner dignity as the sons and daughters of God. The healing of a leper, which we examined in the last chapter, was a typical example of the Lord's approach. On many occasions, his extraordinary powers of observation and empathy were augmented by the charismatic gift of infused knowledge.[6] The Spirit enabled him to transcend the limitations of sense knowledge to know the hidden truth about people, e.g. that the Samaritan woman at the well wasn't married. (cf. Jn 4:1-43)

Jesus wanted to be intimate with the apostles

Jesus had a strong desire to relate to the apostles with even greater intimacy. Not only did he lovingly focus his attention on their innermost selves, he wanted to disclose his deepest self to them. 'I have called you friends,' he declared, 'because I have told you everything I have heard from my Father.' (Jn 15:15) When we recall that Jesus' identity was inseparable from his awareness of God, he was saying in effect that he wanted to be completely open with the twelve. But his best efforts ended in frustration. This became quite obvious on the occasion when Philip said, 'Show us the Father.' Jesus was clearly irritated and disappointed when he replied that to know him was to know his Father. (Jn 14:8-12) St Paul was later to explain why this lack of communication was inevitable: 'It is only a person's own spirit within him that knows all about him.' (1 Cor 2:11) In other words, while I may have a direct awareness of myself, I can only have a partial, indirect knowledge of another person. This remains true no matter how much she tells me about herself. Like all of us, Jesus had a growing and direct awareness of his own subjectivity. We have seen how, as a result of receiving the Spirit's anointing, he also seemed to enjoy an increasingly direct awareness of the subjectivity of his Father. There was no barrier between them, except the limitations imposed by human nature itself. It was precisely this direct experience of God that Jesus couldn't convey to his apostles. They understood the things he said to a certain extent, but they couldn't stand inside his skin. So they couldn't share in his intimate relationship with the Father.

Over a period of time, Jesus appears to have concluded that his words, no matter how eloquent, would not be enough. Only the Holy Spirit would be able to lead the apostles and the disciples into the truth about God. But Jesus realised that he couldn't give the Spirit to them. As a result, he began to talk in a mysterious and paradoxical way. On one occasion he said: 'The Spirit is *with* you now, soon he will be *within* you.' (Jn 14:17) This was a statement of fact, in the sense that while Jesus was with the apostles the Spirit was with them. This was so because Jesus was the Christ, i.e. the anointed One who was filled with the Spirit. It was also a promise, in the sense that Jesus was saying that a time would come when the same Holy Spirit would be poured out on his apostles and disciples. Then it would dwell within them. 'The Holy Spirit,' said Jesus, 'whom the Father will send in my name, will teach you everything and remind you of all that I have said to you.' (Jn 14:26) Afterwards, they would have 'that mind which was in Christ.' (1 Cor 2:16) Jesus said, in a paradoxical way, that he would have to leave his followers in order that the Spirit might be given to them: 'It is better for you that I go away, because if I do not go, the Helper will not come to you. But if I go away, then I will send him to you.' (Jn 16:7) In saying this, Jesus was referring to his forthcoming death and resurrection. They would be the necessary prelude to the sending of the Spirit.

It is clear that Jesus saw his death as a sacrifice of friendship. 'The greatest love a person can have for his friends,' he said, 'is to give his life for them.' (Jn 15:13) The Holy Spirit was the life of his life, breath of his breath. By his death on the cross, Jesus would be able to yield up his Spirit to the Lord. Then the Father would pour out the same Spirit on all those who trusted in his Son. So the last words that Jesus spoke on the cross, 'Into your hands I commend my Spirit,' (Lk 23:46) were a necessary preparation for Pentecost. On that momentous day, the promises were fulfilled. The apostles, together with Mary and the other disciples were immersed like sponges in the Spirit, until they were filled with the utter fullness of God. (cf. Eph 3:19) Their relationship with Jesus was transformed. He was no longer the anointed One who was *with* them. They were consciously aware that he was living *within* their hearts through their faith in him. (cf. Eph 3:17) It is said that, after his resurrection, Jesus could walk through the walls of a room. Having received the Holy Spirit, the believers felt as if Jesus had walked through the walls of their bodies to make his abode within them. They could say with St Paul: 'We no longer live, Christ Jesus lives in us.' (Gal 2:20)

The sending of the Spirit and intimacy with God

As a result of their baptism in the Spirit at Pentecost,[7] the believers were transformed. Firstly, like the disciples on the road to Emmaus, their eyes were opened and they finally recognised that Jesus was the Son of God, the Lord of heaven and earth. As St Paul put it: 'Nobody is able to say, "Jesus is Lord" except in the

Holy Spirit.' (1 Cor 12:3) Secondly, their sense of identity was radically changed. While Jesus had always been God's Son by nature, they became his adopted children. As a result, they began to experience the Father in the way that Jesus had. Writing to the Christians in Rome, Paul said: 'You received the Spirit of adoption, enabling us to cry out, "Abba! Father!" The Spirit himself joins with our spirit to bear witness that we are children of God.' (8:15-16) Thirdly, like Jesus before them, the apostles and disciples had access to the mind and will of God. Writing to his fellow Christians, St John said: 'You do not need anyone to teach you; since the anointing God gave you teaches you everything.' (1 Jn 2:27) St Paul said something similar when he wrote: 'What no eye has seen nor ear heard ... God has revealed to us through the Spirit. For the Spirit searches everything, even the depths of God ... Now we have received not the spirit of the world, but the Spirit which is from God ... *We have the mind of Christ.'* (1 Cor 2:9-16) Fourthly, the apostles and disciples had a Spirit-filled power both to proclaim and to demonstrate the good news of salvation in Christ, even to the point of healings and miracles. As representatives of the community, the preachers were to bear anointed witness to the Lord whose Spirit was the innermost source of their union of mind and heart. (cf. Acts 2:43-45; 4:32-36)

Evangelisation in the early Church was an intimate activity. We know that the inspired words and actions of Jesus published and made known that which was innermost in the mind and heart of God. He wanted the apostles to do the same when they were enlightened by the Spirit. For example, he said that the the good news was like light. It illuminated the deepest depths of a person. As the word of God penetrated to the point where the spirit and psyche meet, it revealed the most secret thoughts and emotions. (cf. Heb 4:12) So Jesus said: 'Your whole body is filled with light, and not darkened at all. It will be light entirely, as when the lamp shines on you with its rays.' That being so, the disciples should not hide their inner light from others; rather they should allow it to shine forth: 'No one lights a lamp and puts it in some hidden place or under a tub; they put it on the lamp-stand so that the people may see the light when they come in.' (Lk 11:33-37)

The proclamation of the Gospel had a unique ability to reach into the most intimate recesses of those who heard it. St Paul tells us that if the word of God is being preached at a Christian meeting, 'when some unbeliever or ordinary person comes in, he will be convinced of his sin by what he hears, his secret thoughts will be brought into the open, and he will bow down and worship God, confessing, "truly God is here among you!" (1 Cor 14:24-26) Jesus promised the disciples that, just as his proclamation of the Good News of God's unconditional love had been accompanied by deeds of power, so would theirs. In Jn 14:12 he says: 'Very truly, I tell you, the one who believes in me will also do the works that I do, in fact, will do greater works.' Before his ascension into heaven he said: 'These are the signs he promised that will be associated with believers; in my name they will cast out devils ... they will lay their hands on the sick, who will recover.' (Mk 16:17-19) In his first letter to the Corinthians, Paul referred to demonstrations like these as 'epiphanies,' i.e. events that manifested and revealed the intimate depths of God's saving love.

INTIMATE RELATIONSHIP WITH CHRIST

I was born at the end of World War II. When I was reflecting upon the significance of that event some time ago, it struck me that it must have been an extraordinarily intimate experience for my mother, as for any woman who gives birth. After nurturing me in her womb for nine months, she finally published and made known that which was innermost in her body. Two or three days later I was baptised, when, following my physical birth, I was born again from a spiritual point of view. This was made possible by the fact that on the cross, Christ, like a divine mother, had borne me in the womb of divine compassion. In biblical Greek the word for *compassion* is *splanchna*, meaning 'inward parts'; it is related to the Hebrew *rahamim* which refers to the 'maternal womb' of Yahweh. By his sufferings on the cross, Christ went into a painful travail of love, longing to bring forth sons and daughters to God. (cf. Rom 8: 22-23) His saving death was a movement of the womb of God, while his resurrection finally published and made known that which was innermost in the mind and heart of God. The passageway leading from his tomb to the world outside was like a birth canal through which I could pass from spiritual darkness to new life in the Spirit. Like any baptised infant I was incorporated into the mystery of Christ and became one of God's people. The original sin with which I had been mysteriously tainted was cleansed. I was rescued from the power of darkness, and became an adopted child of God. (cf. *Christian Initiation*, General Introduction, 2) In principle at any rate, reception of the sacrament empowered me to acknowledge that Jesus was Lord, that God was my Abba, Father, and to overcome sin in my life. It also entitled me to receive revelation and guidance from the Holy Spirit and to proclaim and to demonstrate the coming of God's 'civilisation of love,' much as the apostles had done, even to the point of healings and miracles.

Christians believe that all this, and much more besides, is implicit in the sacrament of baptism and the other sacraments which build upon it, i.e. confirmation and the eucharist. But when we look at our own lives and the lives of Christians round about us, we might be tempted to think that the claims made for the sacraments of initiation are exaggerated. Quite often the lives of baptised people don't seem to be all that different from those who haven't been baptised at all. I have seen statistics which suggest that promiscuity among Christians is much the same as the rate for non-Christians, agnostics and atheists. If they were put on trial for being Christian, there mightn't be enough evidence to find many Catholics and Protestants guilty! How come there can be such a discrepancy between the claims of Christian theory and the realities of Christian practice? I think that we can begin to answer this challenging question by making a distinction between baptism as a theological event and as an experiential one.

Receiving and experiencing the Spirit

There is an example of what I mean in Acts 8:14-18. Philip the evangelist had preached the good-news to some Samaritans. They had come to believe in Christ and were baptised. 'Now when the apostles at Jerusalem heard that Samaria had received the word of God, they sent to them Peter and John, who came down and prayed for them that they might receive the Holy Spirit; for it had not yet fallen on any of them, but they had only been baptised in the name of the Lord Jesus.' This text poses a problem. We believe that people receive the Holy Spirit at the moment of baptism. Nevertheless, even though the Samaritans had been baptised, we are told that 'the Spirit had not yet fallen on any of them.' The apostles could come to this conclusion because they assessed the situation from an *experiential* rather than a *theological* point of view. Instead of denying that these believers had received the Holy Spirit, they were noting the fact that it had no discernible effect upon them. So they prayed, that they might come into a transforming awareness of God, similar to the one experienced by the apostles themselves on the first Pentecost.

Surely it is much the same for modern Christians? We receive the Holy Spirit in baptism. That's a theological fact. However the power and potential of the divine indwelling needs to be released and actualised at a conscious level if it is to have the transforming spiritual effects that we have noted already.[8]

There are two reasons which account for the fact that it takes a lifetime to appropriate in experience the graces we received at the moment of baptism. Everything in the natural order needs time to develop its potential. For example, a newborn baby may be endowed with a very high IQ and all kinds of talents, such as outstanding musical ability. However, none of this will be apparent in the first two or three years of its life. But as time passes, the child's latent abilities will begin to declare themselves, until they become more fully and consciously developed in adult life. It seems to me that the same is true from a psycho-spiritual point of view.

Think of Jesus. From the moment of his conception, he was divine by nature as God's only Son. The Church teaches therefore that Jesus had two natures, one human the other divine. Consequently, some theologians believe that from his birth onwards, Jesus experienced two forms of knowledge. From the point of view of his human nature he was like the rest of us. He had to learn about himself, the world and God in a step-by-step sort of way. However the same theologians argue that, because he had a divine nature, Jesus enjoyed the beatific vision of God at the same time. That would imply that he knew all things in God.

There are at least two problems with this point of view.

Firstly, while it may make theological sense, surely it is psychological nonsense. Secondly, to maintain that Jesus knew everything as God, seems to contradict the teaching of the scriptures. Luke tells us that after the finding in the temple, Jesus increased in wisdom and years. (Lk 2:52) The author of the letter to the Hebrews tells us that Jesus was like us in all things, except sin. (cf. Heb 4:15; 5:7)

I have long accepted an alternative theological viewpoint which believes that when he became man, Jesus renounced his right to omniscence. I'd agree with St Cyril of Alexandria who wrote: 'We have admired Christ's goodness in that for love of us he had not refused to descend to such a low position as to bear all that belongs to our nature, included in which is ignorance.'9 This would imply that he only got to know his real self, i.e. his inner glory as God's Son, by the kind of on-going process of transcendental knowing which we have described in earlier chapters. Because he was sinless, however, Jesus had no interior impediment or block to this dynamic, which enabled him to know his divine self in the intimate awareness of God's presence and love. It would seem that his baptism in the Spirit was a breakthrough experience which inaugurated him into a profoundly new awareness of his identity in God.

Intimacy in the lives of God's adopted children
While Jesus was God's Son by nature, we became his sons and daughters by adoption. Our heavenly Father can see and love in each one of us what he sees sees and loves in Jesus. (cf. *Preface for Sundays in Ordinary Time VIII*) The Holy Spirit has endowed us with an inner capacity for the kind of conscious intimacy with God which was enjoyed by the kenotic Christ who emptied himself of his divine omniscience. Like him, we are invited to become increasingly aware of the love of God for our innermost selves, and of the presence of God's love within our hearts. We have already noted how this becomes possible through a deepening relationship with the Lord through intimacy with the world and with other people. They can mediate the presence, both of the God of love and of the love of God.

However, we are unlike Jesus in one vital respect. While

he was tempted like us, he never sinned, never impeded his ever-growing awareness of God within. On the other hand we have been blinded by the sin of the world and our own personal sins. Sadly, we are virtually unable to see and acknowledge our 'inner glory,'[10] i.e. our true identities in Christ. In chapter five, we saw how self-intimacy is blocked to the extent to which we are un-aware of the shadow side of our personalities. It is blocked in an even more serious manner as long as we are unaware of our sins. It is only when we are aware of both the shadow and our sinful-ness that we can open up our darker depths to the loving mercy of God. Then like the prodigal son who had come to his senses, we can return inwardly to our spiritual home, i.e. the self, where the Lord is present and waiting with compassion and love.

Christian intimacy and attitudes to sin

Christian intimacy is restored when we can acknowledge our wrong-doing and experience both the Lord's forgiveness of our sins and his unconditional love for us as his children. The Bible insists that we need God's help in order to grow in self-awarenes by means of an examination of conscience. In the Old Testament we read: 'The heart is devious above all else, it is per-verse – who can understand it? I the Lord test the mind and the heart .'(Jer 17:9-10) In the Book of Wisdom we are told that, 'You Lord correct little by little those who trespass, and you remind and warn them of the things through which they sin.' (Wis 12:2) Aware that this was true, the psalmist prayed: 'Probe me, Yah-weh, examine me, test my heart and my mind.' (Ps 26:2) In the sac-rament of confession, the priest echoes these sentiments when he prays: 'May the Lord who enlightens every heart, enlighten yours, to know your sins and to trust in his mercy.' In chapter four, we noted how the Lord can answer these prayers by allow-ing us to endure all kinds of trials and tribulations. Needless to say there are many other ways in which he can enlighten us, e.g. by means of a scripture text, a good sermon, an inspiration, etc.

I have found that, for one reason or another, e.g. an un-conscious fear of God, many of today's Christians fail to examine their consciences, either with or without the help of God. They seem to suppress a sense of personal sin. Inevitably, their pseudo-innocence and lack of self-intimacy lead to formal rather than intimate relationships with the Lord. Other Christians are willing to admit their sins alright, but they do so on their own by examining their consciences without the help of God. Instead of seeing sin in intimacy terms, as a failure to respond to the love of the Lord, they see it in terms of abstract moral principles, as a failure to keep the law. So rather than looking at their sins in the light of their relationship with God, they tend to look at God in terms of their relationship to sin.

From a psychological point of view, this kind of negative dynamic can usually be traced back to childhood. Many parents gave the impression that their love was conditional. It depended on their children's willingness to do as they were told. Their words, tone of voice, gestures, etc, said to them, 'We'll love you more if, if you behave ... if you don't shout in anger ... if you don't fight with your sister,' etc. Not surprisingly, reactions like these gave rise to the mistaken belief that they were lovable for what they *did* and not for *who they were*. Because experiences of this kind helped to form their images of God, they felt ever afterwards, albeit at an unconscious level, that God's love was like the love of their parents, i.e. conditional in nature. Whenever they failed to keep the law, they believed consciously or unconsciously that the Lord of justice would withdraw his love from them and mete out his punishments either in this life or in the next.

Many people like these have come to me in the sacrament of reconciliation. I have noticed a number of things about their confessions. Because Church law says that they should be honest about the number and nature of their sins, they have a strong desire to comply with that requirement. It is only by doing so that they can win back the love and approval of God. They are sorry for their sins, not because they withdrew their love from God, but because they are afraid that God has withdrawn his love from them. This mistaken belief evokes the kind of self-doubt and separation anxiety that they may have felt in childhood. Despite the fact that they believe that they can only get back into God's good books by making a detailed confession, they can find it hard to tell the truth about their weaknesses. Many older people will talk in vague terms about the 'sins of their youth'. While they might want to tell me about things like masturbation, heavy petting, sex outside marriage, etc, they are often too ashamed to do so. Not only do they hate their sins, they obviously hate themselves for having committed them. And deep down they seem to suspect that, if I knew what they had been up to, I'd turn against them, just as they believe the Lord has done. It is really painful to have to watch their inward struggle. It becomes clear that, rather than believing in the unconditional mercy and love of God, they are placing their faith in their own ability to make a 'good' confession.

Normally, I try to reassure such troubled people by telling them that there is no need to rake over the sins of the past; the Lord who sees them all, forgives them all. The only thing they have to do is to place all their confidence in God. God will do the rest, will forgive all their sins and forget them.' (cf. Heb 8:12) Sometimes, scrupulous penitents will interrupt me even when I'm speaking such words of reassurance. 'Oh, Father, I forgot something else...' and they go on to tell me about another sin. It becomes clear that they are listening to their obsessive fears and preoccupations instead of paying attention to my words or to the Lord. While I gladly give them absolution, I realise that in all probability, nothing has changed. Some penitents won't feel forgiven because they have failed to tell every sin in microscopic detail. Others will feel relief rather than peace when they feel that they have 'won back' the love of God as a result of absolution. But in either case there is no significant change in the way in which they relate to God. They still see things in relatively impersonal terms such as justice, duty and conditional love. What bedevils penitents like these is the fact that, instead of placing all their trust in the mercy and love of God, they are scared off by his justice.

There are two possible reasons for this. Firstly, we form our image of God by internalising our childhood experience of parental power and authority. Given the fact that none of our parents was perfect, it is inevitable that we experienced at least some conditional love. And then sometimes we would have formed the mistaken impression that there were strings attached to the love of our parents. In either event, we would have come to the conclusion that God was like a demanding parent, hard to please and quick to punish. Psychologists have discovered that an image like this, with its associated negative feelings, is largely unconscious. But as long as it is unrecognised at a conscious level, it will tend to exert a negative influence on our relationship with the Lord. Secondly, negative images of God are sometimes reinforced by parents, teachers and priests who talk about Christianity in a moralistic way. Even when this isn't the case, negative images of God will tend to cancel out the effects of a good Christian education. This can become apparent during a time of crisis.

Negative images of God

Recently a woman told me that she felt that God allowed her five year old son to be killed by a drunken driver because she wasn't a good mother. The fact is, she is an excellent one. But even if she wasn't, it would be a pretty vicious kind of God who would punish her by killing her innocent son. What this tragic episode reveals is the fact that despite her conscious convictions about the love of God, she was still being influenced by an unconscious image which is laden with notions of conditional love, and harsh justice.

Not long ago a widow told me about her husband's death from cancer. 'Father, why did God do this to me? My husband was such a good man and a church-goer. He prayed regularly and he tried to keep the commandments. There is a man down the road who has been in prison twice, he drinks heavily, and never darkens the door of a church. Why wasn't he taken? It's just not fair.' While these sentiments are understandable, they reveal a very questionable image of God. He is seen as the Just One who's love is conditional. He should reward people if their behaviour is good, and punish them if it is not. In other words, dependence on one's own good works replaces faith in Christ as the means of salvation.

It seems to me that we will fail to appropriate the graces we received in baptism to the extent that we consciously or unconsciously expect justice rather than unconditional mercy from the Lord. Those who expect justice put the emphasis on what they must do in order to win salvation, e.g. make a thorough examination of conscience and a detailed and accurate confession. They overlook the all-important fact that we are not saved by what we do for God, but rather by our faith in what a merciful God does for us. The Bible does teach that God is just. In Rev 2:23 the Lord says, 'I am the one who searches minds and hearts, and I will give to each of you (i.e. on judgement day) as your works deserve.' But the Bible also teaches that God is merciful. For example Jesus declared, 'I came not to judge the world but to save it.' (Jn 12:47)

A God of justice or a God of mercy

It would seem, then, that we sinful human beings can only enter into an intimate relationship with Christ when we manage to resolve the tension between the justice and mercy of God. This dilemma lies at the heart of the Judaeo-Christian religion. I have often prayerfully pondered it. Over the years I have discovered a number of ways of approaching it. But perhaps the perspective that has influenced me the most, is one described by St Thérèse of Lisieux. Apparently a certain Sr Febronie told Thérèse that she was afraid of death. Having read the saint's autobiography and letters, I have imagined that their conversation went someting like this. 'God will judge me on the basis of the things I have done and failed to do,' said Febronie, 'I'm scared that I will be found wanting and punished.' 'Why be afraid of God?' replied Thérèse, 'Rely on his mercy and love and all will be well. Remember what the scriptures say, "There is no fear in love, but perfect love casts out fear; for fear has to do with punishment." (1 Jn 4:18) You have tried to love God. After all you have prayed every day, received the eucharist, and gone to confession on a regular basis. Why should you be afraid? Trust in God and you will have nothing to worry about.' 'That's all very fine,' replied Sr Febronie, 'you always talk about the love of God, but you cannot deny that God is a just judge.' To which Thérèse replied, 'Sister, I know and believe that God is just. But remember, being just doesn't only mean being severe in punishing the guilty; it also means recognising good intentions and rewarding virtue. So, if you want divine justice, you will get divine justice. The soul gets what it expects from God.' Thérèse teaches that we are the ones who decide, we are the ones who make the choice.[11] Either we choose to believe in the justice or the mercy of God.

Apparently, Thérèse was upset by Sr Febronie's dilemma.

Sometime later she created a parable in an attempt to convey her heartfelt conviction about the saving mercy of God.[12] Once again I have adapted it in my own way. A rabbit was contentedly eating grass in a field. Suddenly it pricked up its ears. It could hear the distant sounds of a bugle blowing, dogs barking and horses galloping. It looked over its shoulder in fear. It could see a king together with his courtiers. Evidently they were out hunting. Already the dogs had picked up her scent and were heading in her direction. So the rabbit took off across the fields as fast as she could. Eventually, however, she ran out of energy. She could go no further. Soon the dogs had surrounded her. They snarled viciously and bared their teeth. They were waiting for the king who was already dismounting, to slay the rabbit. Then they would pounce and tear her carcass to bits. She looked up at the king. His hand was on his sword. He was about to draw it. The rabbit thought to herself: 'If I don't do something quickly, I'm finished!' Suddenly, she used her remaining energy to jump up on to the king's outstretched arm. With eyes full of desperation and pleading she looked into the eyes of the king. When his gaze met hers, something melted in his heart. His sword-grip weakened. To the disappointment of the dogs and the surprise of the courteirs, he began to stroke the rabbit in a loving way. 'I'm bringing this little creature back to the court,' he announced, 'my children can play with her.'

Thérèse said that, in this parable, the rabbit is the soul. The dogs are our sins which pursue us and threaten to devour us. The king is the Lord. The sword is his justice, which in justice he is entitled to use against us. 'But there is a fatal flaw in the heart of the king,' says Thérèse, 'If you look only into the eyes of his mercy, expecting only mercy, you will receive only mercy'. This profound intuition sums up the good news of the gospel. The conflict between God's justice and mercy is resolved. Yes, God is just and he will judge the living and the dead on the day of judgement. But meantime we live in the age of unconditional mercy. If we bypass the justice of God to rely entirely on his mercy, we will receive nothing but mercy in this life and on judgement day. Thérèse's conviction echoes the teaching of St Paul. In Rom 8:1 he says: 'For those who are in Christ Jesus, there is now no condemnation.'

The experience of divine forgiveness enables the shadow

self and the sinful self to come into what St Ignatius calls 'an intimate knowledge of our Lord.'[13] By removing sin, it also removes the main obstacle to a growing awareness of the deeper self which results from a transcendental relationship with the God of unconditional love and whose presence is mediated in a symbolic way by people, events, and natural things. Through them he seems to say to the innermost self: 'I love and accept you just as you are, shadow and all. You don't have to change to win my love. You don't have to improve or give up your sinful habits. Obviously I would want you to do so because they separate your true self from me. But that is not a condition for receiving my love and approval. That you have already, before you change, even if you never change. Believe what I am saying to you, and accept my love into your heart of hearts, so that you may know that I dwell within you.'[14]

As one opens up one's deepest self to the revelation of God's love in this anointed way, one shares in the dynamics of Christ's Spirit-filled relationship to his divine self and his heavenly Father. It seems to me that this kind of Christian intimacy, which goes beyond the dynamics of the natural psyche to focus on the spiritual self, is one of the key issues in contemporary spirituality.[15]

Notes
1. *Redemptoris Missio*, par. 42.
2. *De Trinitate*, VIII, 2, 3; col .948.
3. *De Trinitate*, IX, 12, 18; col. 972. For a fuller treatment see, V. J. Bourke's, *Augustine's Quest for Wisdom*, Bruce, Milwaukee, 1945, 203-223.
4. *Disputations*, IX, de Potentia, 9.
5. *A Midsummer -Night's Dream* , V, i, 7.
6. For more on this charismatic gift, see my *Maturing in the Spirit*, Columba Press, Dublin, 1991, chap. 3, sec. 2, par. 2.
7. cf. Mc Donnell & Montague, *Christian Initiation and Baptism in the Holy Spirit*, Michael Glazier, Collegeville, 1991, 23-37.

8. For more on this subject see my *Maturing in the Spirit*, Columba Press, Dublin, 1991, chpt 2.
9. *PG* 75, 369, Quoted by R. Brown in *Jesus God and Man*, Macmillan, N.Y., 1967, 102.
10. St Bernard of Clairvaux, *Twelve Steps of Humility and Pride, & On Loving God*, Hodder & Stoughton Christian Classics, London, 1985, 85-88.
11. Bernard Bro, *The Little Way: The Spirituality of Thérèse of Lisieux*, DLT, London,1979, 63.
12. *Ibid*, 79-80.
13. *Spiritual Exercises*, (104).
14. cf. A. de Mello's, *Sadhana*, Gujarat Sahitya Prakash, India, 38.
15. cf. Entry on Spirituality, in *The New Dictionary of Theology*, Gill & Macmillan, Dublin, 1990, esp. 983-986.

CHAPTER 11

Prayer as self-disclosure

So far in this book, we have seen how self-intimacy helps us to get in touch with our personal experience. Interpersonal intimacy schools us in the arts of self-disclosure and loving attention to the inner lives of other people. Not only are these two forms of intimacy a pre-requisite for prayerful intimacy with God, they find their fulfilment in this way. Indeed we could say that we are no closer to God than we are to our true selves and our closest neighbours.

Speaking of intimate relationships with spouses or friends, St Aelred wrote: 'God is friendship ... I would not hesitate to attribute to friendship anything associated with charity, as for instance, he who abides in friendship abides in God and God in him.'[1] The way we relate to others determines the way in which we will pray. If our human relationships are close but formal, it is almost inevitable that our prayerful relationship with God will be much the same. But if some of our relationships are intimate, our prayerful relationship with God will tend to be more personal. There are many outstanding images of what I mean in the Bible. We will mention just two of them.

Biblical images of prayerful intimacy

In Ex 33:7-12 we have a wonderful description of how Moses, the friend of God, used to pray. Firstly, he would go to the tent of meeting. It was a symbol of the private room of the heart mentioned by Jesus in Mt 6:6. Secondly, the tent would be overshadowed by a cloud which was reminiscent of the Holy Spirit which would later envelop our Lady in Lk 1:35. Thirdly, Moses, as leader of the chosen people, would publish and make known to the Lord the deepest concerns of his heart on their behalf. Then we are told that the Lord would publish and make known his thoughts, feelings and intentions by revealing them to his prophet. As the text puts it, 'Yahweh would talk to Moses face to face, as a man talks to his friend.'

Apart from being one of my favourite verses in the the Old Testament, these words are a succinct description of the very essence of prayer as an openness to divine revelation. In the gospels, Jesus is depicted as the new Moses. Like the recipient of the old covenant, Jesus was pre-eminently a man of prayer. Over and over again, we are told how he went apart in order to commune with the divine presence within the tabernacle of his own subjectivity. There he would pour out his deepest thoughts and emotions to the Father. The scriptures allow us to eavesdrop on a number of occasions. His prayerful out-pourings in the garden of Gethsemene and on the cross are two archetypal examples. The author of the letter to the Hebrews says that, 'during his life on earth, he offered up prayer and entreaty, with loud cries and tears, to him who could save him from death.' (Heb 5:7) As we saw in the chapter on Christian intimacy, the Father revealed his presence and his word to Jesus on an on-going basis.

How prayer was described by the saints

When we examine examples like these, we can notice that they describe prayer as a loving dialogue between a person and the Lord. Over and over again the saints advert to this point. St Gregory of Nyssa said that 'prayer is a conference or conversation of the soul with God.'[2] St John Chrysostom said that 'prayer is discussion with the divine majesty.'[3] St Thomas Aquinas wrote: 'For friends to converse together is the proper condition of friendship. People's conversation with God is through contemplation.'[4] St Francis de Sales wrote: 'Prayer is a colloquy, a discussion, or a conversation of the soul with God. By prayer we speak to God and God in turn speaks to us. We aspire to him and breathe in him; he reciprocally inspires us and breathes upon us.'[5] Finally, there is St Teresa of Avila's classic description: 'Prayer is nothing other than an intimate friendship. It is a frequent heart to heart conversation with him by whom we know ourselves to be loved.'[6]

These descriptions of prayer highlight a few important points. Firstly, as Teresa says, prayer is a conversation 'with him by whom we know ourselves to be loved.' The extent to which a person feels loved by the Lord, is the extent that he or she will have both the inclination and the ability to pray. That is why it is so important for every adult Christian to have the power, in Paul's words, 'to be rooted and grounded in love,' (Eph 3:17) and to be able to say, 'I live by faith in the Son of God, who loved me and gave himself for me.'(Gal 2:20) This inner conviction can come either in a gradual way, because of things such as regular prayer and occasional retreats, or rapidly as a consequence of a sudden spiritual awakening. This occurs in the lives of many people, e.g. as a result of experiencing what Charismatics describe as 'Baptism in the Spirit.'[7] It is a religious experience which inaugurates a new and decisive awareness of God's loving presence and activity in one's life. It results in a strong sense of relationship with the person and the words of Jesus. That feeling of closeness enables one to talk to him as a trusted friend.

Secondly, the saints describe prayer as a two-way conversation which involves interrelated elements. There is my self-disclosure to God, and God's self-disclosure to me. Whereas attention to the manifestation of God is the highpoint of prayer, self-disclosure is important because, like John the Baptist, it prepares the way for such Christian revelation.

We will take a brief but incomplete look at the dialogic nature of prayer. In doing so, we will be overlooking many other of its important aspects. In this chapter we will begin by focusing our attention on two types of self-disclosure. Firstly, there is the willingness to reveal one's thoughts and feelings to God. Secondly, as we shall see, both true and false experiences of God can help to disclose the positive and negative contents of the hidden self. This will occur as a person engages in a regular examen of consciousness,[8] one that discerns what was going on during a time of prayer.

Why self-disclosure is important in prayer

When they first hear about the importance of self-disclosure in prayer, many people say, 'Why should I tell God things about myself which he already knows?' I often suspect that such a question is rooted in an unacknowledged reluctance to make the effort that's required to grow in self-awareness or to reveal oneself to the Lord. In any case, there are a number of good motives for trying to do so. To adapt the words of the fourth weekday preface of the Mass, God has no need of our self-disclosure, yet our desire to reveal ourselves to him is itself God's gift. Our act of self-disclosure adds nothing to his knowledge, but helps us to draw closer to the Lord. There are at least three reasons why this is so. The impulse of love is to give. The geatest gift that we can give the Lord, as to any person, is the gift of our true selves. This dynamic is at work in intimate prayer. Added to that is the fact that we will only feel truly accepted and loved by God when we know that God accepts and loves us as we really are, and not as we have pretended to be. Finally, self-disclosure in prayer ploughs the field of the heart in readiness to receive the seed of God's loving self-disclosure. The extent to which we exercise control over the dialogue by failing to express our feelings and desires, is the extent to which we will be closed to the in-breaking of God's word.

What to disclose in prayer

In his *Spiritual Exercises*, St Ignatius of Loyola, encourages those who wish to pray to begin by getting in touch with their God-prompted desires which are ultimately oriented toward conscious relationship with the Lord. Indeed one author has written: 'The Exercises are a way through which we find out for ourselves what it is we want most deeply.'9 Ignatius felt that, at the very beginning of each and every period of prayer, 'we should ask our Lord for what we want and desire.' For example, in par. 104 he says the motive that informs a prayerful reading of the scriptures is a desire to gain 'an intimate knowledge of our Lord, who has become human for us, that we may love him more and follow him more closely.'

Spiritual directors point to the fact that when he met people for the first time, Jesus would often focus in on their desires. By doing this he showed respect for their individuality, dignity and freedom. At the same time, he also helped them to get in touch with the anonymous workings of the Spirit in their hearts. By attending to their replies, Jesus was able to discover the will of God in their 'holy desires'. That understanding would help us to interpret what Jesus meant when he said, 'I only do what I see the Father doing.' (Jn 5:19) For example, in Jn 1:38, he turned round and said to the two young men who were following him,

'What are you looking for?' In Mk 10:51, Jesus said to blind Barti-maeus, 'What do you want me to do for you?' and again in Jn 5:6, Jesus says to the man who had been ill for thirty eight years, 'Do you want to be made well?' What is striking is the fact that in each case he responds to the desires of these people as the expression of the Father's will for him. He invites the young men to become his disciples and he heals Bartimaeus and the crippled man at the pool side.

Incidentally, it is interesting to note that having asked the mother of Zebedee's sons, 'What is it you want?' (Mt 20:21) he turns down her ambitious request because he discerns that it is motivated by a worldly rather than a God-prompted desire.

Once we get in touch with our deeper desires, especially the ones that have a trancendent self-forgetful dimension, we should express them honestly and openly to the Lord. Not only do such desires have a unique ablity to energise our prayer lives, they save us from the perils of self-absorption and prepare us to receive the inspirations of the Spirit.

PROBLEMS IN PRAYING

Excessive self-reference is one of the commonest problems. It tends to inhibit prayer as self-disclosure and loving attention. We have already noted how the pain of being unable to accept them-selves or to be themselves can prevent some men and women from forgetting themselves in out-going love for others. One of the most familiar forms of self-absorption in prayer, is the gravita-tional pull exerted by unresolved feelings such as anger, fear, guilt, mistrust, unworthiness, etc. As long as they remain un-acknowledged and unexpressed they tend to draw our attention away from the Lord by bringing it back to ourselves.

Unhealthy introspection

Some conscientious Christians engage in a good deal of unhealthy introspection. Sometimes they will do this during their prayer times. Instead of revealing their thoughts, feelings and concerns to the God who is present, they go on thinking about themselves in the presence of God. There is a distinct lack of self-disclosure in this form of religious naval-gazing. Growing self-knowledge fails to escape the magnetic pull of egocentricity to be brought into conscious relationship with the Lord. A woman might decide to read the passage in Mk 1:9-16 which describes the very first words spoken by Jesus: 'The time is fulfilled, the kingdom of God has come near; repent, and believe in the good news.' As she ponders this important proclamation her attention is caught by the word *repent* rather than by the preceeding announcement which proclaimed that the kingdom of God was at hand.

I may say in passing that such a biased perception is often influenced by feelings of unworthiness evoked by a perfectionist conscience and negative images of God. They can remain unrecognised for years in the unconscious. The woman may be such a person. She begins to indulge in what looks like a very laudable activity, that of examining her conscience. In reality it turns out to be a morbid exercise in self-deprecation and remorse, one which owes little or nothing to a sense of loving intimacy with the Lord. As we saw in the last chapter, instead of strengthening a sense of fellowship with God this kind of approach can have the opposite effect.

Controlling experience

Sometimes people avoid the unsettling implications of divine revelation by adopting a wilful approach to life. We adverted to this kind of self-absorption in the chapter on intimacy as loving attention. Instead of responding to the uniqueness of people and things, they control and edit their awareness. They can do this by interpreting everything in terms of preconceived ideas or by projecting subjective thoughts and symbols on to the objects of their experience. For example, a monk goes for a walk in the monastery garden. He stops for a while to gaze at a huge oak tree. Instead of telling the Lord what he feels about its dappled colours and textures, he might regard it as a living example of the evolutionary development of nature, which is itself like a tree. Over the millennia, it has reached out its branches in the form of many different species of animal and plant. Or he might see the tree as a symbol of the Trinity. The trunk and branches would be the Father, the sap would be the Spirit, and the leaves that sprout in Springtime would be a sign of Christ rising from his tomb of death at Easter. These may be lovely sentiments, but instead of letting the oak be itself, the monk arbitrarily imposes his ideas on to it. Instead of being admired and appreciated for itself, the tree is used as a screen on to which this wilful cleric projects the contents of his mind in a self-absorbed way.

Being out of touch with one's feelings

If prayer is to be realistic and personal, we need to be in touch with our feelings and to express them to the Lord. One has only to read the psalms to see the truth of this statement. Over and over again, the psalmist pours out his heart to God. Spiritual writers have also stressed the importance of what they call, 'the affections' in prayer. Jonathan Edwards, the outstanding theologian of the spiritual awakening in eighteenth century New England, wrote: 'As in worldly things, worldly affections are very much the spring of men's motion and action; so in religious matters the spring of their actions is very much religious affection: he that has doctrinal knowledge and speculation only, without affection, never is engaged in the business of religion,'[10] or prayer for that matter! We have already noted how our emotions are the fingerprints of subjectivity. They reveal what we really perceive, value, and believe as opposed to what we imagine we perceive, value and believe. When we understand their immediate causes, e.g. grief on hearing of an aunt's death, we may also touch in to a remote cause such as unresolved grief to do with a parent's death during childhood.

As we know, the events of everyday life also effect the way we feel about God. So if we want to be real before the Lord, instead of conforming to some kind of religious ideal, we have to tell him what we really feel about the issues that are important in our lives. They will include such things as our feelings about ourselves, e.g. satisfaction in some achievement; about other people, e.g. gratitude for some great favour; about the events of the day, e.g. distress about a particularly gruesome murder; and about God himself, e.g. appreciation for God's goodness and love. Usually it is not too difficult to share our positive feelings such as joy, love, peace, awe, with the Lord. They find expression in the prayer of thanksgiving, praise, worship and adoration. The trouble arises when we have to come to God, not in our Sunday best, but in the ragged clothes of our anger, fear, guilt, etc, associated as they sometimes are with negative images of God. We will turn our attention therefore to an examination of a couple of the more troublesome feelings that can block our relationship with the Lord.

COPING WITH ANGER IN PRAYER

Normally, two convictions condition the way in which we Christians interpret the events of daily life. Firstly, because of our belief in divine providence, we maintain – mostly in an un-reflective way – that everything that happens is either caused directly by God, or at least tacitly allowed by him. Secondly, because of our belief in justice, we adhere to what has been called the 'just world hypothesis,' which maintains that we get what we deserve. The good are rewarded and those who are evil are punished by God. This notion can be traced back to the Old Testament. When Job suffered misfortune, his friends presumed that his sufferings could only be accounted for by the fact that he was being punished by God for the secret sins he must have committed. In the New Testament, there is another obvious example in the case of the man born blind. The people presume that his affliction must be a form of divine retribution. They ask Jesus, 'Rabbi, who sinned, this man or his parents, that he was born blind?' (Jn 9:2) Jesus replies by saying that neither was at fault.

All of us suffer misfortunes. They can be direct insofar as we have to suffer some kind of adversity such as a heart attack. They can be indirect when someone who is near and dear to us is afflicted. For example, one of our children may be born with a physical or mental handicap, or a relative or friend may have to endure a painful and untimely death. Not surprisingly, we can feel hurt by events like these. Anger and bitterness may well up within. Often it will have an immediate focus. For example, we may feel a real sense of grievance with the doctors and nurses in a local hospital who seemed to fail a relative who was seriously ill. But because of our belief in divine providence and the just world hypothesis, we will usually feel anger with God as well. Consciously or unconsciously we may ask ourselves, 'Why did God allow this to happen, why did he do this to us?' Then we may either blame ourselves by seeing the misfortune as a punishment for sins committed, or we may feel indignant at the unfairness of the whole thing.

As we saw earlier in the book, instead of naming and expressing our anger in an honest way, many of us either ventilate it it in an aggressive fashion, or repress it altogether. I have met many people who felt such aggressive anger against God that they stopped praying, attending church or receiving the sacraments. Their anger led them to hand in their resignation so to speak. They turned their backs on a God, who, in their minds had already turned his back on them.

Aggressive anger

Some time ago a man came to see me during a parish mission. It turned out that he hadn't darkened the door of a church for over ten years. I asked him why he had lapsed. He went on to explain that he and his wife had only one child, a daughter. When she was five years of age she developed leukemia. The man and his wife stormed heaven on behalf of their little girl. At first she experienced a few remissions, but then the disease got worse. 'At that point,' the man said, 'I only asked God to spare my beautiful child from having to suffer pain. But he didn't listen. She died in agony.' 'It must have been terrible for your wife and yourself,' I replied sympathetically, 'In spite of all your prayers, your beloved daughter died a painful death at the tender age of five.' 'You know, father,' he continued, 'I wondered if there was any God there at all. I thought, if you do exist, you are a cruel, uncaring, person. What did my daughter do to you, to deserve such a death? And if you aren't pleased with me and my wife, why take it out on my daughter? After that, I just knew that I didn't want to have anything to do with God, so I stopped going to church or praying.' 'And nevertheless,' I responded, 'here you are ten years later talking to a priest during a mission. Why so?' 'Well, it's like this, father. My anger has died down a bit, so I have decided to give God a second chance!' I must admit I was very moved by what that man shared with me. I could understand why he had felt so bitter. Before we parted, I encouraged him to tell God what he had shared with me. 'I can't explain why your daughter had to die so young,' I said, 'But perhaps God will give you a sense of what he felt about your little girl's suffering and death.'

Repressed anger

Unlike that hurting father, most Christians tend to repress their negative feelings. Their tendency to do this is reinforced either by a fear of divine retribution, or a conscious belief that God is so good and loving that it would be unreasonable to get angry with the Lord. And so, for one reason or another, their feelings of hurt, loss, rage, resentment, etc, are ignored. But of course they don't go away. From the unconscious, they can continue to exert a powerful but negative influence on their intimacy with God. They can prompt a phenomenon which psychologists and spiritual directors call *resistance*. It occurs when a person backs away from relationship. It is usually associated with feelings of coldness and alienation. We may continue to pray and to carry out our religious duties. We go through the motions, but our hearts are not in them. Because God seems distant, unreal and abstract we will suffer from feelings of desolation and dryness of spirit. As long as we fail to acknowledge and to express our negative feelings to God in prayer we will be unreceptive to his self-disclosure.

Recovering and expressing one's anger

In chapter three I proposed a number of ways in which we can grow in emotional self-awareness. At this point we can augment those suggestions by noting two added ways in which we can come to terms with our resentment against God.

I have found that repressed anger can surface when meditating on the scriptures. A few years ago I did an eight day retreat. On the fourth day, my director suggested that I use the account of the great banquet in Lk 14:15-24 as a basis for prayer. Things had being going very well up to that point. I had been aware of an unusually strong sense of God's personal love for me. I'm sure that in recommending the passage he did, my director had hoped that I would recognise that the Lord had prepared a banquet of blessing for me.

When I read the designated verses, however, I was shocked to find that it evoked a lot of anger within. I felt that the king's behaviour was demanding, harsh, vindictive and unreasonable. As I became more agitated, joy gave way to a feeling of coldness towards God. When I told my director about this, he helped me to acknowledge that in the past I had tended to supress any anger I felt toward the Lord. I had often thought that he expected too much from me and that he was almost impossible to please. As we talked, I also realised that, for the same reasons I had often felt a similar kind of resentment towards one of my parents. It was quite a breakthrough to be able, with my director's assistance, to recover, name and understand the causes of my anger.

When I compared the demanding God of this experience with the loving God revealed to me during the first four days of the retreat, I was able to discern what was happening. My anger had been evoked by a negative but unconscious image of God which had been formed in childhood. As soon as I realised that my reaction hadn't been prompted by the Holy Spirit, I was able to re-focus my attention on the God of love who had been revealed to me earlier in the retreat. As soon as I told him about what had happened, my feelings of consolation returned.

Breakdown can lead to breakthrough

Sometimes Christians will be successful for years on end, in repressing their anger against people and God. Then, during a time of adversity, an interior dam bursts and their anger and rage flood out with great force. A few years ago I read how a woman went to a healing week-end which was being conducted by the late Dr Frank Lake. She was on the verge of a breakdown and suicidal. Apparently, this well known Christian psychiatrist advised her to tell God what she felt. She described what happened next in her diary: 'I went alone into the chapel. The panic of what I would do to myself to stop the intolerable pain drove me to my knees, my tongue moving incoherently, my soul stretched tight with a weeping longing. When I was still left alone my very despair drove me to a horror and fury which was unafraid of recrimination. I was staggered by the milk-and-water apologetic God who could not calm this storm, who smiled sympathetically and abstractedly and whom I could not touch. We can bear humans to fall off their pedestals but not God himself. After the first stunning realisation of what God was, my whole mind rose in unity to hate with entire full-blooded, no-holds-barred hatred of the God who had so fooled mankind. Life surged back into every artery and vein, full red blood, as there streamed out from me powerful and unchecked hatred and loathing of a master whose creation had been working wrongly for centuries and who was not wise enough, strong enough or caring enough to mend it. I was livid with his apathy. Didn't he know what his carelessness had done to us? For the first time in my life I dared to demand an explanation.

When none came, I was angrier than I can ever remember being. I turned my eyes on the plain wooden cross and I remembered calvary. I stood in the crowd that crucified him, hating and despising him. With my own hands I drove the nails into his hands and feet, and with bursting energy I flogged him and reviled him and spat with nauseated loathing. Now he should know what it felt like to live in the creation he had made. Every breath brought from me the words: "Now you know! Now you know!" And then I saw something which made my heart stand still. I saw his face, and on it twisted every familiar agony of my own soul. "Now you know" became an awed whisper as I, motionless, watched his agony. "Yes, now I know," was the passionate and pain-filled reply. "Why else should I have come?" Stunned, I watched his eyes search desperately for the tiniest flicker of love in mine, and as we faced one another in the bleak and the cold, foresaken by God, frightened and derelict, we loved one another and our pain became silent in the calm.'[11]

There are a number of points which are worth noting in this powerful account. In the chapel, the young woman's distress became so acute that she couldn't repress her feelings any longer. She surrendered control over her inner experience. Like pent-up lava, her emotions broke through her usual defences . She tells us that for the first time she was able to express 'a fury that was unafraid of recrimination.' This remark implies that for years she had repressed her resentment against God. Evidently she was afraid of being punished for feeling that way about the Almighty. No doubt, at a conscious level, this young woman had thought of God as loving and kind. However, in the heat of the moment, her previously unconscious image of God, as a vindictive tyrant, revealed itself. It was probably formed during her childhood. For example she may have had to placate a bad tempered father by repressing all of her own negative feelings. If she didn't, he might have become violent.

The young woman says that in her moment of crisis she was disillusioned with God. As her conventional notion of a loving deity was swept away by the force of her anger it was replaced by another false image, that of a useless, apathetic God, one who didn't seem to care about her or the world. It was this God who evoked her fury and hate. There was a great danger that her extremely negative feelings might have led to intense self-absorption. Not so in this case. The young woman vehemently expressed her manic bitterness and rage to the Lord. It was a moment of great intimacy in so far as she was publishing and making known that which was innermost in her broken and hurting heart. It is precisely because she unburdened herself in this way that she opened up at a deep level of her personality to the possibility of divine revelation. It began to occur when she noticed the face of the crucified Christ. As she says, 'on it twisted every familiar agony of my own soul.' As her attention was absorbed by the Lord, the Spirit began to publish and make known that which was innermost in God's heart. He revealed that he was suffering in compassionate solidarity with her and yearned for a loving response. In the light of this intimate encounter with the living Lord she not only experienced interior peace, she was able to discern why her other images of God were really false ones.

Surely William Blake was correct, both from a human and a religious point of view, when he wrote: 'I was angry with my friend, I told my wrath, my wrath did end. I was angry with my foe, I told it not, my wrath did grow.'[12]

COPING WITH FEAR IN PRAYER

Spiritual writers suggest that next to sin, fear and anxiety are the greatest enemies of the spiritual life.[13] St Ignatius says, 'For those who are advancing in the way of perfection it is characteristic of the evil spirit to harass with anxiety, to afflict with sadness, to raise obstacles backed by fallacious reasonings that disturb the soul.'[14] From a psychological point of view, one could say that most of our fears originate in the egocentric ego. As I have noted on a number of occasions in previous chapters, its defensive attitude can inhibit loving intimacy with God in so far as it is wilful, mistrustful and unreceptive.

Over the years I have become convinced that feelings such as anxiety, worry, apprehension, dread, fear, timidity and terror are the most deepseated of our negative emotions. Quite often presenting, or surface feelings such as anger, guilt, jealousy, envy and bitterness, have their roots in fear. For example, a woman feels jealous because she is *threatened* by the fact that another woman is friendly with her husband. A worker feels envious of a colleague's talents and success, because he's *afraid* that when he is compared with her he will be judged to be inferior. A young man feels guilty about injuring a child as a result of his careless driving. He is *fearful* for the child, will she ever recover? He is *afraid* for himself, what will others think of him? How will he be punished when his case gets to court? A missioner gets angry with God because he has allowed many of his people to be killed in an earthquake. He feels hurt on behalf of the victims and their surviving relatives and friends. But deep down he also feels *afraid* of an unpredictable universe and a God who fails to conform to the expectations of the 'just world hypothesis'. If prayer is to be intimate, we need to name our fears, to understand their causes, and to disclose them to the Lord.

Common reasons for fearing God

Many people suspect that if they surrendered control over their inner experience by disclosing it honestly to the Lord, anything could happen. That prospect scares them. If the Lord began to reveal himself to them, they fear that they might have no control over what he might say. He could say anything, ask them to do anything. He could challenge their basic attitudes to themselves, undermine their emotional preoccupation with their work, overturn their basic social assumptions. They could be left in a confused state lacking integration and confidence. So to protect themselves, they may try to control their experience of the Lord and let him say only what they can safely hear.

A few years back, a woman came to see me during a

retreat. She said that she was a conscientious Catholic and a member of a prayer group. Nevertheless, she was finding it very hard to pray. We chatted about the problem for a while. 'Did you ever find it easy to pray?' I asked. 'Oh yes,' she replied, 'everything was fine up until about nine months ago.' 'Did anything significant happen in your life around that time?' I enquired. There was an embarassed silence and the woman said, 'Everyone thinks that I'm happily married. My husband and I keep up appearances for the children's sake, but in actual fact we have never been suited to one another. Then about a year ago John came into my life. He is separated from his wife. After meeting him a number of times, I realised that I felt strongly about him. Unlike my husband he had a way of making me feel how special I was. What's more, he told me that he was in love with me.' 'How did you respond?' I asked. 'Well, I had to admit to myself that I was in love with John and felt strongly attracted to him from a physical point of view. But I knew that it would be wrong for us to make love. And so far, we haven't, thank God.'

As the woman spoke, I could sense both her love for her friend and her desire to do nothing dishonourable. 'Sexual abstinence must be difficult when John and yourself feel so strongly about one another,' I responded. 'It sure is father. I sometimes feel that we won't be able to resist much longer.' 'Have you ever talked to God about the relationship?' I asked. 'I have asked God to help me on many occasions,' replied the woman. 'That's good,' I said, 'but have you told the Lord what you feel about your marriage, about John, about your sexual feelings, and so on?' There was another embarassed silence. Then the woman responded, 'Father, I couldn't talk to God about things like that.' 'You have told me,' I said reassuringly, 'why couldn't you talk to the Lord about them?' 'Because ... because I know what God would say.' 'You know what he would say?' 'Yes, father, he would tell me I will have to break off my relationship with John, and I think I couldn't bear that to happen. He is the best thing that has ever happened to me.' Her remark reminded me of one novelist's wry observation that 'in the beginning was the word and the word was no!' Implicit in this woman's reaction was yet another negative image of God, that of a kill-joy. She feared that if she revealed her deeper feelings to him, she would receive a divine admonition which would order her to sacrifice the most precious thing in her life. I encouraged her to disclose everything to the Lord. 'None of us can know what the Lord is going to say. God's not that predictable. In any case if you don't tell him what you are feeling,' I added, 'your prayer will continue to be dry and unsatisfying. It's not surprising when you think about it. If you refuse to open your real self to the Father, he won't be able to reveal his real self to you. And when he does, you will realise how much he loves you. In the light of that love you will know what to do next.'

I met that woman again a few years later. When I asked her how things had worked out, she was able to tell me that she had done what I had suggested. In spite of her fears she had poured out her heart to the Lord. Immediately she felt that he loved her and understood what she was going through. That reassurance had given her the desire and the power to continue to abstain from sexual intercourse with John. Not only that, her prayer life was revivified. Meantime both she and John decided to apply for annulments. Eventually both of them were sacramentally united when they were quietly married in Church.

How God can help us to identify our fears

Spiritual directors encourage people not to dig for the kind of unconscious attitudes which were impeding the woman's relationship with the Lord. Such an introspective process is inevitably self-centered. Better to ask God to bring any obstacles to mind. Meantime we should disclose the feelings of which we are consciously aware. Then the Lord will enlighten us in his own good time by enabling us to recognise deep-seated fears that may be blocking relationship with God.

This can come about with the help of a discerning spiritual director, confessor or confidant. A few years ago I adopted this approach myself. There was something lacklustre about my relationship with God. I asked to be enlightened about anything that might have been coming between us. I seemed to get an answer when I was away on holidays in Portugal. One afternoon as I was returning from the beach, I had what seemed to be a vivid and unexpected experience of God. I suddenly became aware of the fact that the Lord was truth personified. I also had the sense that, although I would be prepared to argue about issues with any fallible human being, there was no point in arguing with the Almighty. God was always right. Suddenly, I felt a surge of anger. I felt squashed and insignificant in the presence of Absolute Truth. It seemed to hover ominously above me in an oppressive way. I felt like a slave who had to submit without question to his all-knowing master. I felt a surge of defiance. This shocked me, and quickly I felt guilty. I thought to myself, 'I'm like the fallen angels who told God that they would not serve him.' I resolved to repent, and asked God to give me the grace of humility.

Sometime later, I reflected on this experience as part of an examen of consciousness. Two things occured to me. Firstly, the God of absolute truth seemed strangely impersonal, cold and distant. Secondly, the experience failed to evoke any of the feelings that one would normally associate with the action of the Holy Spirit, such as joy and peace. On the contrary, all my feelings were agitated, disturbed and negative. Very quickly I realised that I had got in touch with another of my false images of God, one which had probably been formed in early childhood.[15] As a result, I recognised where the fear and distrust which had often inhibited my relationship with the Lord had probably originated.

I have already referred to some other false images of God, especially intimidating ones which picture him as a harsh judge who punishes those who fail to please. Resistance melts as we disclose to God the fearful feelings associated with false images like these. As one's inner being is exposed in this way to the loving gaze of the Lord, one experiences a new depth of intimacy with God.

The fear of the Lord as religious awe

There is a healthy form of religious fear. It is mentioned in Ps 1:7 and Ps 111:10. 'The fear of God ,' they say, 'is the beginning of wisdom.' In *The Idea of the Holy*, Rudolf Otto maintained that any genuine experience of the holiness of God evokes uncanny feelings of awe, reverence, and religious dread. Otto uses these words 'to denote a quite specific kind of emotional response, wholly distinct from that of being afraid, though it so far resembles it that the analogy of fear may be used to throw light upon its nature.'[16] In Is 6:1-10, the prophet recounts such a peak experience when he became intensely aware of the Mystery and Holiness of God. While it fascinated and attracted him, at the same time he was overwhelmed by the awfulness of it, 'Woe is me,' he cried out, 'I am lost!' In the light of God's great holiness, the prophet was aware of his own unholiness, and his need for purification.

Hopefully, we too will have such prayerful encounters with God. Indeed they are the life blood of true religion, providing it with depth, conviction and energy. Needless to say, rather than being a block to relationship with God, 'holy fear' is an intimate response to him.

Reactive fear

Vivid religious experiences are often followed by an unholy fear. It causes people to back away from relationship with the Lord because they are intimidated by the implications. Spiritual directors refer to this kind of resistance as a 'counter-movement,' i.e. one that tends to move away from intimacy with God. If it is repeated time and time again, it's called a 'counter-current.' For example, a directee tells her director about a wonderful and consoling experience of God in prayer. Then in subsequent meetings it becomes apparent to the director that the woman's prayer has become heady, dry and boring. There are a number of reasons why this might happen. Happiness is scarey because it is gratuitous and therefore beyond our personal control. As Sam Keen has suggested, we human beings have a love affair with pain. Most of us seem unable to tolerate three days of uninterrupted happiness.

If the directee's ego could talk, it might explain her resistance by saying something like this: 'Yes the experience was wonderful and consoling, just what I had been longing for, a deeper, more profound realisation of my identity in God. But it was a bit too much. It made me afraid. I had been used to looking at myself in a fairly negative way. My experience of God's love challenged all that. At first I welcomed the change, then it became a bit unnerving. As the saying goes, the devil you know is better than the devil you don't know. I just found it hard to believe that I'm lovable without having to do anything to earn that approval. I'd be better off going more gradually. No sense in rushing into anything. Who knows, God may ask me to do something very difficult, e.g. to endure a painful experience, to make a big personal sacrifice, or to do something very demanding. Just remember the lives of the saints and you will know what might happen. St Teresa of Avila got sick every day, St Augustine had to sever his relationship with his mistress, St Thérèse of Lisieux had to suffer an excruciating death in her mid twenties! I'll just back off for a while. Then I'll pick up again when I have regained my self-control.'[17]

Overcoming resistance

A genuine experience of the Mysterious Other can override the influence of negative images of God and the self. It does this for a while, and then as the fearful implications of change became apparent, both the negative images of God and the self, tend to reassert themselves. The person becomes a veritable 'brain on stilts.' He or she does this by moving away from an awareness of intimate relationship with the Lord, only to take refuge in talk and thought about God. There are a number of ways of overcoming an impasse like this. Firstly, by admitting one's fears and their causes to oneself. Secondly, by recalling and trying to relive the prayer experience that evoked the resistance in the first place. Thirdly, be getting back in touch with one's God-prompted desire for God. Fourthly, these three forms of self-intimacy find prayerful expression when that which is innermost is published and made known to the Lord. Unless one can relinquish control over one's inner life by means of self-disclosure, it is unlikely that the heart will experience the God who reveals himself to those who wait for his coming with loving and sustained attention. It is to this all-important subject that we turn our attention in the final chapter.

Notes
1.   On Christian Friendship, op. cit ., Bk 1, par. 70, 66.
2.   Oratio I, de oratione dominica , n. 2. P.G., 44:1123.
3.   Homiliae in Genesim, homilia 30, n. 5. P.G., 53:280
4.   IV Contra Gentes, 22, in Gilby's, St Thomas Aquinas: Theological Texts, Oxford, 1955, 209.

5. *Treatise on the Love of God,* Vol II, Tan, Rockford, Ill., 1963, Bk 6, chap. 1, 268.
6. St Teresa, *Life,* viii.
7. cf. C. Kerr, *The Way of Peace,* Hodder & Stoughton, London, 1990,131-132; P. Collins, *Maturing in the Spirit,* chap. 2; Mc Donnell and Montague, 316-342.
8. cf. P. Collins, *Maturing in the Spirit* , chap. 11.
9. M. Hebblethwaite, *Finding God in All Things,* Fount, London, 1987, 76.
10. *Treatise Concerning the Religious Affections,* Banner of Truth, Edinburgh, 1986, 30.
11. Frank Lake, *With Respect:A Doctor's Response to a Healing Pope,* DLT, London, 1982, 43-44.
12. *Songs of Experience, A poison Tree* , st 1.
13. St Francis de Sales, *Introduction to the Devout Life,* pt. 4, sec. 11.
14. cf. *Spiritual Exercises,* [315]; Bill Barry, *Paying Attention to God: Discernment in Prayer,* Ave Maria Press, Notre Dame, 1990, 31.
15. On the formation of God images in childhood, cf. A. M. Rizzuto, *The Birth of the Living God: A Psychoanalytical Study,* Chicago Univ. Press, 1979, esp. chap. 10.
16. Rudolf Otto, *The Idea of the Holy* , OUP, London, 1958, 13.
17. cf. Gerald May, *Care of Mind Care of Spirit; the Psychiatric Dimensions of Spiritual Direction,* Harper & Row, N.Y., 1982, 45-48; 75.

CHAPTER 12

Prayer as attention

It seems to me that the feelings of anxious fear, which we discussed in the last chapter, are the most intimate response of un-redeemed human nature to its presence in the world. They disclose a sense of fundamental threat to one's personal welfare and existence. It can be evoked by one or more of four interrelated things. Firstly, there is fear of stepping off the cliff edge of existence into what Milton calls 'the dark womb of uncreated night,' where one's personality is annihilated in death. Secondly, there is fear of guilt and condemnation. The judge is that part of oneself, i.e. conscience, which knows everything we do and are and can give a negative judgement which is experienced as guilt. Thirdly, there is the fear of emptiness and meaninglessness which is rooted in the suspicion that, despite its apparent meaning, the universe and everything in it, including oneself, is ultimately absurd.[1] Fourthly, there is a fear of complete vulnerability, powerlessness and loss of either control or influence over one's own life or the lives of others. Through these four forms of anxious fear, our deepest nature publishes and makes known its most inward sense of contingency as it relates to a created world which isn't the adequate explanation of its own existence.

Pathological forms of anxiety are rooted in the more fundamental forms of threat that we have just described. Neurosis, for example, is a synonym for non-experience, a way of avoiding the threat of non-being by avoiding threatening aspects of being itself. I believe that this sense of ontological anxiety, i.e. the kind that is evoked by the threat of non-existence, is the birthplace of the God-prompted desires that we have examined earlier in the book. They reach in a transcendental way beyond the narrow confines of the individualised self in a deep-seated longing for God. All the great spiritual teachers have been aware of the fact that fear cannot be got rid of by personal effort, but only by the ego's absorption in a cause greater than its own narrow interests. Absorption in any cause will rid the mind of some of its fears; but only absorption in the knowledge and love of him who lives 'beyond the stars' can rid us of all fear. As scripture says, an awareness of the love of God tends to drive out all fear. (cf. 1 Jn 4:18)

Total absorption in God was not only a central characteristic of Jesus's relationship to his Father, it was also a fundamental aspect of his teaching. He said that the ego had to die to its pride, worldly attachments and illusions of self-sufficiency, if it wished to know God and to rely on his providence. (cf. Jn 12:24) With this kind of trusting relationship in mind, Jesus said, 'Therefore do not worry, saying, "What will we eat?" or "What will we drink?" or "What will we wear?" for it is the gentiles who strive for all these things; and indeed your heavenly Father knows that you need all these things. But strive first for the kingdom of God and his righteousness, and all these things will be given to you as well.' (Mt 6:31-34) In his Gifford Lectures in 1953-54, John Macmurray said: 'The maxim of illusory religion runs: "Fear not; trust in God and he will see that none cf the things you fear will happen to you;" that of real religion, on the contrary, is: "Fear not; the things that you are afraid of are quite likely to happen to you, but they are nothing to be afraid of."'[2]

TWO APPROACHES TO GOD

How can God publish and make known his divine nature to us in such a way that he would satisfy our religious desires and allay our fears? The fathers of the first Vatican Council said that the reality of God was beyond the grasp of the human mind, it is 'he who is ineffably exalted above all that is or can be thought of outside himself.'[3] The Fourth Lateran Council taught that the reality of God could be indirectly and partially grasped by the human mind, 'between the Creator and the creature no similarity can be expressed without including a greater dissimilarity.'[4] The tension between the knowability and the unknowability of the Lord has given rise to two complementary types of spirituality in the Christian Churches.

Firstly there is the *apophatic* approach. It is *consciousness*, rather than *content* oriented[5] and stresses the unknowability of God. His infinite nature cannot be grasped by either reason or imagination. God is best understood in a negative way without the aid of concepts, images, and symbols. This form of religious intimacy is epitomised by St John of the Cross, who wrote: 'To reach satisfaction in all, desire its possession in nothing. To come to the knowledge of all, desire the knowledge of nothing. To come to possess all, desire the possession of nothing. To arrive at being all, desire to be nothing.'[6] In recent times Thomas Merton and, to a lesser extent, Karl Rahner were eloquent proponents of the need to approach God by the austere way of negation.

Secondly, there is the *kataphatic* approach. It is *content* rather than *consciousness* orientated[7] and stresses the knowability of God. God is best understood in an indirect way by means of images and symbols. The word *symbol* comes from the Greek meaning 'thrown together.' As we noted in chapter two, an object has symbolic power when it can intimate or indirectly make known that which is innermost in another dimension of meaning. Because of their holistic and revelatory capacity, symbols can transcend the normal multiplicity of rational sense experience to reveal the Mysterious Unity that sustains all things in being. While the meaning of symbols is not accessible to the rational mind, it can be comprehended by the spiritual power of the intuitive mind. Unlike rational concepts, symbolic images tend to evoke an affective response. If an experience has a religious dimension, feelings will be evoked which cannot be accounted for by the immediate object of attention. Their presence would incline one to believe that they had been evoked by the awareness of the mysterious Other. Because of their unique ability to mediate transcendent meaning to the inner self, symbols are the language of religious intimacy.

I suppose it would be true to say that Sts Ignatius of Loyola and, to a lesser extent, Teresa of Avila were proponents of this *kataphatic* approach to God. In our own time, people like Carl Jung, Ira Progoff and Roberto Assagioli have shown that the archetypes of the unconscious, especially the God archetype, become conscious by means of symbols. Images, whether within the psyche or outside in the enviornment become symbols of transcendence in so far as they give content to the God archetype.

While *kataphatic* and *apophatic* spiritualities may stress the importance either of God's knowability or unknowability, they usually include elements of the other approach. It seems to me that we begin to open ourselves to the self-disclosure of God by means of the *kataphatic* orientation, and later on we can graduate to a more *apophatic* one.

Religious desires

God-prompted desire for God is the only power capable of bringing the soul into intimate relationship with the divine. This will be true to the extent that our religious yearnings are unrestricted in three interrelated ways. Firstly, they need to be unfettered by worldly attachments. That's why St Ignatius says, 'Insofar as any created things hinder our progress toward our goal, we ought to let go of them.'[8] Secondly, we have already noted how our desire for God is helped by the kind of self-disclosure that reaches beyond the constraints of self-absorption by revealing one's deepest thoughts and feelings in an intimate way to the Lord. Thirdly, our desire for God will be satisfied when we can pay sustained attention to created reality, e.g. nature, people, the scriptures, art, etc, as so many mirrors of wonder, which can reflect and mediate the presence of the Beyond in the midst of our everyday lives.

Prayer as attention

We have already examined the dynamics of intimacy as loving attention in chapter eight. I think it would be true to say that this kind of attention is the key to genuine prayer; as soon as it ceases, prayer ceases also. Simone Weil supported this point of view when she wrote: 'Prayer consists of attention. It is the orientation of all the attention of which the soul is capable toward God. The quality of attention counts for much in the quality of the prayer. Warmth of heart cannot make up for it. It is the highest part of the attention only which makes contact with God, i.e. when prayer is intense and pure enough for such contact to be established.'[9] This kind of contemplative attention can be exercised during fixed times of formal prayer, e.g. while hearing Mass. But it can also be exercised at any time in an informal way, e.g. while taking a walk in the countryside or in a local park. If we have a constant and attentive desire for revelation we can meet with the God of surprises in any situation, at any time. In the rest of this chapter we will look at some typical examples of how the Lord can publish and make known his divine self to us. I should say in passing that, because I have done so elsewhere, I will not be dealing with the important subject of receiving guidance in prayer.[10]

MEETING THE GOD OF NATURE

Our need for an intimate relationship with the natural world has been a recurring theme throughout this book. The Great Artist can reveal himself through the work of his hands, so to speak. I became a priest as a result of such an experience. When my time in secondary school came to an end I went on a hitch-hiking holiday with two friends. In the course of our travels, we visited the picturesque town of Kinsale on the south coast of Ireland. During our stay there, I can remember sitting on a wall that overlooked the sea. In the twilight I could see some twinkling lights of the nearby town which was about two miles away. Below me was the vast expanse of the sea. Suddenly and spontaneously everything assumed a symbolic significance. The town seemed to represent the world and all it could promise. The ocean represented the infinity and absolute call of God. For my part, I felt that I was suspended between the Lord and the world, time and eternity. Deep down I knew I had to make a choice. Would I continue to pursue my worldly ambition by becoming a doctor, or would I give in to the persistent but unwelcome thought that I was being called to be a priest. In that moment of heightened awareness, when I felt at one with the world, God and my deeper self, I knew that I would have to give the priesthood a reluctant try. I entered the seminary a few days later.

The world is charged with the grandeur of God

There is a wonderful example of intimacy with God, through nature, in the *Autobiography* of St Thérèse of Lisieux. She and her sister Céline used to enjoy chatting together. 'Those were wonderful conversations we had every evening, upstairs in the room with a view,' reports Thérèse. 'Our eyes were lost in the distance, as we watched the pale moon rising slowly above the trees. Those silvery rays she cast on a sleeping world, the stars shining bright in the blue vault above us, the fleecy clouds floating by in the evening wind – how everything conspired to turn our thoughts towards heaven! How beautiful it must be if the obverse side of it was so calm and clear!'

Having recounted the religious experience enjoyed by herself and her sister Thérèse goes on to reflect on its nature. 'Perhaps it's silly of me,' she says, 'but that opening-up of our hearts has always reminded me of St Monica and her son at Ostia, rapt in ecstasy as they contemplated the wonderful works of the Creator. I feel as if we'd received graces belonging to the same high order as some of those bestowed on the great Saints: as the *Imitation* says, God has two ways of making himself manifest; he shows himself to some people in a blaze of light, to others under a considerable veil of symbols and signs. Well, of course it was only this second kind of revelation he saw fit to give to Céline and me, but how light and transparent it seemed, this veil which hid him from our sight!' Finally, Thérèse goes on to answer the questions that spiritual directors like to ask, i.e. what did you feel when the Lord revealed himself to you? And what did you notice about the nature of God? 'How could there be room for doubt?' says Thérèse with the conviction of those who speak with the authority of deeply felt experience. 'How could there be any need for faith or hope? It was love that taught us to find, here on earth, the Bridegroom we searched for. He came upon us alone, and greeted us with a kiss: henceforward we need fear no contemptuous looks.'[11]

Evidently, Thérèse and Céline enjoyed a relationship of mutual intimacy. No doubt they spoke to one another about their desire for God. Following that 'opening up of their hearts' by means of mutual self-disclosure, their attention was increasingly absorbed by the evening sky. Not only were they aware of its beauty, their God-prompted desire for God was satisfied when they became vividly aware of a mediated presence of merciful love. It is interesting to see that Thérèse identifies her experience as a *kataphatic* one. It was made possible by the power of symbols to intimate what God was like.

I should say in passing that God's presence is not always that easy to discern. For example, a man has just told his spiritual director about a memorable walk in the midst of the burgeoning life of a forest. He says, 'Suddenly I was astonished at the abundance of all that life, and I thought to myself, "I'm not alone," and I just stood there listening.' The director says, 'Listening?' 'Listening to the silence,' responds the directee. 'That's a strange thing to say, isn't it?' the director responds, 'Would you like say more about it?' To which the directee replies, 'It was as though the silence was full of life and was telling me something. As though something was being said that I couldn't make out. As though someone responsible for all that life were speaking.' In a quiet voice the director says, 'As though someone were speaking?' 'Yes,' replies the directee, 'and telling me ... well, after a while it sounded as though there was care for me. As though I were a swimmer immersed in care for me.'[12] By concentrating on the directee's affective responses in the forest, the director helps him to notice that his feelings were not only evoked by the immediate environment, they were in part a response to a mediated presence, a Someone, who cared for nature yes, and also for the directee. Rightly, T. S. Eliot says that 'We had the experience but missed the meaning, and approach to the meaning restores the experience.'[13] It is only when we reflect on our experiences, e.g. of nature, either on our own or with the help of a spiritual director, that we will discern whether God was revealed or not.

MEETING GOD IN HUMAN RELATIONSHIPS

I love those gospel stories which tell us how different people were suddenly enlightened. While they payed attention to the humanity of Jesus, that which was innermost in his identity was published and made known to them in a moment of intense intimacy. The Samaritan woman at the well had been talking to Jesus for quite a while when she said, 'I know that the Messiah – that is, Christ – is coming; and when he comes, he will explain everything.' Those words were the prelude to her moment of enlightenment when Jesus made this self-disclosure: 'That is who I am, I who speak to you.' (Jn 4:26-27) On another occasion, Jesus asked the apostles who they thought he was. Having offered a few conventional opinions, Peter was enlightened by the Spirit to intuitively recognise the truth: 'You are the Christ,' he said, 'the Son of the living God.' (Mt 16:16) After his resurrection, Jesus appeared to a number of people who at first didn't recognise who he was. For example when Mary of Magdala met Jesus outside his tomb, she thought that he was a gardener. But as soon as Jesus called her by name, she was enlightened and as a result came to see who he really was. (Jn.20:16)

Meeting Christ in the Eucharistic Community

St Luke never met the earthly Jesus. In his gospel, he asks the question: after the ascension how do believers meet the risen Lord? He gives his answer in the account of the two disciples on the road to Emmaus. It seems to be a liturgical text. By leaving Jerusalem, members of the community withdraw from the hassles of life. They hear the scriptures being recalled by a stranger, who then goes on to explain their messianic and prophetic meaning, i.e. the liturgy of the word. Finally, they share a meal together and recognise Jesus in the breaking of bread, i.e. the eucharist. As soon as they enjoy this moment of spiritual intimacy, the Lord disappears. The disciples notice that as they were involved in these activities of the eucharistic community, their hearts burned within them because, unknowingly at first, they were in the company of Jesus. He himself had said, 'Where two or three meet in my name, I am there among them.' (Mt 18:20) His presence had been mediated by the community, as it shared the scriptures, the homily and the eucharist. (cf. Lk 24:13-36)

St Paul learned about the presence of the risen Jesus in the Christian community when he was enlightened on the road to Damascus. 'He fell to the ground, and then he heard a voice saying, "Saul, Saul, why are you persecuting me?" "Who are you Lord?" he asked, and the answer came, "I am Jesus, whom you are persecuting." (Acts 9:4-5) In other words, Jesus was present in those members of the Christian community that he had arrested and mistreated. After this revelation, it is not surprising to find that St Paul taught that the community of believers is the body of Christ, e.g. 'Christ's body is yourselves, each of you with a part to play in the whole,' (1 Cor 12:27) and 'Christ is the head of the body, that is, the Church.' (Col 1:18) The apostle to the gentiles says that Jesus manifests himself by means of the fruits (cf. Gal 5:22) and gifts of the Spirit which are present in the community. (cf. 1 Cor 12:4-12; Rom 12:4-9; Eph 4:9-14)

All of these points have profound implications from a

religious point of view. If we want an intimate relationship with the Lord, we should pay loving attention to one another. In this connection I can recall some words written by a man in a concentration camp:

> I sought my God, I could not find him,
> I sought my soul, it evaded me,
> I sought my neighbour and found all three!

We will go on to look at some of the ways in which the Lord can reveal himself through our intimate relationships with one another.

The Mystical Body of Christ

St Paul adverts to a very real barrier to interpersonal intimacy in a verse we have already quoted: 'What person knows a man's thoughts except the spirit of the man which is in him?' (1 Cor 2:11) In other words, while we have a direct awareness of our own subjective experience, we can only have an indirect awareness of the subjective experience of another person. However, from a theological point of view, we can say that when each person is consciously united to Christ, e.g. a husband and wife, a number of things happen. To the extent that they are open to the activity of the Spirit within their respective personalities, they share in the subjectivity of the Lord by 'having the mind of Christ.' (1 Cor 2:16) Surely that means that, if the two people are anchored in God by means of their conscious relationship to Jesus, they can overcome their separateness as individuals by 'having the same thoughts, sharing the same love, and being one in soul and mind.' (Phil 2:2)

What I'm implying, therefore, is the fact that Christian relationships have quite a different potential for mutual intimacy than their merely human counterparts. I would go so far as to say that ecstatic experiences of interpersonal love can have a quasi-mystical dimension. Is it any surprise therefore, that St Paul compares the union of a Christian husband and wife to the intimate union of Christ with his Church, (cf. Eph 5:23) i.e. one of identification and unity?

Our desire to see Jesus more clearly, can be satisfied when we pay attention to the the acceptance, understanding and

217

approving love of a spouse, friend, confidant or stranger. We noted a number of examples of this type of experience earlier, especially in dealing with the healing power of intimacy. When we experience the love of another person or persons in this way, all kinds of feelings can be evoked in the heart, e.g. joy, relief, peace, release, well-being, healing, affirmation, etc. However if we reflect on such an experience afterwards, with or without the help of a spiritual director, we may come to consciously realise and acknowledge that some of our affective responses had been evoked by the awareness of a presence that was mediated by the attitudes, words and deeds of the other person. By looking into his or her merciful and loving eyes, we may have ended up looking into the eyes of the One who lives within our brothers and sisters. As William Blake once wrote:

> For Mercy has a human heart,
> Pity a human face,
> and Love, the human form divine,
> and Peace, the human dress. [14]

It would seem that we Christians are called to share the gentle and compassionate love of Jesus which is published and made known in and through our intimate human relationships and to share that love with any other people we meet.

MINISTERIAL COMPASSION AND THE HEART OF GOD

Over the years I have met with the Risen Jesus on a numerous occasions as I have tried to respond to the needs of other people. During parish missions we try to visit the sick and the housebound. On one occasion the parish priest asked one of my companions and myself to see a male parishioner who was dying from cancer in a local hospital. Before meeting the man, we happened to meet his wife. We were deeply moved as she told us, with tears and sobs, about the terrible pain her husband was enduring. Then we visited the man. We could see the suffering etched on his face. Again we were moved. We put our hands on his head and began to pray for him. As I sensed his distress, strong feelings of compassion welled up within me. I felt that the Lord was with us and that he would bring relief to the cancer patient. And so he did. From that moment until his peaceful death some time later, the man experienced no more pain. As I have reflected on that encounter and many others like it, I have felt that the Lord has been saying within my spirit: 'It is I who suffer in the people you meet, for I am in travail within them. The compassion you feel is a share in my compassion, and your desire to bring them help and healing is a share in my desire for them.' In other words, as I have payed loving and compassionate attention to brothers and sisters in the Lord, I have felt at one with Jesus. At moments of intimate identification like that, I believe that Jesus has published and made known his feelings, attitudes and desires within me.

Meeting the God of another's experience

Ministerial intimacy of a Christian kind can take another form. As I have listened to people, and paid sustained attention to their experience, I have sometimes found myself paying attention to the God of their experience. I can recall an occasion when I visited a poor couple who lived in a caravan on the roadside. The man of the house, so to speak, told me that he and his wife were the parents of no less than nineteen children. Then pointing to his spouse he said, 'You know, father, my wife nearly died a few years ago. She lay unconscious for weeks in the hospital. The doctors told us that she had no hope of recovery. Well, me and the children prayed for her every day. Then six weeks later she regained consciousness. Thanks be to God, here she is today. Father, they say that men can heal,' and then turning and pointing to a picture of the Sacred Heart he said with great conviction, 'There is the only Man who can heal anyone.'

Then he went on to tell me that he was from the town of Kilkenny. 'When I was a boy, he said, 'there was a *duine le Dia* in the parish, if you get my meaning father.' I told him that I was aware that mentally handicapped children were referred to as 'one of God's people' in the Irish language. 'Well, the children used to make fun of this boy and call him names. One Sunday, we were all at Mass. The priest was preaching his sermon, when this young lad came into the church. He walked down the main isle and gawked at the people. They began to giggle in a distracted way. Then a cloud moved away from the sun, and a huge beam of light flooded through the window, right across the sanctuary. The boy was fascinated by it. He approached it slowly. The people laughed out loud when he began to take his coat off, with the intention of hanging it up on the sunlight. But there was a gasp of disbelief when he stood on his tippy toes and throwing his coat over the beam of light, it hung there in the air!' While there was an impish grin on the man's face as he told his story, I knew that it was a parable that conveyed some of his deepest religious convictions.

When I left his caravan I could feel a great joy within my heart. It lasted for days. As I reflected on that memorable encounter, I realised that my joy had been evoked by the man's *magnificat*. It was as if he had said:

My soul magnifies the Lord,
my spirit rejoices in God my Saviour.
He has done great things for me.
He heard my prayers and the prayers of my children
when he rescued my wife from the jaws of death.
He confounds the smugness of the strong
and does great things for the poor
who count for little in this world.
He can make an overcoat hang on a beam of light,
because nothing is impossible to my God!

By paying attention to the God of this man's experience, he had become the God of my experience also, one who published and made known something of his wonderful inner life to me. By listening to a brother or sister, we may end up listening to the Lord. As Heb 13:2 observes: 'Remember to welcome strangers ... there were some who did that and welcomed angels without knowing,' i.e. the bearers of God's word.

INTIMACY WITH GOD IN PRIVATE PRAYER

Freud argued that the way in which we experience adult relationships is conditioned by the ones we experienced in childhood. He wrote: 'The nature and quality of the human child's relations to people of his own and the opposite sex have already been laid down in the first six years of life ... All of his later choices of friendship and love follow upon the basis of the memory-traces left behind by these protoypes.'[15] I'm sure there is a lot of truth in

what Freud says. However, I don't believe that our experience of
adult intimacy is completely pre-determined by our childhood
relationships. Erickson has shown how the dynamics of adult intimacy can have a healing effect of a retrospective kind, one that
can undo some of the negative attitudes and feelings which were
imbibed in the first years of life. The kinds of relationships we
have been examining could have that salutary effect from a
psychological point of view.

Ana-Maria Rizzuto has argued that the same childhood
relationships can also have a spiritual effect. In her book, *The Birth
of the Living God*, she examines how children form their images of
God. Apparently research has shown that they are largely determined by the love of our parents and childhood carers. She
writes: 'The mirroring components of the God representation find
their first experience in eye contact, early nursing, and maternal
personal participation in the act of mirroring ... When the child is
able to connect the word God to his experiences he will utilise his
experiences of the mirroring phase for his first elaboration (of an
image of what God is like).'[16] When we have positive experiences
of adult intimacy, the people who look at us, with eyes filled with
love, not only reinforce the positive God images formed in childhood, they can also challenge and weaken the influence of negative God images which may have been formed at the same time.
In other words, by means of their contemplative attitude, other
Christians become role models of the Father's love.

It seems to me that when we are praying in private, the
influence of those human looks of love become remembered sacraments which, consciously or unconsciously, are used by God to
mediate his love to us and for us. It is yet another example of the
way in which God's grace builds on our nature and human experience.

Contemplating the love of God

Every now and then, I use the following exercise in
prayer. I begin by recalling these words of scripture: 'God is love,'
(1 Jn 4:16) and 'As the Father loves me, so I love you.' (Jn 15:9)
Then I recall this moving prayer of St Paul's: 'I pray that you may
have your roots and foundations in love, so that you, together

with all God's people, may have the power to understand how broad and long, how wide and deep, is Christ's love. Yes, may you have the power to understand how broad and long, how high and deep, is Christ's love. Yes, may you come to know his love – although it can never be fully known – and so be completely filled with the very nature of God.' (Eph 3:18) Then I imagine that Jesus is kneeling before me with a towel around his waist. I notice, as St Teresa of Avila used to recommend,[17] that he is looking at me with eyes filled with love and humility. He is not there to tell me what he wants. Rather he wants to know what my God-prompted desire might be. I tell him that I want to experience his love in a deeper way than ever before, so that I might return it to him and to the people I meet.

Sometimes when I do this exercise I recall the way in which I have looked at people with great appreciation and approval, and I think, 'That's only a shadow of the way in which the Lord is looking at me at this moment.' On other occasions I call to mind the way in which loving friends and acquaintances have looked at me. As I re-live the experience, I realise that their appreciation and approval was only a faint reminder of God's intense love for me.

While there have been many occasions when my heart has seemed impervious to the action of God's grace, there have been precious moments when I have become consciously and vividly aware of the love of God, which has been poured into my heart by the power of the Spirit. (cf. Rom 5:5) While it is true that the Lord uses the imperfect love that people have shown us to mediate his love to our hearts, it is equally true that the experience of God's perfect love in prayer has a unique inner effect. Not only does it affirm our true identities in Christ, it heals the ill-effects of defective loving in childhood and adult life, thereby empowering as to love as we have been loved. St Aelred of Rievaulx points to the reciprocal relationship that exists between human and divine love and how they intersect in prayer: 'From the sweetness of fraternal charity one takes wing to fly aloft to the more sublime splendour of divine love, and by the ladder of charity one ascends to the embrace of Christ himself; and again one descends to the love of the neighbour.'[18]

Contemplating God's word in scripture

When we pay prayerful attention to the scriptures, the Lord can publish and make known his inner nature to our hearts. Jesus said: 'The words I have spoken to you are spirit and they are life.' (Jn 6:63) The Spirit which is the intimacy of God, is like a surgeon's knife, it exposes that which is innermost to the Presence and inspirations of the Lord. In the Greek New Testament the words *rhema* and *logos* are both translated as 'word'. From a linguistic point of view, nuanced descriptions can be given to each of these words. And even if their meanings overlap in the Greek of the New Testament, they can be distinguished one from the other in experience. When the 'word' is a verb, i.e. the word of God that is spoken as 'a statement' to me, it is *rhema*. [19] When the 'word' is a noun, i.e. the word of God in itself which is objectively and universally true, it is *logos*. As we contemplate the scriptures, God's *logos* word becomes his *rhema* word spoken into our hearts. It is this utterance that reveals both the Lord and his will to us, thereby strengthening our trust in him. As St Paul says in Rom 10:17: 'Faith comes by hearing, and hearing by the (*rhema*) word of Christ.' There is an example of what I mean in the Annunciation account. Mary said to the Angel Gabriel: 'Be it done unto me according to your (*rhema*) word.' (Lk 1:38)

The Benedictine method

In the Western Christian tradition, there are two notable ways of praying the scriptures, the Benedictine and Ignatian. In his Rule, St Benedict encouraged his brethren to engage in the *Lectio Divina*. It consisted of four sequential steps of reading, meditation, prayer and contemplation. Writing about its purpose he said: 'The Holy Scripture is the well of Jacob from which waters are drawn which will be poured out later in prayer. Thus there will be no need to go to the oratory to begin to pray; but in reading itself, means will be found for prayer and contemplation.'[20] Having placed oneself in the presence of God, one asks in the words of a hymn, 'to see in the scriptures, the Saviour's face, to hear his word and heed his calling, know his will and grow in grace.' Then one goes on to read a chosen passage slowly, reverently and attentively, two or three times. Afterwards, one meditates on, and ponders the hidden meaning in a striking image, phrase or word. As it begins to evoke a personal response in the heart one stops thinking about the text in order to talk to the Lord about it, i.e. prayer as self-disclosure. The person asks for the grace of achieving intimacy with God.

Speaking about the relationship of meditation to prayer, Guigo II, a medieval author, wrote: 'When meditation busily applies itself to this work, it does not remain on the outside, it goes to the heart of the matter. When the soul is set alight by this kindling it deduces how sweet it would be to know by experience, yet it can find no means of its own to have what it longs for. So the soul, seeing that by itself it cannot attain to that sweetness of knowing and feeling that which it longs for, it humbles itself and betakes itself to prayer.'[21] God responds to this cry for help. Guigo goes on to say: 'The Lord, whose eyes are upon the just, whose ears can catch the very meaning of their prayers, does not wait but breaks in upon the prayer by bestowing the precious gift of contemplation.' We will return to this point in a moment.

The Ignatian method

The method of scriptural prayer proposed by St Ignatius of Loyola was similar in many ways to the Benedictine approach. He hoped that the person using his approach will, slowly and gently, enter into the spirit of Jesus Christ and come to know him more intimately, love him more deeply, and follow him more closely. One takes a long loving look at Jesus in the light of the concrete circumstances of one's own life, thoughts, feelings, etc. Whereas Benedict recommended rational consideration of the meaning and implications of a text, Ignatius proposed a more imaginative approach. In his *Spiritual Exercises* he encourages people who use his method to make a mental video of a gospel scene by seeing the persons involved [106]; then listening to what they say [107]; and finally, considering what they do [108] in as much concrete detail as possible. Ignatius encouraged people to tell God about their personal responses, e.g. their feeling reactions, and he adds, 'According to the light that I have received, I will beg for grace to follow and imitate more closely our Lord.'

[109] He also encouraged people to return to the same meditation two or three times in order to deepen their awareness of the Lord. In the Ignatian view, as soon as there is true consolation, i.e. an inner increase in hope, faith, charity, and joy, meditation turns to contemplation, even though the subject matter remains the same.

During a directed retreat, a woman named Anne uses the nativity text in prayer. She describes how she approached it. 'I tried to begin by looking at the people in the scene. By "looking" I don't mean just observing or imagining externals, such as features or clothes, but trying to get "inside people's skins" and feel what they were feeling. These feelings might be joy, or love or peace – more or less anticipatory feelings at the time of my birth; but I was often surprised by my unexpected feelings – such as anxiety, or discomfort or displeasure at my intrusion.' When asked if any highlights stood out for Anne as a result of praying about Christ's infancy, she replied, 'On the first occasion the realisation that Jesus had moved out of the security of his divinity into our humanity for people like myself filled me with a sense of awe that anyone could be so loving. This in turn, seemed to pull out of me, in a new way, a conviction that I had been created to move out in love for others.' Anne says that, when she came back to the text, it had a different effect. 'Looking at Christ (i.e. the contemplative attitude perhaps) I felt a sharp contrast between us. His love for people turned my annoyance at having to spent time with two visitors some time earlier in the day, into a sense of shame, which I shared with him (i.e. self-disclosure). Then I felt I too was being loved. At some stage it seemed to me that I was touching the manger (i.e. moment of contemplative awareness), and the conviction began to grow and deepen within me that here was the meaning I was searching for in my life (i.e. her God-prompted desire for God was being satisfied). I found myself saying to Christ the words of Albert Camus:

Don't walk in front of me, I may not follow.
Don't walk behind me, I may not lead.
Walk beside me, and just be my friend.[22]

As we pray the scriptures, in either a Benedictine or Ignatian way, we may enjoy moments of contemplation. Reasoning gives way to rapt attention to Christ. The person doesn't have to make any effort. Truths that were intellectually known before assume a new significance and depth of meaning. The heart spontaneously reacts with feelings of consolation which are the sure mark of the Spirit's action.

A few years ago, I was invited to speak at a conference in Italy. When I got to Rome, en route to my destination I was suffering from high anxiety. What would I say to the conference? Would my interpreter be able to cope? Would I be able to find out what buses and trains I would need to get to my engagement? I had a blinding headache. My body was like a wound-up spring. Finally, I turned to the Lord and poured out all of negative feelings to him, while asking for his help. Could he perform a miracle and cancel the conference? I didn't think that was likely! After a while I recalled a scripture text in Is 41:10: 'Fear not, I am with you, I will uphold you with my victorious right hand. I will strengthen and uphold you,' that was just what I needed to hear. Those words gave me hope. I asked the Lord to carry out his promise. Nothing seemed to happen. I felt disappointed and let down and told the Lord as much. Then I went back to the text and noticed, as if for the first time, that the Lord had said: 'Fear not, be not dismayed.' Perhaps this was not a word of advice, but rather the Lord's command. As I sensed the power and the goodness of God, I said to him, 'Be it done unto me according to thy *rhema* word. If you want me to be courageous, I will be courageous. I'll take on the whole of Italy if necessary. But you must help me.' Well, it was like a miracle. I had no sooner uttered the words when a great cloud of peace seemed to descend upon me. My headache disappeared. My tension melted. Stress was replaced by a quiet confidence in the Lord. It was never to desert me. I sailed through the conference without a worry. As I have reflected on that memorable experience, I have come to suspect that it contained a moment of contemplative intimacy with Christ as the Victorious One. I seemed to get a deep sense not only of his power, but also of his love and his desire to help me. What else could have accounted for so much on-going consolation and peace?

The apophatic approach to God

So far I have been describing *kataphatic* forms of prayer

and contemplation. As people develop spiritually, they can come to realise that God is so mysterious, that he is infinitely beyond the images and concepts which we use to describe him. So some people let go of them, often as a result of an experience of the dark night of the soul. By withdrawing his consolations, the Lord allows some of his faithful and dedicated followers to experience aridity in prayer and on-going desolation of Spirit. While it is a very painful experience the person can carry on as normal in his or her everyday life. God has a purpose in allowing this to happen. God wants us to experience our own poverty and to see more clearly that his consolations cannot be earned or controlled. St John of the Cross sees the dark night of the soul as a time when the inner senses of understanding and imagination are purified.[23] During this period of desolation, ideas and images do nothing for people. Their feelings don't react, so they have to cleave to the One who is beyond idea and image with the naked commitment of the will. Ironically, it is in moments of this kind, that people experience a deep form of intimacy with the incomprehensibility of God in the cloud of unknowing.

You may recall how, earlier in the chapter, St Thérèse referred to the fact that God can reveal himself to some people in 'a blaze of light'. She was referring to the ironic fact that, during the dark night of the soul, such people may be spiritually illuminated. When the desolation lifts, those same people may be more content with a form of contemplation which has more to do with loving faith in the Mystery of God, than with any rational or imaginative content. This would be the *apophatic* approach.

A short examen of consciousness

St Ignatius believed that a period of prayer should normally be followed by a review period during which one would try to notice what had happened. I have found that the following four questions are helpful.

1. When was I most aware of the Lord's presence during my period of prayer, or during the last few days as the case may be? e.g. while attending mass, praying in private, reading the scriptures, ministering to someone else, talking to another person, enjoying nature, etc.

2. What did I feel when the Lord revealed his presence to me?

Were my feelings positive ones, e.g. peace, joy, well-being, hope, gratitude, encouragement, etc? In Ignatian language, feelings like these are known as 'consolation' and are usually evoked as a result of the Spirit's activity.
Were my feelings negative ones, e.g. anger, oppression, morbid guilt, anxiety, agitation, sadness, restlessness, mild depression, etc.? In Ignatian language, feelings like these are known as 'desolation' and are not evoked by the Spirit. They have their origin in the unconscious. Sometimes they can be due to illusions and/or false inspirations prompted by the evil spirit.

3. What did you notice about the Person of the Lord that would account for the feelings that were evoked within you? How was he for you, what was he like? e.g. was he loving, attentive, accepting, understanding, etc, or impersonal, distant, demanding, judgemental etc.? These are the most important questions in a review of prayer and/or religious experience.

4. How did you decide to respond to the presence or the inspirations of the Lord? Did you tell him what you felt, e.g. appreciation, gratitude, etc.? And did you make any resolution which might have enabled you to express in action the implications of your growing relationship with Christ, e.g. to be for others what the Lord is for you, such as compassionate, generous, etc.

Conclusion

T. S. Eliot has written: 'We shall not cease from exploration, and the end of all our exploring will be to arrive where we started.'24 And so it is in this book. It began by looking at the authority and importance of religious experience especially in modern culture. We suggested that intimacy was the key which would unlock its meaning. We looked at the nature and importance of self-intimacy and some of the means that can be used to grow in such self-awareness, e.g. the examen of consciousness above. We went on to indicate how self-intimacy is necessary if we want to grow in intimacy with nature and other people. By the same token, interpersonal intimacy and closeness to nature help us to grow in self-awareness. Finally, we saw how personal and interpersonal intimacy are necessary if we want to enjoy an intimate relationship with the Lord. As that which is innermost in our inner selves, nature and other people, is published and made known to us, so God uses these disclosures as the iconography of revelation. In and through them he intimates to our hearts what is innermost in his own mysterious depths. As we grow in intimacy with the Lord, our transcedental awareness illumines and transforms the way in which we experience all of the other intimate relationships in which we are involved.

As we reflect on the implications of such religious experience, we see that the intimacies we have explored have to be woven together into a seamless garment of connectedness. To paraphrase T. S. Eliot, 'Love is the unfamiliar Name behind the hands that weave this shirt of flame.'[25] The great St Paul puts it this way: 'Clothe yourselves with (this) love, which binds everything together in perfect harmony. And let the peace of God rule in your hearts, to which indeed you were called in one body.' (Col 3:14-15)

Notes

1. Paul Tillich, *The Courage to Be*, Fontana, London, 1971, 48-61.
2. Quoted by Bill Barry in *Paying Attention to God*, Ave Maria Press, Notre Dame, 1990, 29.
3. *Meditations on Priestly Life*, Sheed & Ward, London, 1974, 13.
4. Karl Rahner ed., *The Teachings of the Catholic Church*, Alba House, N.Y.,1966, 99.
5. cf. G. May, *Will & Spirit: A Contemplative Psychology*, Harper & Row, N.Y., 1982, 108.
6. K. Kavanagh & O. Rodriguez eds., *The Collected Works of John of the Cross*, Inst. of Carmelite Studies, Washington D.C., 1976, 67.
7. May, *ibid*, 108.
8. Principal and Foundation, *Spiritual Exercises*, [23]
9. *Waiting on God*, Fontana, London, 66.
10. For more on this subject see, *Maturing in the Spirit*, chap. 7.
11. Trans. R. Knox, The Harvill Press, London, 1958, 134-135.
12. cf. Connolly & Birmingham, The Art of Spiritual Direction,

Human Development, No. 1, Spring 1987, 16-17.

13. Dry Salvages, *Four Quartets*, line 93.
14. Songs of Innocence, *The Divine Image*, st. 3.
15. The Dissolution of the Oedipus Complex, in *SE* 19, quoted in Rizzuto, *The Birth of the Living God*, Chicago, 1979, 30.
16. *Ibid*, 188.
17. A. de Mello, *Sadhana: A Way to God*, Gujarat Sahitya Prakash, Anand, 1979, 113-114.
18. *Spiritual Friendship, op. cit.*, 129.
19. *Theological Dictionary of the N.T.*, ed. Bromily, Erdmans, Grand Rapids, Mich., 1985, 505-511. C. Farah Jr. in Mc Nutt, *The Power to Heal*, Ave Maria Press, Notre Dame, Ind., 1977, 229-232.
20. *Specululum monachorum I*, PL 184:1175, quoted by J. Leclercq in *The Love of Learning and the Desire for God: A Study of Monastic Culture*, SPCK, London, 1978, 90.
21. Quoted by D. Stanley in *I Encountered God: The Spiritual Exercises with the Gospel of John*, Gujarat Sahitya Prakash, India, 1986, 12.
22. Mary Guy, A 19th. Annotation Retreat Experience, *Review for Religious*, Nov-Dec.1984, 892-893.
23. cf. Toner, *A Commentary on St Ignatius' Rules for the Discernment of Spirits*, The Institute of Jesuit Resources, St Louis, 1979, App. II, 271-282.
24. Little Gidding, in *The Four Quartets, op. cit*., l. 240.
25. Little Gidding, *op. cit.*, l. 208.

Index